Territorial Cohesion and the European Model of Society

Territorial Cohesion and the European Model of Society

Edited by Andreas Faludi

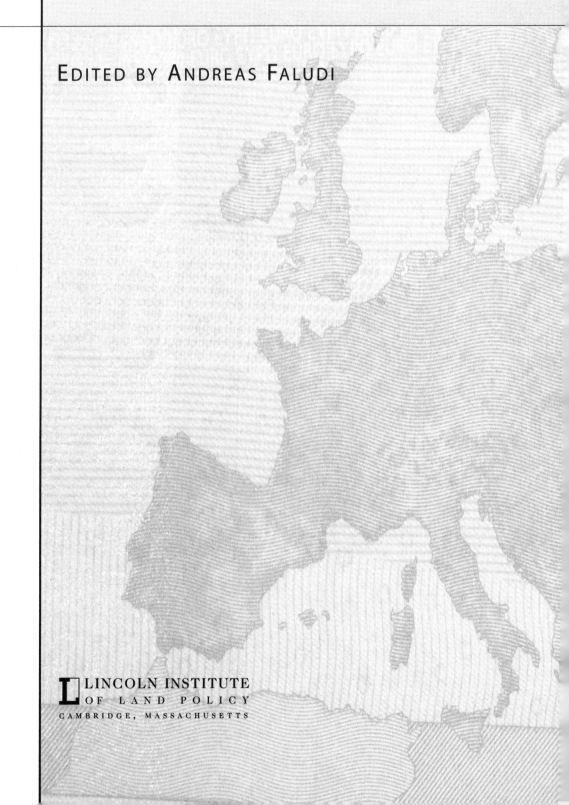

LINCOLN INSTITUTE
OF LAND POLICY
CAMBRIDGE, MASSACHUSETTS

Library of Congress Cataloging-in-Publication Data

Territorial cohesion and the European model of society / edited by Andreas Faludi.
    p. cm.
  Includes bibliographical references and index.
  ISBN-10: 1-55844-166-2
  ISBN-13: 978-1-55844-166-8
  1. Regional planning—Europe. 2. Land use—Europe. 3. Intergovernmental
cooperation—Europe. I. Faludi, Andreas.
  HT395.E8T467 2007
  307.1'209—dc22   2006039569

Designed by Janis Owens, Books By Design, Inc.

Composed in Janson by Books By Design, Inc., in Cambridge, Massachusetts. Printed and
bound by Webcom in Toronto, Ontario, Canada. The paper is Legacy Offset, a recycled,
acid-free sheet.

MANUFACTURED IN CANADA

Contents

Foreword

The publication of this volume offers an occasion to revisit an earlier work, *European Spatial Planning*, also edited by Andreas Faludi and published by the Lincoln Institute of Land Policy in 2002. It is now seven years since 2000 and the conception of that work, and time to take stock of developments on both sides of the Atlantic. Then, the European Union (EU) had 15 member states. Now, since May 2004, it has 25, and it will soon have 27. Then, the European Spatial Development Perspective had just been adopted at Potsdam. Ahead lay the drafting of European constitution under the direction of former French president Valéry Giscard d'Estaing. But the constitution, unanimously adopted by the EU member heads of state, would later be rejected by voters in France and the Netherlands, foiling ratification and leading to a period of "reflection."

One of Lincoln Institute's goals for the earlier book was to familiarize American planners with the European approach to transnational planning, and possibly to apply analogous transboundary thinking to planning across state lines within the U.S. federal system. The difficulty of such a conceptual transfer was acknowledged, and it is thus gratifying to note the considerable recent interest in the United States in a new "megaregional" planning strategy that crosses all sorts of boundaries—municipal, metropolitan, state, and even national borders.

In this volume, based on papers first presented in Vienna in the summer of 2005, the authors have taken up territorial cohesion as a kind of successor concept to spatial planning and spatial development. The question posed is whether there are lessons for planners in the United States (and more broadly North America) to be found in the European experience, and, more tentatively, whether it is possible to reflect back to Europe any useful insights based on an American view of the world. The title indicates that foundational ideas about Europe (with its distinct "model of society") lie behind the concept of territorial cohesion, which can be understood as a goal of spatial equity that tends to favor development-in-place over selective migration to locations of greater opportunity.

This approach is counterposed to an American social model that is seen by some Europeans as a subspecies of what has been called "Anglo-Saxon ultraliberalism." From the western side of the Atlantic, one observes that the equity principle behind territorial cohesion appears to be diametrically opposed to the efficiency principle based on free mobility of labor. It is a strategy based on "need" rather than "potential," as one "Anglo-Saxon" participant in the Vienna conference put it. A willingness to make this trade-off between potentially higher productivity and a particularly rooted conception of place is indicative of the difference between the two models of society.

Paradoxically, the threat of labor mobility within the EU, embodied in the footloose and not entirely apocryphal idea of the "Polish plumber" taking jobs in France, was a factor in the rejection of the treaty to ratify the European constitution, which would have enshrined the principle of territorial cohesion. The political challenge for the EU, which is not (at least as of yet) the "United States of Europe," has, of course, increased with its expansion, adding not just more territory, but dramatically less prosperous populations with a propensity to migrate within the EU.

Returning to the challenge of westbound transferability, apart from the obvious legal, political, social, and cultural differences between the United States and the European Union, it is often noted that EU25 contains a population 50 percent larger than the United States within less than half the land area, yielding a population density of almost 300 per square mile versus only about 85 per square mile in the United Sates. Yet the more urbanized parts of the United States are beginning to approach European densities: the 14-state Northeast megaregion, for example, with approximately 52 million people in 188,380 square miles, weighs in at more than 275 people per square mile, suggesting that at least physical planning around infrastructure, especially high-speed rail, could be informed by European precedents.

Inspired by the European spatial planning approach, academic planning departments and regional and state planning organizations across the United States have begun to explore a new kind of megaregional planning that extends across state lines into vast territories containing significant urban and natural systems: infrastructure *and* ecostructure. In some parts of the country, involvement in these protoplans extends to elected officials and the business community. There is even a nascent national planning initiative, "America 2050," that is looking to shape policy across the megaregions. These efforts are beginning to tackle questions akin to those addressed by the Europeans through the territorial cohesion objective: how to deal, for example, with the decline of older industrial cities, or the continuing depopulation of the Great Plains. It is too early to judge what the results will be, but perhaps not too soon to tip our hats to Andreas Faludi and the "roving band" of European planners who inspired this new way of thinking.

Armando Carbonell
Chairman
Department of Planning and Urban Form
Lincoln Institute of Land Policy

Preface

In 2000, as a European Fulbright Fellow at the Graduate School of Design at Harvard University, I was able to renew my contact with the Lincoln Institute of Land Policy. In June 2001, I convened the seminar "European Spatial Planning" at the Institute. This gathering of European scholars and practitioners led to publication of a Lincoln Institute book of the same title in 2002.

Two participants in that first seminar, Armando Carbonell, a Lincoln Institute senior fellow, and Robert D. Yaro, president of the Regional Plan Association of New York, New Jersey, and Connecticut, were sufficiently inspired to organize a master's studio at the University of Pennsylvania, where they both teach, to look into formulation of an American Spatial Development Perspective (ASPD), an allusion to the European Spatial Development Perspective (ESDP), which emerged from the European experiences of the 1990s. Thus, the 2003–2004 master's class considered the spatial implications of U.S. population and economic growth until 2050.

Based on this work, the Lincoln Institute, together with the Regional Plan Association, sponsored a meeting in September 2004 at the Rockefeller Brothers Fund Conference Center in Pocantico, New York, where the American Spatial Development Perspective was presented.[1] At that meeting, the idea of a follow-up to the seminar "European Spatial Planning" was hatched. It was decided to hold the second seminar in Europe in 2005.

Meanwhile, the University of Pennsylvania master's class of 2004–2005 took the American Spatial Development Perspective a step further under the flag of "America 2050," exploring the implications for the Northeastern Megalopolis, a conscious reference to the 1961 classic by Jean Gottman, *Megalopolis* (Twentieth Century Fund). Another class at Georgia Tech was working with Professor Catherine Ross, looking at the Piedmont Atlantic Metropolis in the southeastern United States. (There have been similar such exercises by master's classes since.) The American Spatial Development Perspective was the topic as well of a well-attended roundtable at the

[1] See A. Carbonell and R. D. Yaro, American spatial development and the new megalopolis, *Land Lines* 17, no. 2 (2005):1–4.

Association of European Schools of Planning Congress in Vienna in July 2005, the venue of the second Lincoln seminar. The papers in this volume originate from that second seminar.

Since publication of the ESDP in 1999, the European planning discourse has taken a new turn—it is increasingly couched in terms of a policy to achieve "territorial cohesion." The papers in this volume shed light on various aspects of this new concept. Suffice it to say that by emphasizing territorial cohesion, its European proponents want to, among other things, find answers to why whole regions are losing their populations because of globalization and to how this loss exerts disruptive effects on communities. Relocating does not raise many eyebrows in the United States, but Europeans are less inclined to move after jobs and are more likely to consider having to do so as an imposition. Right or wrong, Europeans assume that they have something akin to a birthright to a settled life in familiar surroundings. This is the "soft" side of Europe that some bemoan and others value.

The intuition underlying the initiative for the second seminar was that territorial cohesion is closely linked to what former president of the European Commission Jacques Delors has called the "European model of society." Thus the title of the Vienna seminar was "Territorial Cohesion and the European Model of Society." When the idea was being formulated, the European model of society was still a topic mostly for insiders. However, the topic has erupted since. The reason for this is that at the end of 2004, a new European Commission under José Manuel Barroso took office under the banner of a program reviving the Lisbon Strategy adopted in 2000. The Lisbon Strategy had been about turning Europe into the most competitive region globally. The Barroso Commission planned to put in place a range of measures to promote economic growth and labor participation (sluggish growth being seen as the Achilles' heel of Europe). Progress was to be measured by a range of indicators. Member states were also to submit annual progress reports to the European Commission for its comments.

His approach, however, caused much concern, first in the European Parliament, where Barroso had to forcefully defend his program, and later in Europe generally. Opponents feared that his strategy might be at the expense of the European model of society. Arguably, this concern played a role in French and Dutch voters rejecting the Treaty establishing a Constitution for Europe in May and June 2005, only weeks before the Vienna seminar. The model was also invoked in the acrimonious debate over the Financial Perspectives 2007–2013 on the agenda of the European Council of Heads of State and Government, a multiannual framework for the budget of a European Union that now has 25 members and is slated to expand to 27 in 2007, with more candidates, including Turkey, waiting in the wings.

During the second half of 2005, and thus after the Vienna seminar, British Prime Minister Tony Blair was on the receiving end of criticism for his alleged ultraliberal views, as well as for his refusal to put the British budget rebate, negotiated years before, on the line. Chairing the European Council of Heads of State and Government under the rotating presidency of the EU, he put the European model of society—also called "social Europe"—on the agenda of an informal summit at Hampton Court near London. But the meeting was overshadowed by the issue of the Financial Perspective, the resolution of which—such as it is—had to wait until mid-December 2005. (The required approval of the European Parliament came in May 2006, after some further concessions from the member states.) The implications of all this for territorial cohesion policy still have to be worked out, but in retrospect the decision to hold the Vienna seminar on Territorial Cohesion and the European Model of Society in July 2005 appears to have been opportune.

The European model of society as a concept was fairly new to most of the participants in the seminar, who were handpicked for their expertise on territorial cohesion and to represent various European traditions. The seminar, graciously hosted by the Austrian Institute for Regional Studies and Spatial Planning (ÖIR), also included participants from the Lincoln Institute of Land Policy and the Regional Plan Association, augmented by researchers dealing with metropolitan development in the United States or familiar with the European scene.

This is not the end of the discussion on territorial cohesion. Much will depend on the rapidly changing currents of European politics. In particular, the budget deal referred to above was realized only by means of the promise of a fundamental discussion of wholesale reforms starting in 2008. Cohesion policy is the second largest item, next to the EU's Common Agricultural Policy. At present, the planning experts concerned are scrambling to formulate arguments for territorial cohesion policy to be factored into the equation. The hope is that this publication will clarify some of the deeper underlying issues by articulating the relationship of territorial cohesion to the European model of society, elusive though the concept may sometimes seem.

Andreas Faludi
Delft, The Netherlands
July 2006

Chapter 1

The European Model of Society

ANDREAS FALUDI

> Europeanization is fascinating as an alternative to the American way, not the least to Americans critical of America.
> —ULRICH BECK,
> "An Empire of Law and Consensus," *International Politics*, 2005

The absence of large-scale planning in the United States stands in contrast with Europe and its "bold plans and investments designed to integrate the economies of and reduce the economic disparities between Member States and regions, and to increase the competitiveness of the continent in global markets" (Carbonell and Yaro 2005, 1). At a meeting in February 2005 of the Green/European Foreign Alliance group in the European Parliament, the American public policy analyst Jeremy Rifkin even saw the European vision of the future as "quietly eclipsing the American Dream" (EuActive 2005b), and the British foreign policy analyst Mark Leonard (2005) pointed out why Europe would run the twenty-first century.

Is there a specifically European model of society? At the informal meeting of the European Council of Heads of State and Government of the European Union member states at Hampton Court in October 2005, the issue was discussed. In his position paper, the Belgian economics professor André Sapir (2005) claimed that there is not one European model but four, and in his evaluation of the models' efficiency and equality, he found that only the Nordic model—everybody's darling at present—scored high on both criteria.

Sapir discussed practical arrangements, but the European model is also a normative concept standing for moderating the pursuit of economic growth and competitiveness with concerns about social welfare and equity; sustainability and governance also are factored in for good measure. These concerns overlap with those articulated under the flag of territorial cohesion such as equity, competitiveness, sustainability, and good governance (Faludi

2005, 5). The concept of territorial cohesion is found in Article 16 of the Treaty establishing the European Community on services of general economic interest (Official Journal 2002). The Commission of the European Communities (the European Commission) links such services to the European model of society (Berrod 2003). But the Convention on the Future of Europe has gone beyond this linkage, proposing territorial cohesion as one of the objectives of the European Union (EU) on a par with economic and social cohesion. After all, "people should not be disadvantaged by wherever they happen to live or work in the Union" (CEC 2004a, 27). Territorial cohesion also relates to the Lisbon Strategy under which the EU has set itself the goal—now receding into the future—of "becoming the most competitive and dynamic knowledge-based economy in the world" (European Council 2000; see also Faludi and Waterhout 2005 and chapters 3 and 6 in this volume). This Lisbon Strategy aims to achieve sustainable economic growth, with more and better jobs, greater social cohesion, and respect for the environment.

Reconciling competitiveness and equity has already been central to the European model as conceived by Jacques Delors, president of the European Commission from 1985 to 1995, but the meaning of the European model remains contested. Recognizing the variety of relevant arrangements, Hemerijck and Ferrera (2004, 249) nevertheless see a common approach "built around a solidaristic commitment that society should not abandon those who fail. . . . Institutionally, the model is marked by high degrees of interest organization and comprehensive negotiation between governments and social partners over conflicts of interest. Patterns of social partnership based on trust encourage social capital to overcome particularistic interests."

Other authors emphasize diversity. Esping-Andersen (2002, 25) thinks it is "fruitless to contemplate a single design for all nations even if they face similar problems. . . . [A]ny realistic move towards common objectives must presume that such, if accepted will be adapted to national practice." Even so, the European model is playing a prominent role in the struggle over the development of the EU, in particular where Europe rejects the U.S. model. As Portugal's secretary of state for European affairs, Francesco Seixas da Costa, said in the European Parliament in 2000, "We are not sure that the American model, which is a radical model, one of deep injustices, one which has introduced factors of great social injustice and great marginalization and exclusion, is the model for the future. We do not want this model for Europe" (as quoted by Martin and Ross 2004, 326).

Indeed, the outcomes of the French and Dutch referendums that stopped ratification of the Treaty establishing a Constitution for Europe in its tracks are said to have stemmed in part at least from the fear that the constitution does not do justice to the European model (Lamy 2005; Lang and Majkowska 2005; Ricard-Nihoul 2005), but perhaps one should not make too much of this observation. Harvard scholar Andrew Moravcsik has commented wryly that engaging European citizens "will not necessarily create rational (let alone supportive) debate, because those with intense preferences about the EU tend to be its opponents" (as quoted by Boucher 2005, 7).

Taking Sides on the European Model

Advocates of the European model wish to strengthen the EU's powers to match the entrenched market-making policies such as removing barriers to free trade. Others see little reason to go beyond the creation of a level playing field. This "ultraliberal" view is often associated with Britain, regarded by many Europeans as "a virtual Trojan Horse in Europe"; the "more *dirigiste* attempt to create a new European order" is associated with France (Siedentop 2000, 140, 151). The issue has erupted around the European Constitution and the "Financial Perspectives 2007–2013," the multiannual budget of the EU (Menon and Riseborough 2005; on the EU budget, see Begg 2005 and chapter 6 in this volume).

According to Siedentop (2000, 156), the ultraliberal view forgets that any truly liberal capitalist government "will always have to address itself to social arrangements which impede mobility, both social and geographical. . . . The creation of a single European market implies, therefore, coordinated state action to foster reasonable equality of opportunity." Delors, too, thought the "*laissez-faire* approaches of Anglo-Saxon liberalism missed an essential matter. Markets existed within specific broader 'models of society' which moralized individuals and structured preferences" (Ross 1995, 46). Not concerned with the EU, Etzioni (1990, 182) makes the same point: "The question hence, is how to provide a context that is strong enough to contain competition but not so powerful to undermine it." Esping-Andersen (1990, 14–15) describes this point of view as the institutional approach, insisting "that any effort to isolate the economic from social and political institutions will destroy human society. The economy must be embedded in social communities in order for it to survive." Hemerijck and Ferrera (2004, 249–250) claim that, in fact, the European model contributes to competitiveness in that it "can reduce uncertainty, mitigate social conflict, and enhance adjustment capacity and readiness to accept change, bear more risks, acquire specialized skills, and pursue investment opportunities" (see chapter 3 in this volume).

This notion of a humane social order based on a mixed economy, civilized labor relations, the welfare state, and a commitment to social justice has its roots in the Social Democrat–Christian Democrat mainstream of continental European politics. Indeed, the

> conviction that European capitalist societies both were and ought to be different was shared by the mainstream. It was also the core of the political project to which Delors had devoted most of his life. In it societies were more than markets, citizenship more than consumption, and government

more than an economic traffic squad. People belonged to moralized collectivities which negotiated with one another for the good of all. Citizenship involved solidarity with others. Government, beyond stimulating economic activity to provide welfare, should craft a wide range of public goods, not only because of market failures and "externalities," but in response to demands for solidarity. (Ross 1995, 46)

This view is in contrast to the neoliberalism of, for example, former British prime minister Margaret Thatcher, who quipped that she did not know society, only individuals. Her view is an individualistic one. Individualism is one of the principles that, according to Huntington (2005, 41), constitute the "American Creed." The ultraliberal charge against the European model is that with its emphasis on welfare it is costly, among other reasons, because it does not give incentives for people, especially those at the lower end of the labor market, to work and is thus detrimental to competitiveness. A Swedish report—quoted by Republicans with glee during the U.S. election campaign of 2004—puts the American competitive advantage in stark relief (Bergström and Gidehag 2004). It found that only tiny Luxembourg in the EU could rival the richest of the American states in terms of gross domestic product (GDP) per capita. The authors admit that GDP is a crude measure that misses the output of the black economy, which is said to be significant in Europe's high-tax states. GDP also overlooks the value of leisure or a healthy environment or the way in which prosperity is spread across a society. Still, higher GDP per capita allows Americans to spend $9,700 more a year than Europeans on cars, TVs, computers, and other goods.

Exchange rate changes make such comparisons difficult, according to Haseler (2004, 70–71). His claim is that "by 2002, a rough calculation would place the per capita incomes of Luxembourg, Denmark, the Netherlands, and Sweden slightly ahead of the USA, those of the reunited Germany, France, the UK, Belgium, and Finland at roughly equal, and the rest lower." Esping-Andersen (2002, 11) casts more light on the comparison of incomes by pointing out that the average American is likely to spend more on health care than do Europeans. This only goes to show that such comparisons are difficult to make. While otherwise defending the U.S. record, Huntington (2005, 30–31) admits that "more Americans . . . work longer hours, have shorter vacations, get less in unemployment, disability, and retirement benefits, and retire later, than people in comparable societies." Indeed, the fact is that according to "'quality of life' indicators used by the UN Development Programme . . . all the EU countries rank extremely highly, alongside the US and Japan. And in the UN's Human Development Index . . . the EU countries also do extremely well" (Haseler 2004, 71).

Rifkin (2004, 71) duly mentions the reasons given by economists for Europe's alleged poor performance as "the governments' inflexible labor policies, anti-entrepreneurial biases, overtaxation, and burdensome welfare programs—so-called 'Euroschlerosis,'" but he points out that economists forget that America's recent economic growth has not come without a steep price tag in the form of record consumer and government debt. Similarly, Schubert and Bouzon (2005, 33) offer the reminder that "Europe . . . has a positive financial balance sheet with respect to its development. Both the external (balance of payments) and internal balances (public finances) are good. . . . While the US, in contrast, has recorded higher economic growth in recent years, its growth has come at the cost of financial sustainability." Todd (2003, 179) is even more scathing: "The American system is no longer able to provide for its own population. More seriously from a European perspective, the constant attempts to foist the liberal model onto the strongly rooted and state-centred societies of the Old World is in the process of blowing them apart. . . ." Indeed, some, not only in France where Todd comes from, but also in the rest of Europe, see the American system as a menace to European ways of doing things.

The magnitude of the actual differences between European social and political thought and that of the United States is, however, a moot point. As Peyrony points out in chapter 4 of this volume, Henri de Saint-Simon, a supporter of the colonies in the American Revolution, was greatly impressed by the fledgling United States. Moreover, ever since the writings of political observer Alexis de Tocqueville, Europeans have drawn inspiration from American political thought and practice. Siedentop (2000, 199) even asserts that "the universalism of the Declaration of Independence and the Constitution . . . captures the character of European civilization more successfully perhaps than any political document that Europe itself has produced." Finally, in contemplating the future of Europe, Haseler (2004, x) draws on American federal history, because "the basic similarities are too striking to be set aside . . . [:] a continent-wide system, similar issues of federal-state relations, similar population size, similar level of economic and cultural development, similar ethnic divisions and, notwithstanding recent divergences . . . similar ideology and values."

Based on these and other similarities, the American judge Mark C. Christie (2005) holds up the "Madisonian federal model" for Europe to follow. Indeed, when preparing for the Convention on the Future of Europe, former French president Valéry Giscard d'Estaing went to Washington to study the history of the U.S. Constitution (Norman 2003), and at the opening of the Convention on the Future of Europe he stated in a reference to the events of 1787 that the convention was "Philadelphia." Likewise, the drafters of the U.S. Constitution drew on the European Enlightenment, and so Europe and the United States have much in common. In fact, the Oxford historian Timothy Garton Ash (2004) points out that the differences between America and Europe are less than one may be inclined to think and that the two have a joint interest in promoting the values of the free world.

Further complicating matters is the complexity of the political land-scape of the United States as pointed out by Ash (2004, 67). Europeans may be at odds with the current U.S. administration, but there is passionate opposition to it from within an increasingly polarized United States as well. Reacting to statements made by the U.S. political analyst Robert Kagan (2003) about Americans being from Mars and Europeans from Venus, Reid (2004) and Rifkin (2004) invoke the European model as a wake-up call for America. They ventilate that ultimately its "soft" power will prevail over the "hard" power of the United States, and European authors claiming to have deep sympathies for the United States but also misgivings about its current course—authors such as Haseler (2004) and Todd (2003)—agree. Siedentop (2000, 183–184) even suggests a kind of "Marshall Plan in reverse" that would reinforce American idealism to help the "old Northeastern Establishment in the United States to adjust to the movement of population and wealth South and West, while defending European values against excessive straying of American attention towards the Pacific basin."

Yet in fact the European model is being invoked against the United States, with the French leading the way. French support for European arrangements "has always been accompanied by arguments and rhetoric designed to establish that only by organizing itself can Europe contain American influence" (Siedentop 2000, 171). Superficially, the aversion is to hamburgers and Hollywood as symbols of global capitalism and its reckless-ness toward people and their livelihoods, but also toward nature, cultural heritage, and regional identity. As a French chief planner has said, Euro-peans are rooted in the soil. They are not footloose, as are "the much more nomadic peoples of the North American Continent" (Guigou 2001, 4; see also Todd 2003, 178). Huntington (2005, 50) confirms that the "manifesta-tions of territorial identity are weak or missing in America." According to this author, Americans have generally not developed attachments to particular localities, nor have they linked themselves as a people with any particular national site or, to the same extent as other peoples, identified themselves with their overall territory. In chapters 2 and 4 of this volume, however, Robert and Peyrony demonstrate that territorial roots are impor-tant to Europeans. Resisting the decline of territorial integrity stemming from the migration foisted on them by economic disruptions is one of the rationales of French-style and, as far as the French are concerned, European planning as well.

Because of these roots of Europeans in their soil, it is not surprising that, as Robert claims in chapter 2, food plays a critical role in defining European culture and identity. By way of contrast, "Americans have a diffi-cult time understanding the close cultural relationships Europeans have toward rural life, farming practices, food cultivation, processing and consumption," which is one reason why Europe objects to genetically manipulated food (Rifkin 2004, 321). Rifkin (2004, 332) also claims that almost everyone he knows in Europe "among the professional and business classes has some small second home in the country somewhere—a dacha usually belonging to the family for generations." He thinks that this way of life helps to explain support for organic farming and sustainable development. Todd contends similarly that the deepest divergence between Europe and the United States is that European (and Japanese) societies have evolved from the labor of generations of miserable peasants experiencing wealth only belatedly. He goes on to observe:

> All of these societies maintain as part of their genetic code, as it were, an instinctive comprehension of the notion of economic equilibrium. On the level of moral practice one associates it with the notions of work and compensation, on the level of accounting with the notions of production and consumption.
>
> American society, on the other hand, is the recent outcome of a highly successful colonial experience but one not tested by time—it developed over three centuries, thanks to the importation of literate workers to a world rich in minerals and other natural resources, and agriculturally productive, thanks to its virgin soil. America seems to have understood that its success stems from a process of one-sided exploitation and expenditure of wealth that it did not create.
>
> The strong understanding that Europeans, the Japanese, or any other people of Eurasia have about the necessity of an ecological balance and of a commercial balance is the outcome of a long peasant history. . . . America has always grown by playing out its soils, wasting its oil, and looking abroad for the people it needed to do its work. (Todd 2003, 177)

Support for global agreements such as the Kyoto Protocol is part of the same rhetoric, as is support for the United Nations. The discussion between the "unilateralist" United States and the "multilateralist" European Union has reached a stage at which there is concern about how to manage their mutual relations. Be that as it may, in Europe's dealings with the United States the rhetoric of the European model is potent. In internal European discussions, however, it is less evident that a European model exists. Europe is diverse. Indeed, the opening sentence of the European Spatial Development Perspective reads: "The characteristic territorial feature of the European Union (EU) is its cultural variety, concentrated in a small area" (CEC 1999, 7). And Article 151.4 of the Treaty establishing the European Community cites preserving diversity as a Community concern. Thus in his Hampton Court position paper, Sapir (2005) identified four European models. One can argue, however, that synthesis is achieved by means of the process in which diverse models go through the sieve of European politics. For example, it is said that the European social model is not an extrapolation of the models of the EU member states; "rather, it is rooted in a set of constitutional policy principles, works with a floor of social guarantees, operates a regime that forces national systems to communicate with each other and pursues a set of wider aspirations" (de la Porte and Pochet 2002, 290).

This process relates to how European arrangements come about. Under the "'Community method," the Commission has the exclusive prerogative to submit proposals for legislative acts to the Council of the European Union (also known as the Council of Ministers) and subsequently the European Parliament for approval, after which they become European law. Naturally, before all this comes to pass much mutual learning is required. European Commission president Jacques Delors was acutely aware of this learning process and is the subject of the next section.

The Influence of Jacques Delors

In her book-length examination of Jacques Delors, Drake (2000) demonstrates the continuity of Delors's thinking. She paints a complex but attractive picture. Rather than seeking power, Delors invoked a "working model of society in which an enlightened (because educated) citizenry would fulfil its potential within rational (understandable, accessible and transparent) democratic structures." He was "far more at home in the language of rational and expert diagnosis, prognosis and remedy than with the rhetoric of political promise" (Drake 2000, 26, 29). Likewise, Haseler (2004, 78) found him to be a "technocrat with a broad historical vision." These observations call up the Saint-Simonian tradition in French politics, which Peyrony mentions in chapter 4 of this volume.

In the late 1950s, while Delors was laboring in the French Planning Commissariat, a "blueprint for a society began to take shape in his own mind and in the networks he was beginning to weave." Although his political home was on the left, he became a member of the political cabinet of the Gaullist prime minister Jacques Chaban-Delmas with responsibility for, among other things, transforming industrial relations, a duty that "chimed well with . . . his desire to create and reinstate the role of social 'intermediaries' such as the trade union movements" (Drake 2000, 35, 38). It was at this point that he began to think in terms of a "new society."

In 1979 Delors was elected to the European Parliament, and in the early 1980s he served as French finance minister. This service "represented a continuation of his activity and reputation as a 'moderniser' on the French left, acting within liberal capitalism, and standing aside from the class struggle of the traditional left." However, his

> experience of government office only served to underline the contradictions that he had always experienced between the desire to change society, and the constraints inherent in the political means of doing so, and in his own temperament. His forty years of professional life in France had been heavily skewed towards roles where he hoped to bring about change through influence in the form of ideas, expertly researched, effectively

communicated to the appropriate channels, and delivered by others. The flaw in this formula in France was that his ideas were often distorted or dropped in the political process. . . The same formula, in the very different setting of the EC, was to meet with greater success, before indirectly contributing to similar sorts of political constraints. (Drake 2000, 44–45)

Indeed, Delors "went to Brussels as . . . a 'rational European,' a pragmatist predisposed towards the neo-functionalist analysis of European integration, tempered with idealistic if not abstract hopes." Some suspected him to have arrived with a ready-made plan for a European society. However, in his maiden speech to the European Parliament Delors recognized that both pragmatism and imaginative vision had their limits and that a combination of both was required (Drake 2000, 46, 99). He also began to refer to Europe rather than to the European Community, presenting it as a "polity in the making." And this may continue to be the case now that ratification of the constitution aiming to finally settle the issues in European integration is being called into question (Milton and Keller-Noëllet 2005, 114).

Pragmatism and vision were Delors's hallmarks. After watching Delors's political cabinet in action, the American specialist on French politics George Ross observed that Delors and his Commission "were practiced in scanning their environment, seeking things that were malleable, avoiding those which were implacable, and moving step by step towards the goal of a sustainable 'European model of society'" (Ross 1995, 11). The feeling was, however, that Europe needed to take dramatic steps to become more competitive—a theme slated to remain on the agenda. At the same time, Europe ought not to open itself up to the full floodtides of the international market. Instead, steps should be taken "to make the Community into a regional economic bloc whose synergies and economies of scale would stimulate European innovation. The fruits of new economic successes could then be directed towards perpetuating the 'European model of society.' Europe would then stand—practically—as a humane combination of institutions and ideas that could stimulate market success while simultaneously promoting social solidarities designed to ameliorate the harshness of market relations" (Ross 1995, 4).

This viewpoint implied that the European Community had to become like a state. And, in fact, Delors was leaning toward a form of European federalism. Although Delors's spectacular achievement was the Single Market, he saw no contradiction between pursuing competitiveness and enhancing the European model of society. However, the Community would have to take on tasks normally performed by states. In describing this thinking, Ross invokes the metaphor of the Russian doll first used by François Lamoureux, Delors's deputy *chef de cabinet*. Accordingly, the Single Market would make people realize that additional measures were needed, which is why adherents of the European model wish to give more powers to the EU. These measures would include doubling the Structural Funds and thereby turning regional or cohesion policy into serious business, while bringing this policy at the same time under a unique "multi-governance regime" (Hooghe and Marks 2001). Cohesion policy is part of the state building that, according to this dialectic, follows from market integration—which is why it is anathema to ultraliberals.

These elements and the rest of the "Delors package" took shape in the wake of the Single European Act of 1986. Just after the package was made public, Delors said in the European Parliament,

> It is self-evident that a large market without internal frontiers could not be completed or operated properly unless the Community had instruments . . . enabling it to avoid imbalances interfering with competitiveness and inhibiting the growth of the Community as a whole. . . . [T]he ship of Europe needs a helmsman. . . . The large market without internal frontiers cannot, by itself, properly be responsible for the three main functions of economic policy: the quest for greater stability . . . [,] the optimum allocation of resources to obtain the benefit of economies of scale and to stimulate innovation and competitiveness and the balanced distribution of wealth allowing for individual merit. (As quoted by Ross 1995, 41)

In the early 1990s, after the signing of the Treaty on European Union (Maastricht Treaty), Delors presented a second package, Growth, Competitiveness, Employment (CEC 1993). The first Danish vote on the Maastricht Treaty had been negative, the French had accepted the treaty only with an almost imperceptible majority—far smaller than the percentage rejecting the Treaty establishing a Constitution for Europe in 2005—and the United Kingdom was still under the Conservatives with their Euro-skeptic wing. As the title suggests, Delors's second package, also in the form of a white paper, focused on employment. Anticipating the birth of the EU's Lisbon Strategy in March 2000, it identified the root of the employment problem: competitiveness, or rather the lack thereof. A remarkable aspect of this white paper was the launch of the Trans-European Networks (TENs), in the eyes of many a key to achieving territorial cohesion. However, for this initiative, like others, the member states refused to give the Community the necessary instruments.

Delors did succeed, though, in other measures—above all, the European Economic and Monetary Union (EMU). In his 1995 book, Ross described the evolution of this policy, and a more recent book coauthored with Andrew Martin builds on experiences with administering EMU since its introduction. According to Martin and Ross (2004, 1–2), the European Central Bank (ECB) has more autonomy than any other EU institution, whereas authority over welfare state and employment relation institutions remains in the hands of the member states. At the same time, there is "an EU polity that sharply separates authority over macroeconomic policy from that governing social models. The two domains are highly interdependent, however. Macroeconomic policy significantly affects the burdens on and resources available to social policy."

This relationship between domains is not unlike the relationship between the Single Market policies aiming to create a level playing field, on which the EU is strong, and the market-correcting policies, on which the EU is weak (Scharpf 1999; 2002). Thus, "the question is whether the macroeconomic foundations of the European social model will be maintained" (Martin and Ross 2004, 2). The theory is that the EMU will boost growth and thereby ensure the survival of the model, but in fact the EMU's dedication to price stability may keep employment low. The outcome is not predetermined, however. "National politics of social model change may refract the pressures generated by EMU in directions that preserve high degrees of social protection and labor rights" (Martin and Ross 2004, 3).

In their conclusions, Martin and Ross paint two scenarios: one in which the Lisbon Strategy is succeeding and one in which it is not, leading to a "war of attrition" of the ECB against the European social model. However, the authors believe that "most Europeans are determined to stand by the social models that they built earlier. . . . But the central threats remain continuing low growth and high unemployment. . . . It therefore cannot be ruled out that these will create conditions . . . that would sap the European models by stealth" (Martin and Ross 2004, 329–330). In the end, then, Delors's European model may fall victim to his other brainchild, the EMU.

Finally, it is impossible to understand Delors without taking into account his French roots. Siedentop (2000) credits the French élite with a vision of a Europe modeled on France—a vision it pursues with great effectiveness. Siedentop is concerned about the accumulation of power in Brussels, but he does not see it as the result of conspiracy, but rather "a matter of habit and attitude induced by the powerful administrative machine at the disposal of the French élite. When the French executive has decided that it wants something, it gets its way" (Siedentop 2000, 107). As Haseler (2004, 133) points out, "French governance has kept a meritocratic brake on mass democracy."

Yet Siedentop acknowledges that there have been changes in French political culture. The reforms under way represent "an institutional move away from the fabled tutorship of the state" (Siedentop 2000, 111). However, "the process of decentralization initiated in France . . . testifies to what the French have long considered a weakness of their own bureaucratic and *dirigiste* form of politics. It has been a conscious attempt to create a wider political class and thereby give French public institutions a deeper anchor in local opinion and local interests—in fact, to promote the kind of intermediate associations that would work against the disjuncture of élite opinion and popular opinion which has, at frequent intervals since 1789, led to revolutionary upheaval" (Siedentop 2000, 129).

An example of decentralization is the insistence on stakeholder participation in French regional development policy and the influence such
participation has had on EU regional policy (Faludi and Peyrony 2001;
Faludi 2004). However, creating a wider, more open political class takes
time. Meanwhile, the insider joke is that Brussels is the last refuge of the
French centralizers, the *Jacobins*: "The slow work of decentralization in
France may already look like ominous writing on the wall to the French
élite. How tempting, then, to turn Brussels and the European Union into a
refuge for *dirigiste* habits and attitudes which may at last have had their day
in France itself" (Siedentop 2000, 143). "Over-integration" has contributed
to the draining away of idealism from European integration (Siedentop
2000, 220), a reminder of the growing unease, not to say skepticism, about
European integration leading to the rejection of the Treaty establishing a
Constitution for Europe in 2005.

The European Model After Delors

After Delors, European leaders had no stomach for another Commission
president with his flair. But his successor, Jacques Santer from Luxembourg,
and the Santer Commission resigned over allegations of cronyism, to be
followed by a Commission under former and again present Italian prime
minister Romano Prodi. During his term, the European Council adopted
the Lisbon Strategy. When it fell on stony ground, Prodi set up various
panels to find ways of resuscitating it, which was, according to Peuziat
(2004), a common strategy of Commission presidents. The rest of this
section describes briefly the findings of these panels.

The Sapir Report

In July 2002, Romano Prodi appointed a High Level Study Group to review
EU-level economic instruments for their suitability for economic governance in the context of enlargement. The Belgian professor of economics
André Sapir—the same one who later wrote the position paper for Hampton Court—was asked to chair the group.

The group's report, which came out in July 2003, claims that the Single
Market has been a success, the remit of competition policy has widened,
and, even more remarkable, the European Economic and Monetary Union
has resulted in the 12 (as from 1 January 2007, when Slovenia will have
joined, 13) member states having the same currency, the euro (Sapir et al.
2004). Low inflation and lower budget deficits also have been achieved, but
those achievements have been accompanied by lower growth. Moreover,
the context has changed. Rather than economies of scale and an industrial
structure dominated by large firms with stable markets and long-term
employment patterns, today's world requires greater mobility, more retrain-
ing, greater flexibility of labor markets, more external finance (in particular

equity finance), and higher investment in both R&D and higher education—themes that are receiving greater attention in the EU.

The report also points out that the present combination of low growth
and high public expenditure is no recipe for success. Growth is of para-
mount importance for the sustainability of the European model. If anything, developments in demography and technology and globalization are
increasing the demand for social protection. And enlargement poses additional challenges. The income gap between the new member states and the
current EU is much larger than during any other round of enlargement.
Convergence, then, is more than ever the key to success. The new member
states have high levels of human capital, but they also have a legacy of old
industries, environmental damage, and poor public administration.

The report recommends transforming the EU system of economic
policy making and of modes of delivery. In that vein, the report also addresses
transport infrastructure requirements. In commenting on the report, Pelkmans and Casey (2004) point out that the Trans-European Networks are a
responsibility (a competence in EU parlance) shared by the Community and
the member states. But the result falls short of expectations. They conclude

> that the division of powers on cross-border infrastructure is wrong in the
> EU. The costs of a lopsided assignment . . . are very high, be it for the
> patchwork of "national" railways, the great inhibition of member states to
> invest in true transit systems of motorways with a European network in
> mind, the cross-border interconnectors in electricity and air traffic control
> networks. . . . The "need to act in common" is very strong for cross-border
> infrastructure . . . and bilateral cooperation is necessarily inappropriate in
> those cases where "missing links" ought to be identified in a European
> (transit and network) perspective. (Pelkmans and Casey 2004, 16)

Pelkmans and Casey also regard the argument—relevant to the conduct of
cohesion policy—that the future convergence fund should be allocated to
countries, not regions, as convincing. They view richer countries obtaining,
as they do under current arrangements, financial assistance from the
Community coffers which they have filled with their own contributions in
the first instance under *juste retour* considerations (Begg 2005) as a useless
form of pumping around money and castigate the swiftness with which
Commissioner for Regional Policy Michel Barnier and his colleague from
agriculture, Franz Fischler, condemned the recommendations as "a pure
case of protection of turf and/or power, rather than the outcome of a reflection on what would be best for EU growth in the longer run" (Pelkmans and
Casey 2004, 21). Regional representatives have criticized the Sapir Report
as well. In fact, an impressive coalition has rolled into action (Peuziat 2004).
Regional and local authorities recognize that not only will they benefit from
an EU cohesion policy, but, because of the insistence on their involvement

as stakeholders, such a policy will also enhance their standing in relation to the national governments.[1]

The Strauss-Kahn Report

This report is different from the much better known Sapir Report. The Prodi Commission established a roundtable, A Sustainable Project for Tomorrow's Europe, to examine the European model of development. The roundtable was chaired by Dominique Strauss-Kahn, former finance minister in the French Socialist government of Lionel Jospin. The report of the roundtable, issued in 2004, insists that a shared European model of society exists and that it is based on the inviolability of human rights, the humanist model of man, a view of culture as first and foremost an instrument for human development and not as a commodity, a model of sustainable development, and a multilateralist vision of the international order. The report recognizes that these concepts are not unique, but asserts that the European model expresses them in unique ways. It points out that Europe is thus a "community of values," but admits that it "is not yet fully formed: like the sense of national belonging . . . feeling European is a sense which is under construction. The community will be consolidated by the creation of a political Europe. . . . [A] political Europe and a European identity each stimulate the growth of the other. But the principle is clear: there can be no political Europe without a European community of values; a political Europe cannot be created unless a European people emerges" (CEC 2004b, 33).

This process is under way, and it is gradual. However, the Strauss-Kahn Report points out that because "there is no political embodiment of the European model by the European Union, the model is not properly defended." Thus, it is necessary to build a "political Europe": "the European Union is out to recreate a virtuous circle for the endangered European model. To do this, the report suggests changing paradigm and adding to the current approach of remedial action one of creating new opportunities. . . . The European model of justice now has to do more than simply correct unwanted effects caused by society . . . : it must attack problems at the root" (CEC 2004b, 16, 17).

To this end, the EU must be given a political arm: political institutions, public life, and a feeling of belonging. However, there "can be no democracy without a *demos*, without a European people" (CEC 2004b, 19). The report then boldly claims that, although Europeans are not always aware of it, this *demos* exists for the simple reason that it shares a model of society. This chimes well with Haseler's argument that a "European superpower would . . . offer a different western model for both the economy and

---

[1] The Sapir Report was the subject of a policy debate in the October issue of *Regional Studies*, with Hall (2005) presenting the Commission's case for the continuation of a comprehensive regional policy.

society. Europe's so-called 'sclerotic' welfare societies, so criticized by Wall Street . . . are proving more stable than the gyrating, raw, free-market American model. And Europe's social model—of capitalism with a social vision—could become the basis for a continent-wide ideology, a kind of 'European dream' every bit as successful in inspiring future Europeans as was the more individualistic 'American dream' in inspiring Americans" (Haseler 2004, 5). Elsewhere, Haseler (2004, 126) argues that Europe is breaking with the American *idée fixe* about the free market. What the Strauss-Kahn Report does not say—but Haseler does—is that America may thus serve as the "other," allowing a strong European identity to form.

The Reflection Group

The Prodi Commission also formed a group to "reflect on the role that the most deep-rooted values of our shared historical background could play as the binding element of fellowship and solidarity"; it also referred to the "fundamental values at the core of the European venture" (Biedenkopf, Gemerek, and Michalski 2004, 2). The Polish philosopher Krzysztof Michalski who chaired the group talked as well about solidarity and Europe's self-image and how these factors influence Europe's role in the world.

The group concluded that the inspiration behind European integration had been lost and that it was now being identified with economic integration—the ultraliberal version of Europe. However, as a source of inspiration economic integration was "incapable of substituting for the political forces that originally propelled European integration and cohesion" (Biedenkopf, Gemerek, and Michalski 2004, 6). The Lisbon Strategy, too, could not "establish the internal cohesion that is necessary for the European Union; nor, indeed, can economic forces alone provide cohesion for any political identity. To function as a viable and vital polity, the European Union needs a firmer foundation" (Biedenkopf, Gemerek, and Michalski 2004, 6).

After a discussion of the role of religion, the group's report concludes with reflections on Europe's role in the world. This report has received less attention than its predecessors and in particular the Kok Report.

The Kok Report

In 2003 the EU High Level Employment Task Force chaired by Wim Kok, a former Dutch Labour prime minister, published a report with the telling title *Jobs, Jobs, Jobs* (CEC 2003). A year later, at the invitation of the European Council, the Commission established another High Level Group, once again chaired by Kok, to "identify measures which together form a consistent strategy for the European economies to achieve the Lisbon objectives and targets" (CEC 2004c, 5). The group presented its report as the Barroso Commission took office in late 2004. The report pointed out that events had not helped the Lisbon Strategy, but that the European

Union and its members states had "clearly themselves contributed to slow progress by failing to act on much of the Lisbon Strategy with sufficient urgency . . . due to an overloaded agenda, poor coordination and conflicting priorities" (CEC 2004c, 6; see also Milton and Keller-Nöellet 2005, 136). Nevertheless, it found the Lisbon Strategy to be even more urgent than before, because economic growth and employment provide the means to sustain social cohesion and environmental sustainability. In turn, social cohesion and environmental sustainability properly conceived contribute to higher growth and employment.

Like previous reports, the Kok Report endorses the European model, but it expresses concern about its sustainability. In an attempt to assuage those concerned about alleged ultraliberal tendencies, the report states: "The Lisbon Strategy is not an attempt to become a copy-cat of the US—far from it. Lisbon is about achieving Europe's vision of what it wants to be and what it wants to keep in the light of increasing global competition, an ageing population and the enlargement. It has the broad ambition of solidarity with the needy, now and in the future. To realise this ambition, Europe needs more growth and more people in work" (CEC 2004c, 12). The report also reiterates the Sapir Report's concern about the state of infrastructure:

> Europe's level playing field remains cluttered with infrastructural obstacles. For too many companies, accessing areas of the internal market on the other side of the continent is effectively impossible. For others, the non-availability of broadband, either at accessible prices or at all, is an equally significant structural disadvantage compared with competitors elsewhere.
>
> More urgently than ever in the light of enlargement, Europe's internal market needs to be connected. Many of the new Member States are not only on the periphery of the internal market geographically; they are also in desperate need of expanded and modernised infrastructures. (CEC 2004c, 27)

The Kok Report also addresses environmental concerns: "Well-thought-out environmental policies provide opportunities for innovation, create new markets, and increase competitiveness through greater resource efficiency and new investment opportunities. In this sense environment policies can help achieve the core Lisbon Strategy objectives of more growth and jobs" (CEC 2004c, 35).

The report ends by addressing the delivery of the Lisbon Strategy. It points out that individual member states have made progress in one or more of its policy priority areas, but none has succeeded consistently across a broad front. The task is to develop national policies in each member state, supported by an appropriate European-wide framework, "and then to act in a more concerted and determined way. The European Commission must be prepared to report clearly and precisely on success and failure in each

Member State. National and European Union policies, including their budgets, must better reflect the Lisbon priorities" (CEC 2004c, 7).

As noted earlier, the Kok Report came out just as a new European Commission under José Manuel Durão Barroso, a former center-right Portuguese prime minister, was taking office. The European Council warmly recommended the report to Barroso.

The Barroso Commission

Once Barroso assumed office, Socialists in the European Parliament began to look on with dismay as the new Commission president formulated his strategy. During the Convention on the Future of Europe preparing the European Constitution, they had already vehemently defended the European social model. Now the Barroso Commission was said to have a liberal bias—liberal being a word with a distinctly different meaning than in the United States. The fear was that in an all-out effort to pursue the Lisbon Strategy, social and environmental concerns would receive short shrift. Elated by their success in forcing Barroso to withdraw his first proposed team of Commissioners, Socialists tabled a motion calling on him to uphold the European economic and social model. In the ensuing debate, echoing Sapir and Kok, as well as Delors, Barroso retorted that for the model to survive, the EU had to become more dynamic. At the same time, he assured Parliament that he did not want to throw the European model out of the window, but to modernize it—a claim that British prime minister Tony Blair also made in his speech before the European Parliament outlining the intentions of the U.K. presidency of the EU during the second half of 2005 (EuActive 2005b).

Meanwhile, the debate around the European model has become more heated in the wake of the revelation by the Barroso Commission that it intends to give priority to growth. Barroso claims that this priority is a short-term expedience. In doing so, he has invoked the metaphor of his three children. They are the economy, social Europe, and the environment. Each is equally close to his heart, but because the economy is in bad shape, he says it is natural for him to give more attention to the economy. The context for his invoking this metaphor was Barroso's presentation in early 2005 of a "Communication to the Spring European Council" reviewing progress on the Lisbon Strategy. After a review of past achievements, including a "unique participative social model," the communication, titled *Working Together for Growth and Jobs*, points out that progress on the Lisbon Strategy has been mixed at best, because there has not been enough delivery at the European and national levels (CEC 2005a, 4). However, it also points out member states

> need a dynamic economy to fuel our wider social and environmental ambitions. This is why the renewed Lisbon Strategy focuses on growth and jobs. In order to do this we must ensure that:

- *Europe is a more attractive place to invest and work*
- *Knowledge and innovation are the beating heart of European growth*
- *We shape the policies allowing our businesses to create more and better jobs.*
  (CEC 2005a, 5, emphasis in the original)

The communication hastens to clarify that making growth and jobs the immediate target "goes hand in hand with promoting social and environmental objectives. The Lisbon Strategy is an essential component of the overarching objective of sustainable development." The communication then adds for emphasis: "The Commission is fully committed to sustainable development and to modernising and advancing Europe's social model. Without more growth and jobs this will not be possible." It proposes giving Europe's actions more focus in order to mobilize support for change and to simplify and streamline "Lisbon governance": "There should be an integrated set of Lisbon 'guidelines' to frame Member State action, backed by only one report at EU level and only one report at national level presenting the progress made. This will significantly reduce the national reporting burden placed on Member States" (CEC 2005a, 6).

The communication then proposes that the Commission present a Lisbon Action Programme that integrates the existing Broad Economic Policy Guidelines and Employment Guidelines within a new three-year economic and employment cycle. In addition, member states would appoint a "Mr. or Ms. Lisbon" at the government level responsible for member states formulating their National Action Programmes within the framework proposed (CEC 2005a, 11–12).

The communication makes only passing reference to cohesion policy and to territorial cohesion. Territorial cohesion is not yet a recognized objective of the EU. Formal EU territorial cohesion policy will have to wait until ratification of the Treaty establishing a Constitution for Europe, a prospect that is now receding. However, economic and social cohesion are well-established concerns, and thus the Spring Council of Heads of State and Government insisted that cohesion policy be included in the remit of the Lisbon Strategy (European Council 2005a). Meanwhile, the Commission has outlined how cohesion policy will support the Lisbon Strategy (CEC 2005b), this against the backdrop of the Community financial framework for 2007–2013 (CEC 2004d). The European Council of December 2005 agreed with great difficulty on a reduced framework, but without any fundamental reform of either the Common Agricultural Policy (CAP) or the cohesion policy that some member states have worked toward (European Council 2005b).

It is clear that future cohesion policy will be conducted within the framework of "Lisbon governance." But only the future can tell whether territorial cohesion policy will be a major concern. The Commission makes little play of the policy, but it has insisted on including a third objective for future Structural Funds, European territorial cooperation, which would allow it to continue stimulating member states and regions to operate cross-border and transnational policies.

Meanwhile, the Eurobarometer—a kind of Gallup Poll—reports that the vast majority of EU citizens put the environment above growth. Thus, there is a groundswell of support for at least elements of the European model. Further evidence is the results of the French and, less clearly, the Dutch referendums on the constitution, where the desire to preserve a "social Europe" in the face of globalization was a factor contributing to its rejection. Yet this response may have been the wrong one, because, as Milton and Keller-Nöellet (2005, 122) show, the constitution would have preserved the balance between liberal economics and the European social model. But referendums have their own dynamics.

Conclusions: Implications for Territorial Cohesion Policy

Anyone concerned with European issues should take cognizance of the notion of a European model of society—as did the heads of state and government meeting informally at Hampton Court in October 2005. The position paper by André Sapir outlined for the heads of state and government the existence of four European models rather than one, but, somewhat in the vein of the Strauss-Kahn Report and the reflection group, the Commission in its contribution to the discussion claimed that "common European values underpin each of our social models. They are the foundations of our specific European approach to economic and social policies" (CEC 2005c, 4). The Commission then detailed the shared values: solidarity and cohesion, equal opportunities and the fight against discrimination, adequate health and safety in the workplace, universal access to education and health care, quality of life and quality in work, and sustainable development and the involvement of civil society. It also pointed out that European citizens have greater expectations than others of the state, that the European dimension reinforced national systems, and that there was a strong tradition of social dialogue and partnership. Thus, the European model operates as a normative concept. The Commission then documented the threats to this model, underlining Barroso's message of the status quo being no option, but this is not the place to rehash the argument.

On a different but related level, the European model is a conceptual, or perhaps rhetorical, device invoked in discussing European integration. In this sense it does exist, and whoever is concerned with European issues, including those involved in territorial cohesion policy, had better take cognizance. As noted in the introduction to this chapter, shared concerns are equity, competitiveness, sustainability, and good governance. Territorial cohesion balances them with a view toward how they become manifest on various spatial scales where stakeholders face each other for the simple reason that their interests overlap. With this being Europe, stakeholders may also share the same memories of, and attachments to, their environment. The European model as such is more abstract, but animated by the same moral convictions: that the market is not everything and that there are values beyond growth giving legitimacy to intervention by a strong but unobtrusive state "as the only way to create an environment (and food and drink) fit for humans" (Haseler 2004, 126). Neither territorial cohesion nor the European model can be sustained without such intervention.

References

Ash, T. G. 2004. *Free world: America, Europe, and the surprising future of the West*. New York: Random House.

Beck, U. 2005. An empire of law and consensus. *International Politics—Transatlantic Edition. (Special Issue).*

Begg, I. 2005. *Funding the European Union*. London: Federal Trust. http://www.fedtrust.co .uk/default.asp?groupid=0&search=\quot;Funding%20the%20EU\quot.

Bergström, F., and R. Gidehag. 2004. EU versus USA. Stockholm: Timbro. http://www .timbro.com/euvsusa/pdf/EU_vs_USA_English.pdf.

Berrod, F. 2003. Les services publiques à la européennes: Entre subsidiarité et politique de l'Union. *Revue en linge: Etudes Européennes.* http://www.etudes-europeennes.fr.

Biedenkopf, K., B. Geremek, and K. Michalski. 2004. *The spiritual and cultural dimension of Europe: Concluding remarks. Reflection Group initiated by the President of the European Commission.* Vienna/Brussels: Institute for Human Sciences. http://europa.eu.int/comm/ research/social-sciences/pdf/michalski_281004_final_report_en.pdf.

Boucher, S. 2005. *Democratising European democracy: Options for a quality inclusive and transnational deliberation.* Notre Europe Policy Papers No. 17. Paris: Notre Europe. http://www.notre-europe.asso.fr/IMG/pdf/Policy17-en.pdf.

Carbonell, A., and R. D. Yaro. 2005. American spatial development and the new megalopolis. *Land Lines* 17(2):1–4.

CEC —Commission of the European Communities. 1993. *Growth, competitiveness and employment: The challenges and ways forward into the 21st century.* Luxembourg: Office for Official Publications of the European Communities.

———. 1999. *European Spatial Development Perspective: Towards balanced and sustainable development of the territory of the EU.* Luxembourg: Office for Official Publications of the European Communities.

———. 2003. *Jobs, jobs, jobs: Creating more employment in Europe.* Luxembourg: Office for Official Publications of the European Communities.

———. 2004a. *A new partnership for cohesion: Convergence, competitiveness, cooperation. Third report on economic and social cohesion.* Luxembourg: Office for Official Publications of the European Communities.

———. 2004b. *Building a political Europe: 50 proposals for tomorrow's Europe. Report on the round table "A sustainable project for tomorrow's Europe" formed on the initiative of the President of the European Commission chaired by Dominique Strauss-Kahn.* Luxembourg: Office for Official Publications of the European Communities.

———. 2004c. *Facing the challenge: The Lisbon strategy for growth and employment. Report from the High Level Group chaired by Wim Kok.* Luxembourg: Office for Official Publications of the European Communities.

———. 2004d. *Proposal for a Council Regulation laying down general provisions on the European Regional Development Fund, the European Social Fund and the Cohesion Fund (presented by the Commission).* Luxembourg: Office for Official Publications of the European Communities.

———. 2005a. *Working together for growth and jobs: A new start for the Lisbon Strategy (communication to the spring European Council)*. Luxembourg: Office for Official Publications of the European Communities.

———. 2005b. *Cohesion policy in support of growth and jobs: Community Strategic Guidelines, 2007–2013 (communication from the Commission)*. Luxembourg: Office for Official Publications of the European Communities.

———. 2005c. *Communication from the Commission to the European Parliament, the Council, the European Economic and Social Committee and the Committee of the Regions: European values in the globalised world (contribution of the Commission to the October meeting of heads of state and government)*. Luxembourg: Office for Official Publications of the European Communities.

Christie, M. C. 2005. *Political integration in Europe and America: Towards a Madisonian model for Europe*. CEPS Policy Brief No 72. Brussels: Centre for European Policy Studies.

Drake, H. 2000. *Jacques Delors: Perspectives on a European leader*. London: Routledge.

Esping-Andersen, G. 1990. *The three worlds of welfare capitalism*. Princeton, NJ: Princeton University Press.

———. 2002. Towards the good society, once again? In *Why we need a new welfare state*, G. Esping-Andersen, D. Gallie, A. Hemerijck, and J. Myles, eds. Oxford: Oxford University Press.

Etzioni, A. 1990. *The moral dimension: Towards a new economics*. 2d ed. New York: Free Press.

EuActive. 2005a. European dream or Lisbon realities? 16 February. http://www.euractiv.com/Article?tcmuri=tcm:29-135531-16&type=News&_lang=EN&email=50473

———. 2005b. Blair to argue reform case before EP. 23 June. http://www.euractiv.com/Article?tcmuri=tcm:29-141351-16&type=News&_lang=EN&email=50473.

European Council. 2000. *Presidency conclusions*. Lisbon European Council, 23 and 24 March. http://ue.eu.int/ueDocs/cms_Data/docs/pressData/en/ec/00100-r1.en0.htm.

———. 2005a. *Presidency conclusions*. Brussels European Council, 22 and 23 March. http://ue.eu.int/ueD/cms_Data/docs/pressData/en/ec/84335.pdf.

———. 2005b. *Presidency conclusions*. Brussels European Council, 15 and 16 December. http://ue.eu.int/ueDocs/cms_Data/docs/pressData/en/ec/87642.pdf.

Faludi, A. 2004. Territorial cohesion: Old (French) wine in new bottles? *Urban Studies* 41(7):1349–1365.

———, ed. 2005. Territorial cohesion. Special issue, *Town Planning Review* 76(1):1–118.

Faludi, A., and J. Peyrony. 2001. The French pioneering role. In Regulatory competition and cooperation in European spatial planning, A. Faludi, ed., special issue, *Built Environment* 27(4):253–262.

Faludi, A., and B. Waterhout. 2005. The usual suspects: The Rotterdam Informal Ministerial Meeting on Territorial Cohesion. *Tijdschrift voor Economische en Sociale Geografie* 96(3):338–342.

Guigou, J.-L. 2001. Europe and territorial planning. In *Europe and its states: A geography*, A. Bailly and A. Frémont, eds. Paris: La documentation française.

Hall, R. 2005. The future of European regional policy: Issues surrounding "An Agenda for a Growing Europe." *Regional Studies* 39(7):966–971.

Haseler, S. 2004. *Super-state: The New Europe and its challenge to America*. London: I. B. Tauris.

Hemerijck, A., and M. K. Ferrera. 2004. Welfare reform in the shadow of EMU. In *Euros and Europeans: Monetary integration and the European model of society*, A. Martin and G. Ross, eds., 248-277. Cambridge: Cambridge University Press.

Hooghe, L., and G. Marks. 2001. *Multi-level governance and European integration*. New York and Oxford: Rowman and Littlefield.

Huntington, S. P. 2005. *Who are we? America's great debate*. London: Free Press.

Kagan, R. 2003. *Of paradise and power: America and Europe in the new world order*. New York: Knopf.

Lamy, P. 2005. What next? Le mot de Notre Europe. *Notre Europe*. http://www.notre
-europe.asso.fr/article.php3?id_article=802.

Lang, K.-O., and J. Majkowska. 2005. The Netherlands—Europe's new obstructionist?
SWP Comments (German Institute for International and Security Affairs). June. http://
www.swp-berlin.org/common/get_document.php?id=1323&PHPSESSID=970fea0d51
25867a86f70849efee08ec.

Leonard, M. 2005. *Why Europe will run the 21st century*. London: HarperCollins.

Martin, A., and G. Ross. 2004. EMU and the European social model. In *Euros and Europeans: Monetary integration and the European model of society*, A. Martin and G. Ross, eds.
Cambridge: Cambridge University Press.

Menon, A., and P. Riseborough. 2005. *The best laid plans: Britain's presidency and the Council
of the European Union*. Notre Europe Studies and Research No. 42. Paris: Notre Europe.
http://www.notre-europe.asso.fr/article.php3?id_article=811.

Milton, G., and J. Keller-Noëllet. 2005. *The European constitution: Its origins, negotiation and
meaning*. London: John Harper.

Norman, P. 2003. *The accidental constitution*. Brussels: EuroComment.

Official Journal of the European Communities. 2002. *Consolidated treaty establishing the
European Community*. 24 December. C 325. http://europa.eu.int/eur-lex/lex/en/treaties/
dat/12002E/pdf/12002E_EN.pdf.

Pelkmans, J., and J.-P. Casey. 2004. Can Europe deliver growth? The Sapir Report and
beyond. *Policy Briefing* 45. Brussels: Centre for European Policy Studies. http://shop
.ceps.be/BookDetail.php?item_id=1092.

Peuziat, J.-P. 2004. *La politique régionale de l'Union européenne: Entre expertise et réforme*.
Paris: L'Harmattan (Inter-National).

Porte, C. de la, and P. Pochet. 2002. Conclusions. In *Building social Europe through the open
method of co-ordination*, C. de la Porte and P. Pochet, eds. Brussels: P. I. E.—Peter Lange.

Reid, T. R. 2004. *The United States of Europe: The new superpower and the end of American
supremacy*. New York: Penguin.

Ricard-Nihoul, G. 2005. *The French "no" vote on 29 May 2005: Understanding and action*.
Notre Europe Studies and Research No. 44. Paris: Notre Europe. http://www.notre
-europe.asso.fr/IMG/pdf/Etud44-en.pdf.

Rifkin, J. 2004. *The European dream: How Europe's vision of the future is quietly eclipsing the
American dream*. Cambridge: Polity Press.

Ross, G. 1995. *Jacques Delors and European integration*. Cambridge: Polity Press.

Sapir, A. 2005. *Globalisation and the reform of the European social models*. Bruegel Policy Brief
Issue 2005/01. Brussels: Bruegel. http://www.bruegel.org.

Sapir, A., P. Aghion, G. Bertola, M. Hellwig, J. Pisani-Ferry, D. Rosati, J. Viñals, and H.
Wallace, with M. Butti, M. Nava, and P. M. Smith. 2004. *An agenda for a growing Europe:
The Sapir Report*. Oxford: Oxford University Press.

Scharpf, F. 1999. *Governing in Europe: Effective and democratic?* Oxford: Oxford University
Press.

———. 2002. The European social model: Coping with the challenges of diversity. *Journal
of Common Market Studies* 40(4):645–670.

Schubert, C. B., and J. Bouzon. 2005. An agenda for sustainable growth in Europe. EPC
Working Paper No. 18. Brussels: European Policy Centre. http://www.theepc.be
/TEWN/pdf/724290342_EPC%20Working%20Paper%2018%20An%20Agenda%20f
or%20Sustainable%20Growth%20in%20Europe.pdf.

Siedentop, L. 2000. *Democracy in Europe*. London: Penguin.

Todd, E. 2003. *After the empire*. New York: Columbia University Press.

Chapter 2

The Origins of Territorial Cohesion and the Vagaries of Its Trajectory

JACQUES ROBERT

The concept of territorial cohesion has a strange destiny. It has been used extensively in European—and sometimes national—political debates for almost a decade, and it was the subject of intense lobbying before the adoption of the Amsterdam Treaty as well as in the context of the preparation of the European constitution. Now it is included as an objective of European policies in the European constitution (the ratification process of which is seriously endangered after two negative referendums in France and the Netherlands), with the same rank as the objectives of economic and social cohesion. In addition to political difficulties, numerous endogenous and exogenous factors are likely to have strong spatial impacts in Europe and already represent significant challenges for territorial cohesion.

Despite its presence in EU policy making, neither the European constitution nor national legislation provides a precise definition or explanation of the concept of territorial cohesion. Such a definition cannot be derived from current or past practice, because territorial cohesion has so far hardly been applied concretely as an operational policy concept. This lack of application does not mean, however, that territorial cohesion is an artificial concept, very successful in the political debate but empty in its justification and in its possibilities of operationalization.

The Territorial Roots of Europeans

Current views of the "ideal" of territorial cohesion can be better understood by looking far into the past. For Europeans, European citizenship is not yet something to be fully embraced. They identify with their country, but much more with their region of origin. Yet during the last two centuries, numerous exogenous factors forced a large number of Europeans to move away from their home regions. For example, poverty and rapid demographic growth led millions of Europeans to emigrate to North America and elsewhere. Meanwhile, the industrial regions and metropolitan areas spawned by the Industrial Revolution attracted millions of people from rural areas. The two world wars also produced population movements and even the redefinition of some national borders, as well as the lowering of the iron curtain.

All these factors that obliged a large number of Europeans to cut their regional roots could be called the "great European frustration." This commonly shared feeling that occurs when people must leave their home regions emerges only because regional identity factors are extremely strong in Europe. Numerous regions have a cultural heritage that is more than 1,000 years old (and even more than 2,000 years in some regions of Italy and Greece). Cultural traditions generally encompass several centuries, as do cultural landscapes and even gastronomic specialties. During the 1980s, a new "ideology" emerged in the context of European integration: that of a "Europe of the regions."

■ European Integration: A Subtle Balance Among Modernity, Culture, and Traditions

The postwar period, and in particular the period of European integration from the 1960s onward, was a period of reconquest for the right to live and work in the home region. This reconquest was made possible by, among other things, the sustained economic growth. Although population shifts from rural to urban areas were not insignificant, they were not necessarily taking place over long distances, and thus were not likely to generate substantial disruptions in feelings of regional identity. An exception, however, was the out-migration from some southern regions such as Italy, Spain, and Portugal. The implicit but dominating European ideal was therefore to modernize and improve living conditions and styles, while preserving regional cultural traditions and identities. All factors likely to disrupt this subtle balance among modernity, culture, and traditions were considered not only with suspicion, but also even with hostility.

In the context of postwar European integration, territorial issues became strategic by the mid-1970s, at the end of the so-called *Trente Glorieuses*, the 30 years of European prosperity between 1945 and 1975. The first oil shock of 1973 and the subsequent economic recession generated—or more precisely accelerated the emergence of—a new development paradigm. The recession affected many regions severely, but especially the peripheral ones and those with an old industrial tradition. In addition, the first two decades of European integration and the Common Market had obviously favored the most central regions—the area currently called Europe's "pentagon" (London-Paris-Milan-Munich-Hamburg). The new development paradigm was based on the assumption that a strong regional identity and a distinct regional culture facilitate regional economic development and are vital elements of any effort to create an atmosphere of trust, entrepreneurship, and creativity among citizens (Süssner 2002, 199–206). A new, modern, forward-looking European regionalism was superimposed onto older forms of provincialism, clamoring for its "rights to roots." In some regions, the new paradigm led to efficient economic development. An outstanding example has been the emergence of the "Third Italy," the prosperity of which is based on new industrial districts that network a myriad of small enterprises. In this paradigm, culture has played an important part, not only as an inherited asset or as an effort to support creativity and to improve the accessibility of culture for the citizens, but also as a way of strengthening the feelings of solidarity and symbolic community among them.

The genuine regional culture is not just there to be discovered by tourists. Rather, it is under continual construction. Identity, in turn, is constantly being redefined, reconstructed, and reinvented through culture (Burgi-Golub 2000, 211–213). The challenge is to facilitate the interplay between the old and the new, between openness and rootedness, to develop new visions and to free the mind to search for new pathways. The realization of the development potentials of regions has been considered in the new paradigm as strongly dependent upon people's entrepreneurship, their ways of thinking, their forms of social relationships, and their norms and values. The new paradigm has been transforming the regions into social and political spaces for collective action.

In the decades after its creation in the mid-1970s, the new development paradigm had to take on new dimensions. It had to adapt to the new challenges facing economic development, from knowledge-driven growth to global competition. Paradoxically, the wider markets and competition areas became, the stronger was the search for external economies based on intense regional networking and clustering, often encompassing cross-border areas. Numerous public policies, including those of the European Union (EU), were tailored to support the new paradigm. With the emergence of neoregionalist ideologies that were rather ill-equipped to handle the social exclusion and marginalization as well as the interethnic relations so prevalent in contemporary Europe, deviations caused by an overemphasis on regional identities also were observed.

The Search for Territorial Cohesion: A Reactive, Defensive Attitude

The need for territorial cohesion corresponds more with a reactive, defensive attitude toward factors with territorial destructuring effects than with a rationally conceived model of territorial development. The emergence of the concept of territorial cohesion during the 1990s would not have been possible without an accumulation of various factors with real or potential destructuring effects on European regions. Indeed, the quest for stronger territorial cohesion is more properly understood after contemplating the many factors with destructuring effects on territorial development. In fact, the effects of these factors have been growing stronger over the past 10–15 years.

Put simply, factors such as globalization, international integration, liberalization, increased competition, and rapid technological evolution have extremely strong territorial impacts on European regions. Some of these impacts are positive, but a similar number generate asymmetric shocks, territorial marginalization, relocation of businesses, and unemployment. EU sectoral policies also have strong territorial impacts, sometimes detrimental in nature. Other factors threatening the territorial cohesion of an integrating continent are the specific geographical handicaps of certain regions (examples are mountains and islands with poor accessibility and areas with very low population density). Europe's rural areas must cope with serious problems in order to survive. The globalization of the economy and the EU's reformed common agricultural policy have resulted in stronger competition and thus the shrinking competitiveness of European agricultural products. The exposure of these products to the international market and to the recent EU enlargement is threatening the territorial cohesion of numerous rural areas. In such a changing environment, local competitiveness becomes a central issue. A sector or a specific product closely associated with a particular area's identity may become a growth pole for the entire area, ensuring its further survival. The production of nougat in Montelimar (southern France) or of porcelain in Meissen (eastern Germany) illustrates such situations.

The Territorial Governance of EU Policies

The issue of territorial governance of EU policies is a particularly serious one. Community culture, in terms of politico-administrative practices, is excessively sectoral (Robert et al., 2001). History, above all, is to blame. When the Treaty establishing the European Community (Treaty of Rome) was adopted in 1957, the aim was to bring the European states and people closer to each other by means of a limited number of major common policies. But the impacts of these common policies and of related economic integration were not perceived for a long time. Almost 20 years passed before a European Regional Development Fund was created to reduce the regional imbalances generated by integration, and almost 30 years before environmental considerations, as a prelude to sustainable development, could find a place in the treaty.

Curiously, the progress of European integration and the related deepening of common policies were expressed in the hyperspecialization of functions and competences within the Community authorities, and in particular within the European Commission. Because today's Commission has a monopoly on the right to take initiatives, its political proposals necessarily reflect its own culture of sectoral specialization. Thus, this model has been almost identically reproducing itself for several decades. The changes in public interventions and governance that were occurring at the member state level (such as decentralization, territorialization, mediation, and coordination) hardly penetrated the Community authorities. Certainly, some horizontal initiatives emerged—for example, integrated rural development and integrated development of coastal areas—and territorial concepts have been gradually appearing in various sectors of Community policies. But so far such initiatives have remained rather limited, and attempts toward implementing cultural change have been far from strong enough to generate a breakthrough in the dominant stream that remains sectoral.

European integration has, however, reached a stage at which the juxtaposition of two logics that ignore each other can no longer continue without crystallizing in tensions with detrimental effects on integration and on the European identity itself. Parallel to the continuation of the Community sectoral model, a strong structuring of territories can be observed throughout the whole EU that mobilizes not only the public and semipublic structures, but also all the dynamic forces of society. This dynamics is particularly strong in the field of local development, but it also exists in various forms on other scales. The cross-border areas, the communities that organize their destiny within the framework of broad territories or megaregions (such as those bordering the Baltic or the Mediterranean benefiting from Interreg support) need European approaches other than those that result from hypersectoralization of public policies.

Lobbying for Territorial Cohesion

Lobbying for territorial cohesion began in 1994 when the European Commission (CEC 1994) published *Europe 2000+: Cooperation for European Territorial Development*. Also at this time the Informal Council of Ministers for Spatial Planning decided at its Liège conference to prepare a European Spatial Development Perspective (ESDP). The inspiration, which came mainly from France, was made instrumental at the Strasbourg-based Assembly of European Regions, which adopted a resolution on the subject a few years later. Once the support of European regional authorities was obtained, the next target was the EU level.

The preparation of the Amsterdam Treaty (signed in 1997) was an outstanding opportunity. Lobbying was not unsuccessful, but it remained modest. The term *territorial cohesion* was included in Article 7d of the treaty where it deals with services of general economic interest. But because territorial cohesion was obviously not an overarching objective to be respected by all EU policies, the lobbying went on. The concept had no impact on the 2003 Treaty of Nice, but it did have a decisive one in the context of the preparation of the European constitution by the European Convention. Regional authorities were represented in the Convention, and through them lobbyists advanced their causes. The target, then, was finally reached:

Article I-3 enumerating the "Union's Objectives" stipulates: "The European Union promotes economic, social and territorial cohesion as well as solidarity among Member States."

More important than the details of the lobbying process is certainly the spirit underlying it. Several basic concerns can be identified in the rather intricate process that led to the inclusion of the objective of territorial cohesion in the constitution. The first set of concerns is related to the territorial impacts of the globalization process and of liberalization policies. One argument is that the spatial diffusion of the economic and social benefits generated by progress in technology and by increasing trade is slow, whereas, by contrast, the economic distortion effects produced by asymmetric shocks in the context of economic globalization are sudden and may have devastating effects. European policies should therefore be directed toward maintaining an equivalent standard of living in all regions and respecting the various lifestyles found in the European model of society. One specific concern was that European policies were aimed exclusively at increasing competitiveness and at strengthening the economically strongest metropolitan regions at the expense of others.

A second complaint, not totally independent from the first one, is about the territorial incoherence of EU sectoral policies—in other words, about EU governance that ignores the diversity of regions and territories and that does not respect spatial development planning elaborated at lower levels.

Finally, the lobbying efforts also included a warning: Europeans would distance themselves from European institutions if those institutions were not able or willing to recognize the territorial dimension of development and the specificities of regions. This warning largely anticipated the present difficulties encountered in ratifying the European constitution.

The Multidimensional Character of the Concept of Territorial Cohesion

The concept of territorial cohesion is a multidimensional one. Several aspects of the objective of territorial cohesion are related to issues with a regional dimension such as promoting territorial capital and regional identities, increasing the propensity of regions to anticipate asymmetric shocks and to face successfully the challenges of globalization, providing services of general interest, and promoting intraregional integration. Other aspects of the objective of territorial cohesion have to be promoted on a wider interregional or transnational scale. Examples are integrating very remote areas and promoting the connectivity and territorial integration of regions, in particular those facing geographical and other handicaps or those having a cross-border character

Various institutions are now attempting to define the concept of territorial cohesion. The European Commission indicated in its third cohesion report that "the concept of territorial cohesion extends beyond the notion of economic and social cohesion by both adding to this and reinforcing it. In policy terms, the objective is to help achieve a more balanced development by reducing existing disparities, avoiding territorial imbalances and by making both sectoral policies which have a spatial impact and regional policy more coherent. The concern is also to improve territorial integration and encourage cooperation between regions" (CEC 2004, 27).

At the end of 2004, the Dutch Presidency of the European Union organized, in the context of the enlarged EU, a meeting of ministers responsible for territorial development (the last one had taken place in 2001). The goal is to hold similar meetings twice a year organized by each EU presidency, The meetings would tackle operationally the new territorial challenges of Europe, including the need to provide the concept of territorial cohesion with concrete substance and with policy instruments. In its report presented to the other 24 country ministers, the Dutch Presidency asserted that "it is possible to distinguish three distinct but related dimensions of territorial cohesion, a regional/national dimension, a transnational and interregional dimension and a governance dimension" (Dutch Presidency 2004a, 11).

Regional/National Dimension

A widely understood aspect of the concept of territorial cohesion is that of adding a territorial dimension to EU cohesion policy. More specifically, policy makers must recognize territorial imbalances and disparities in addition to socioeconomic imbalances and ensure that policies and strategies take into account specific territorial and cultural characteristics, identities, and the potentials of regions (such as territorial capital), which are central to long-term, sustainable development.

The activation of regional potentials—a recent expression related to the new development paradigm—must take into consideration a wide variety of factors that may act as constraints. It is also important to consider areas in which action can be taken, such as labor markets, production systems, endogenous potentials, R&D and innovation, clusters, urban and metropolitan functions, natural factors and resources, social, cultural, and environmental factors and services of general interest.

Accessibility is an equally important factor that encompasses the broader transport infrastructure, including high-speed trains, as well as the internal connectivity of regions to major transport networks. The search for adequate accessibility must take into account not only the most peripheral regions, which generally lack efficient networks and nodal infrastructure, but also the constraints generated by traffic congestion in the most developed regions of the European pentagon as well as in some metropolitan regions and corridors of the peripheries. Delivering profitable and high-frequency transport services is also a particular challenge for ensuring a high level of accessibility. In the field of telecommunications networks, overcoming the digital divide related to broadband networks is a challenging task as well.

Transnational and Interregional Dimension

The concept of territorial cohesion is often related to the ways in which urban system linkages, economic linkages, and sociocultural linkages combine internal coherence (within a region) and external connectivity. The emphasis is less on the level of development in a place and more on webs of relations among people and firms. Territorial integration is the expression of increased connectivity, a concept going far beyond the pure transport functions. It applies not only to cross-border or transnational areas, but also to the links between one region and its neighbors and between the various parts of a single region. The role of territorial cohesion policies in this respect is to promote key internal and external linkages such as production, information and knowledge, and trade and logistics.

Territorial balance and integration are another objective of territorial cohesion. The main message of the European Spatial Development Perspective was to strive for more polycentricity in the European settlement structure. Such a goal implies identifying possible alternative "global integration areas" on the European continent and promoting their development and prosperity. Another important issue in the context of territorial integration is overcoming spatial fractures and disruptions at the national, cross-border, and transnational levels (including external borders). In this respect, territorial cooperation and networking on all scales are being promoted by EU and national/regional policies, and such policy making will become a major priority in the years to come. On a regional scale, territorial integration is being strengthened through the enhancement of urban-rural relationships and the development of related partnerships.

A particularly important dimension of territorial balance is the distribution of factors of competitiveness across the European territory. According to Cambridge Econometrics, University of Cambridge, and Ecorys-NEI (2004), the main drivers of competitiveness, in line with the Lisbon Strategy,[1] are innovation (research infrastructure and expenditure, technology transfer, networking of high-tech small and medium-size enterprises), entrepreneurship (a risk-taking culture, response to international change, supplies of venture/risk capital, start-ups located in networked sectors with an international orientation), economic governance (the power of public entities to attract and negotiate with international investors and the availability of sufficient public resources such as grants or fiscal powers for attracting foreign direct investment in competitive projects), and internationalization (inflow of global finance, interaction between indigenous companies and global companies via alliances, joint ventures, mergers, knowledge transfer, and recruitment).

---

[1] The Lisbon Strategy, which seeks to make the EU the most competitive knowledge-based economy worldwide by 2010, was adopted by the European Summit held in Lisbon in 2000.

Governance Dimension

The concept of territorial cohesion is also linked to attempts to make public policies more integrated and coordinated in their effects on particular regions and territories. In this respect, the value of the concept is that it puts the territorial dimensions of various EU policies more firmly at the core of EU political discourse. The implementation of territorial cohesion policies should therefore be grounded in balanced, sustainable development, supported by complementary, coherent sectoral policies. The territorial impacts of sectoral policies could be anticipated, thereby preventing undesirable consequences and increasing positive synergy between various EU policies. To be effective, territorial cohesion as a policy objective requires coherence among regional and sectoral policies with substantial territorial impacts, particularly those in the areas of innovation and research, networks, and competition. What must be taken into account is that the governance of EU policies is not only a *multisectoral* process but also a *multilevel* process in which national and, increasingly, regional authorities have a decisive influence. Fulfilling the objective of territorial cohesion requires significant "added value" in the quality of multilevel governance. The final conclusions of the 2004 Rotterdam meeting took account of these proposals: "The Ministers recognised that *territorial cohesion* adds to the concept of economic and social cohesion by translating the fundamental EU goal of balanced and sustainable development into a territorial setting. They recognised that it is both a multi-sectoral and a multi-level concept that can be implemented at regional/national, transnational and European levels" (Dutch Presidency 2004b, 1).

The Outlook for Territorial Cohesion in Europe

What makes the trajectory of the concept and objective of territorial cohesion particularly unusual is the irony that it became a topic of interest at a time when numerous obstacles were mounting to counteract its implementation.

After 10 years of lobbying, territorial cohesion found its greatest opportunity to become a major objective of EU policies, with the same rank as economic and social cohesion, when it was introduced into the text of the European constitution. Yet the unexpected difficulties in the ratification process of the constitution may significantly postpone and even offset this opportunity. Such an outcome does not mean, however, that the expression of territorial cohesion will be banned from public policies. Even though the term itself may not be part of the official EU vocabulary and concrete definitions and applications are still missing, unless the ratification process finally succeeds or a new Treaty takes over the objective of territorial cohesion, the objective is already embedded in various national and regional spatial planning laws, doctrines, and strategies. Territorial cohesion is a basic concept underlying the activities of the informal meetings of ministers responsible for spatial development policies. The Rotterdam meeting of November 2004 was specifically dedicated to territorial cohesion, and the first version of the "Territorial State and Perspectives of the European Union" adopted at the Luxembourg meeting in May 2005 had the following subtitle: "Towards Stronger European Territorial Cohesion in the Light of the Lisbon and Gothenburg Ambitions" (see Luxembourg Presidency 2005). Whatever the political context for recognition of the objective of territorial cohesion, there is no doubt that its implementation will face many challenges in the years to come. Europe's society, economy, and natural resources are subject to long-lasting changes that will make the achievement of territorial cohesion more difficult. For example, the aging of the population will become evident during the coming decade when the numerous cohorts of "baby boomers" born in the years after World War II will retire from professional life. Competition between regions for attracting young, qualified manpower will thus become intense. A significant share of retired people tend to locate in attractive rural areas where new types of infrastructure, facilities, and services will have to be developed, in particular in the housing, health, and culture sectors.

Another important demographic issue that could affect territorial cohesion is immigration. The pressure of potential immigrants is high along the external EU borders, but yet the aging of the population is likely to make immigration to Europe necessary for economic reasons. The challenge will be how to shape a peaceful multicultural Europe. The unsuccessful integration of immigrants will produce not only social and economic tensions, but also spatial problems that will counteract territorial cohesion, such as sociocultural conflicts and growing insecurity in metropolitan areas, the development of gated communities, and further moves by the better-offs away from inner-city areas toward the surrounding rural areas, resulting in growing commuter flows.

In the economic sphere, the acceleration of the globalization process is putting pressure on the evolution of employment in Europe. Many regions are seeing large numbers of enterprises relocate to China and other emerging industrial economies, while imports from low-wage countries are threatening European enterprises that do not relocate. The restructuring of the European economy toward more competitive knowledge-based activities is unavoidable, and it is being promoted in the context of the Lisbon Strategy. This structural adjustment will have territorial impacts. It is likely to be implemented at the expense of the less productive regions, in particular peripheral ones and those with traditional industries. The question is whether in such a context the new development paradigm will be sufficient to maintain an adequate level of territorial cohesion. There are signs that accelerating globalization and its territorial impacts may become a significant political issue in Europe. The obstacles to ratification of the European constitution are very much related to this issue.

Yet another important challenge facing territorial cohesion is rising energy prices. The steadily growing oil prices since 2000 and their acceleration since the onset in 2003 of the war in Iraq reflect an increasing imbalance between supply and demand at the global level. Limitations on the supply side are related to the low level of significant oil discoveries in the past decades and to the probability that oil production will peak between 2010 and 2020. In turn, the probability that energy prices will increase sharply over the next decade is far from insignificant. In territorial terms, such developments could have strong impacts, such as higher transport costs and lowered mobility, negative economic impacts in regions highly dependent on road and air transport (peripheral regions in particular), competing uses of agricultural land for food and biofuels production, and the migration of people toward regions with more favorable climatic conditions (southern and coastal regions). Energy-intensive industries will also be affected by growing production costs. A substantial increase in energy prices is therefore a significant challenge for territorial cohesion.

Last but not least, climate change is also threatening territorial cohesion. The territorial impacts of climate change are multidimensional. The most important impact is the sustained drought in southern Europe, which is causing significant damage to agriculture and cattle breeding, to vegetation and biodiversity because of the growing number of devastating forest fires, to tourism because of water supply constraints, and to energy production because of insufficient water reserves for hydropower. Another threat posed by climate change is the more frequent occurrence of natural hazards such as flooding, which threatens a large number of European regions along main rivers in both the northern and central parts of Europe and in Mediterranean areas. Taken all together, the damage produced by climate change in Europe over the past decade amounts to billions of euros, in addition to the significant loss of human life.

Conclusions

The need to preserve and even strengthen territorial cohesion can be considered a cultural peculiarity of Europe, originating in its history and identity. The process of European integration has brought with it both opportunities for and constraints to territorial cohesion. The prosperity of the postwar period made it possible for many Europeans to live and work in the home regions, a kind of "right to roots."

Although the aspirations of Europeans related to their attachments to their home regions are changing, with young people more inclined to live and work in other regions or even countries and retirees looking for quiet, attractive, sunny areas in which to spend their last years, Europeans are not becoming indifferent to the processes of territorial destructuring. However, the eminently sectoral culture of EU governance has ignored the specificities of European regions, a factor that has led some Europeans to distrust their institutions. A decade of lobbying was needed to include the objective of territorial cohesion in the European constitution. Once that step was taken, popular mistrust threatened ratification of the constitution. In this respect, the fact that the European constitution (and the overarching political objective of territorial cohesion) was rejected precisely by those who are most attached to their home regions or who are most afraid of the destructuring forces originating from the external context, is a significant paradox. It can only be explained by the fact that abstract ideologies related to the European model of society (liberal versus social), instrumentalized by political parties and the media, are significantly more powerful than the more concrete political objectives related to the territory, such as that of territorial cohesion. The new situation that has resulted—characterized by the emergence of new challenges to territorial cohesion (population aging and growing immigration, acceleration of the globalization process, growing energy prices, and the damaging territorial impacts of climate change) in a context in which the objective of territorial cohesion is absent at the EU level—is even more paradoxical. One can observe, for example, that significant political efforts are being undertaken throughout Europe to strengthen metropolitan areas to face the challenge of globalization, while disregarding the territorial imbalances that such efforts may produce.

Even while Europe waits for a solution to the ratification of the constitution or for a new treaty, territorial cohesion remains an objective for the informal meetings of ministers responsible for spatial development as well as for some national and regional authorities. They will all have to ensure that the concept of territorial cohesion does not disappear from EU terminology in the years to come and that it finds solid applications in European regions. They will also have to define how concretely and on which scale territorial cohesion can face most successfully the new challenges of territorial development in Europe.

References

Burgi-Golub, N. 2000. Cultural identity and political responsibility. *Cultural Policy* 7(2): 211–223.

Cambridge Econometrics, University of Cambridge, and Ecorys-NEI. 2004. *A study on the factors of regional competitiveness*. Brussels: European Commission.

CEC—Commission of the European Communities. 2004. *A new partnership for cohesion: Convergence, competitiveness, cooperation. Third report on economic and social cohesion*. Luxembourg: Office for Official Publications of the European Communities.

Dutch Presidency. 2004a. Exploiting Europe's territorial diversity for sustainable economic growth. Discussion paper, EU Informal Ministerial Meeting on Territorial Cohesion, Rotterdam, 29 November.

———. 2004b. *Presidency conclusions*. EU Informal Ministerial Meeting on Territorial Cohesion, Rotterdam, 29 November.

European Commission. 1994. *Europe 2000+: Cooperation for European territorial development*. Luxembourg: Office for Official Publications of the European Communities.

Luxembourg Presidency. 2005. *Scoping document and summary of political messages for an assessment of "The territorial state and perspectives of the European Union: Towards a stronger European territorial cohesion in the light of the Lisbon and Gothenburg ambitions."* Endorsed for further development by the Ministers for Spatial Development and the European

Commission at the Informal Ministerial Meeting for Regional Policy and Territorial Cohesion, Luxembourg, 20–21 May.

Robert, J., T. Stumm, J. M. deVet, C. J. Reincke, M. Hollanders, and M. A. Figueiredo. 2001. *Spatial impacts of Community policies and the costs of non-coordination*. Brussels: European Commission.

Süssner, J. 2002. Culture, identity and regional development in the European Union. In *Informationen zur Raumentwicklung*. Vol. 4/5. Bonn: BBR.

Chapter 3

Territorial Cohesion

The Underlying Discourses

BAS WATERHOUT

Through the recent efforts of the European Commission and the member states of the European Union (EU), the concept of territorial cohesion is taking shape (for efforts of the Commission, see DG Regio and DG Employment 2005; for those of the member states, see Faludi and Waterhout 2005; Ministers for Spatial Development and European Commission 2005). Nevertheless, its meaning has not yet crystallized (Faludi 2005; Zonneveld and Waterhout 2005). Currently, it is even uncertain whether territorial cohesion policy will come about anyway. Now that the French and the Dutch have said "non" and "nee" to the constitutional treaty, its institutional basis seems shaky. At the same time, the concept of territorial cohesion is undergoing various interpretations. This chapter seeks to identify these interpretations and relate them to various European models of society.

Territorial cohesion has been closely linked to the concept of services of general interest,[1] a link that also is made in Article 16 of the Treaty of Amsterdam and the Treaty of Nice, currently the only formal basis for EU territorial cohesion policy. The field of European spatial planning is concerning itself with territorial cohesion as well. Whereas European spatial planning is a game in the margins of formal EU policies played by a small number of officials from the Commission and the member states, as well as some modestly concerned ministers responsible for spatial planning, services of general interest have been the topic of speeches given by former

---

[1] This chapter does not distinguish between services of general interest and services of general economic interest. The latter can be found in Article 16 of the Treaty of Amsterdam. However, generally policy makers speak of services of general interest, without specifying whether they are talking about market or nonmarket services or both (see also CEC 2004b).

presidents of the European Commission such as Jacques Delors and recently Romano Prodi (2002, 2003). There is another difference as well. European spatial planners hope to be taken seriously in Europe by being able to frame their ideas in terms of territorial cohesion, but the provision of services of general interest is a political aim in its own right and will in fact, according to numerous Commission papers, lead to territorial cohesion.

Against this institutional backdrop, this chapter identifies four story-lines underlying territorial cohesion that, between them, might be considered the seedbed for territorial cohesion policy. These storylines are (1) "Europe in Balance"; (2) "Coherent European Policy"; (3) "Competitive Europe"; and (4) "Green and Clean Europe." The relevance of the storylines is explained in the brief introduction to discourse analysis theory that follows. As will become clear in the conclusions to this chapter, the current views on territorial cohesion only address a fraction of these storylines, which, in turn, are grounded in different European models of society.

A Discourse Analytical Approach to Territorial Cohesion

Storylines are part of discourse analysis theory as invoked by Hajer. He defines a discourse as "an ensemble of ideas, concepts and categorizations that are produced, reproduced and transformed in a particular set of practices and through which meaning is given to physical and social realities and which permeates regional, national and supranational policy making circuits" (Hajer 1995, 44). Discourses are therefore more than just a debate or discussion. Seen from a social constructivist viewpoint, they form an institutionalized reality. Without engaging in an extensive literature review, this section briefly describes discourse analysis theory with a view toward the function of storylines in this particular chapter and their meaning for territorial cohesion.

Like those of many other social scientists, Hajer's interpretation of discourse is based on the work of Foucault. Foucault focuses on the way discourses are produced through institutionalized practices. These practices, in turn, influence people's actions and in doing so produce political preferences. With this approach, which is based on laying bare certain linguistic practices or conventions through rhetorical analysis, Foucault fundamentally challenges mainstream political theory, because traditionally political scientists have not focused on institutionalized practices, but instead on institutions, individual stakeholders, and the articulated stakeholder preferences (Peters 2003).

According to Hajer, a problem with Foucault's radically different route is that in his abstract notion of discourse, based as it is on primary linguistic analysis, the role of actors remains ambivalent. In Foucault's way of seeing things, it is difficult to understand how discourses develop and change. After all, although they are influenced by discourses, individual actors always have the option of leaving routines and developing new ones. Inevitably, this flexibility affects discourse, which, as defined by Hajer, is about producing and reproducing certain practices.

To make Foucault's theory more applicable to the study of concrete political events, Hajer introduces the concepts of storylines and discourse coalitions. He calls them "middle range concepts" that fill the gap between Foucault's abstract work and concrete political events. In doing so, Hajer reintroduces the role of agency into discourse analysis, which is necessary to understand how particular discourses emerge, develop, and change. Applied to territorial cohesion, discourse analysis, so conceived, may help one understand how this policy is being shaped and why.

But doing so requires identifying so-called discourse coalitions. Discourse coalitions are "a variety of actors that do not necessarily meet but through their utterances reinforce a particular way of talking that is reproduced via an identifiable set of storylines and discursive practices in a given policy domain" (Hajer 2000, 139). In this chapter, "the given policy domain" is that of territorial cohesion (constituting services of general interest and European spatial planning), and it is in this domain that discursive production takes place.

The key to identifying discourse coalitions for territorial cohesion is storylines and metaphors. Hajer defines storylines "as (crisp) generative statements that bring together previously unrelated elements of discourse and thus allow for new understandings and create new meanings. . . . The importance of storylines for coalition formation is in their essentially figurative or metaphorical nature which allows for a diversity of interpretations. This is why they help constitute a discourse coalition consisting of a variety of actors" (Hajer 2000, 140).

The main reason for the emergence of discourse coalitions is that the storyline binding them together just "sounds right." Actors do not have to share the same belief systems or cognitive understanding; storylines bridge different discourses and tie the actors together. Hajer argues that "not shared belief systems but multi-interpretable storylines are the glue that hold together the coalitions behind transnational policy discourses" (Hajer 2000, 140).

Hajer's theories closely resemble other communicative theories. An example is that of the bridging or hegemonic concepts devised by Kohler-Koch (1999; see also Héritier 1999), which have been applied to analyzing the concept of polycentric development (Waterhout 2002). Indeed, polycentric development, too, is a perfect example of a storyline gathering a variety of actors behind it, uniting those in favor of cohesion and of competitiveness. But, as described later in this chapter, polycentricity has lost some of its discursive power and currently serves just the interests of actors supporting balanced development of the EU territory.

Another well-known theory has been put forward by Throgmorton (1992), who argues that planning is mainly about "persuasive storytelling."

The concepts developed by Hajer provide analysts with the tools they need to discover these "persuasive stories" and link them to a set of actors.

The value of identifying storylines and discourse coalitions for analyzing an emerging policy field such as territorial cohesion is easy to understand. The future of a policy field that lacks a legal basis (and thus norms and standards) and therefore is not pursued by powerful actors depends on the outcome of communicative competition between its potential stakeholders.

Storylines Feeding into Territorial Cohesion

This section discusses the four storylines—"Europe in Balance," "Coherent European Policy," "Competitive Europe," and "Green and Clean Europe"— that between them form the seedbed for the current discussions on territorial cohesion. As will become clear, actors may invoke more than one storyline. There is nothing strange about this. The crucial question is, in the end, to which storyline will they give priority, and will it block or open up opportunities for forming coalitions in support of a consensus around a combination of storylines? With territorial cohesion policy still in the making, this consensus has yet to crystallize. Based on the storylines and the way they develop, it seems possible, however, to identify beforehand some elements that eventually will have to be included in the final policy package. This is the subject of the two concluding sections.

"Europe in Balance"

The storyline "Europe in Balance" combines the thinking of planners who participated in the process of developing the European Spatial Development Perspective (ESDP) with that of lobbyists for services of general interest. Their common objective for territorial cohesion is to level out regional disparities. The storyline is thus related to the traditional objective of the EU, which is to establish economic and social cohesion, and thus to the distribution of EU Structural Funds to which the ESDP tries to add a territorial development rationale.

From the planners' perspective

Reducing regional disparities was a crucial issue during the ESDP process (Faludi and Waterhout 2002). Whereas member states in northwestern Europe were often stressing the importance of core regions for Europe's competitiveness, member states in southern Europe, led by Spain, were emphasizing the need to reduce disparities. They argued that a more balanced Europe would eventually improve Europe's competitive position. A solution was found by invoking the politically acceptable concept of polycentric development, which serves both cohesion and competitiveness objectives (Waterhout 2002). Polycentric development on the EU scale translated into the development of several global economic integration zones next to the existing core area in the northwest (London-Paris-Milan-Munich-Hamburg) known as the pentagon of Europe (CEC 1999). In doing so, it stressed the importance of both the core areas as well as the need for a better balance within Europe.

The concept of polycentric development turned out to be a real winner and was picked up in many policy documents at the European as well as at the member state and subnational levels, as well as in Interreg and the European Spatial Planning Observation Network, or ESPON (Zonneveld, Meijers, and Waterhout 2005). Yet polycentric development is considered a vague political goal and is difficult to operationalize (Davoudi 2003; Peters 2003; Shaw and Sykes 2004; Waterhout, Zonneveld, and Meijers 2005). Also, it seems to be explained increasingly in terms of cohesion, equity, and spatial justice (Baudelle and Peyrony 2005) rather than in terms of competitiveness (CEC 2001d; DG Regio and DG Employment 2005).

Interestingly, the concept was virtually absent from the two recent discussion papers tabled at the informal meetings of ministers at Rotterdam in 2004 and Luxembourg in 2005 (MINVROM 2004; Ministers for Spatial Development and European Commission 2005).[2] Today, polycentric development has been replaced by the new and equally vague concept of territorial capital (described later in this chapter). So for the moment, the "Europe in Balance" storyline, although never totally absent, seems to have lost some ground in the European spatial planning debate.

European spatial planners are not the only ones with a say in the matter, however. Organizations that have always been closely involved in traditional cohesion policy are expressing strong political support for the "Europe in Balance" storyline (a development discussed later in this section), and those organizations are lobbying for a policy safeguarding the provision of services of general interest throughout Europe.

Services of general interest

After services of general interest and territorial cohesion were introduced in Article 16 of the Amsterdam Treaty, a few years passed before the debate about implementing this article took shape. Documents fueling this debate were prepared by the secretariat-general of the European Commission in charge of this dossier. In general, the impression is that the provision of these services will automatically result in more territorial cohesion (see, for example, CEC 2001a, 2001c, and 2004b; European Parliament 2003; Commission Staff 2004; CoR 2005; EcoSoc 2005). The authors of the reports discussing services of general interest regard territorial cohesion as an abstract concept, the meaning of which is barely explained. A typical expression in the European Commission's white paper is as follows: "In the

---

[2] To be more exact, where polycentric development is mentioned it is related only to the regional or national level, not to the European territory or to the political objective of balancing Europe.

Union, services of general interest remain essential for ensuring social and territorial cohesion and for the competitiveness of the European economy" (CEC 2004b, 4).

The wish to guarantee services of general interest refers to the difficulties of living in the outermost, less accessible regions where the provision of services of general interest cannot be guaranteed through the market. Among such services, the European Commission lists the following: electronic communications, postal services, electricity, gas, water, transport and broadcasting (CEC 2004b). Because this kind of policy is particularly relevant for the more peripheral, more sparsely populated, and less accessible regions, it is no wonder that since the mid-1990s the strongest lobbying was conducted by associations such as the Assembly of European Regions (AER), the Conference of Peripheral and Maritime Regions of Europe (CPMR), and the Committee of the Regions (CoR), all of which, according to Faludi (2004, drawing on Husson 2002), have been used by French players to voice their concerns (for a broader account of the French influence, see Tatzberger 2003). At the European Convention, convened to draft the constitutional treaty, the following parties also supported the inclusion of services of general interest (often in combination with territorial cohesion) in the constitutional treaty: Belgium, Italy, Luxembourg, Malta, Portugal, Slovenia, and Spain, as well as Bulgaria and Romania, which are slated to join the EU in 2007. Ten delegates to the European Convention from the European Parliament handed in a joint proposal on general-interest services, while members representing the U.K., Germany, and Austria submitted separate proposals. Some observers of the process—the Committee of the Regions, the European Economic and Social Committee (EESC), and the European Social Partners—also proposed including territorial cohesion in the constitutional treaty under Article I-3.

As indicated by Faludi (2004) referring to Guigou (2001; see also Rifkin 2004), this movement toward territorial cohesion is based on the assumption that Europeans are less nomadic than Americans and more strongly attached to the region in which they were born. Because of different languages, different cultural traditions, and different identities, it is also less easy for the average European to move. Thus, it would follow that, complementary to the growing liberalization of the EU economy and according to certain European norms and values, some kind of policy should be in place to safeguard quality of life where the market cannot provide it. The idea is that, based on European values stressing diversity, people should not be negatively affected in their development possibilities because of where they happened to be born. This point was emphasized by the European Parliament in a resolution on territorial cohesion prepared by the French rapporteur Ambroise Guellec. The resolution argued that territorial cohesion should be "based on the principle of equity between citizens, wherever they live in the Union [and] calls, therefore, for regional development to be founded on programmes which guarantee equality of treatment between the EU's territories, while preserving their diversity, which notably implies appropriate accessibility of services of general interest (SGI) and services of general economic interest (SGEI)" (European Parliament 2005, 2). All these developments provide a clear agenda for territorial cohesion policy, albeit a narrow one confined strictly to the least accessible regions and in which territorial concerns as such do not play much of a role. Such an agenda nevertheless clearly aims to keep Europe in balance.

Europe in balance interpreted in territorial terms: Polycentric development

A broader definition of territorial cohesion that would be relevant to a wider range of European regions is supported by those organizations that always have been closely involved in cohesion policy. Based on several amendments proposed at the European Convention, it is clear that a wide range of actors would like territorial cohesion to contribute to a more cohesive and balanced European territory. For example, Portuguese members of the European Convention specifically focused on the reduction of regional disparities as a rationale for territorial cohesion policy. Their proposal reads: "To promote economic, social *and territorial* cohesion *through policies aiming at reducing inequalities between states and regions*" (European Convention 2003, emphasis in original). The Committee of the Regions, too, views territorial cohesion as a means of reducing disparities. The CoR, one of the most active players in the field of territorial cohesion, has set up a special Commission for Territorial Cohesion Policy to finance studies on the subject (Study Group for European Policies 2002). In an opinion presented to the European Convention, the CoR asserted that "territorial cohesion must be understood as an objective in reducing disparities in development between European regions, to be achieved by reorganising Community territory in such a way as to enable polycentric, harmonious, balanced and sustainable development" (CoR 2003, 4).

Within this view, polycentric development is still being advocated. In making this recommendation, the committee insisted that "polycentric development is impossible without adopting a genuine spatial blueprint" (CoR 2003, 6). This statement must have been music to the ears of those spatial planners convinced that territorial cohesion policy cannot do without a spatial strategy—but not necessarily a blueprint! Considering the current state of affairs, however, this message has never come through (a fact that is touched upon in the section on the "Coherent European Policy" storyline).

Another player with a similar message is the European Parliament. By means of the Schroedter Report (named after the rapporteur, Elisabeth Schroedter) adopted on 6 November 2002, the European Parliament stressed "the need to promote territorial cohesion in Europe so as to prevent the population, economic activities, employment and investments from being concentrated in the wealthier zones of the European Union" (European

Parliament 2002, 8). The European Parliament reiterates this point in two more recent reports by rapporteur Konstantinos Hatzidakis and, as already noted, by Guellec (European Parliament 2004, 2005), both arguing explicitly for polycentric development. Guellec emphasizes that, among other objectives of territorial cohesion, the "initial priority should be given to combating distortions between centre and periphery and disparities at subnational level, so as to strengthen cohesion" (European Parliament 2005, 2).

Thus, the European Parliament, like the Committee of the Regions, relates polycentric development first and foremost with a balanced and cohesive Europe (instead of a competitive Europe, to which polycentric development used to be related, too [Waterhout 2002]). Another issue that has stirred unease in the Committee of the Regions and the European Parliament (a judgment that from the beginning of the ESDP process has underlain the efforts of European spatial planners) is the limited effectiveness of cohesion policy. This unease has become even stronger since publication of the Sapir Report, which, for the sake of stimulating economic growth, advises tossing out the traditional cohesion policy altogether (Sapir et al. 2004). The European Parliament has repeatedly called for account to be taken not only of "the per capita GDP criterion but also [of] other indicators reflecting regional sensitivities and the development difficulties" (European Parliament 2002, 7; see also European Parliament 2004, 2005). This call by Parliament opens the door for a territorial cohesion policy that is based on more sophisticated indicators—for example, those now being developed within the ESPON program.

Clearly, in the view of the European Parliament the concept of territorial cohesion in the constitutional treaty legitimizes a revision of cohesion policy and the development in that context of a completely new kind of policy for the territorial development of the EU territory. The next section further explores the issue of policy delivery.

"Coherent European Policy"

Policy coherence not only makes cohesion policy more effective, but also stands on its own as an issue related to EU sector policies with territorial impacts. The problem with these policies is that, from a spatial perspective, they are not coherent. The focus in this storyline, "Coherent European Policy," is on achieving horizontal coherence—a focus that comes through loud and clear in the documents tabled at the Rotterdam and Luxembourg ministerial meetings (MINVROM 2004; Ministers for Spatial Development and European Commission 2005).

For a long time, horizontal coordination has been a rationale for working on the ESDP. In the minds of the policy makers concerned, the fact that EU sector policies cause unintended territorial impacts was enough of a reason, even in the absence of a formal EU competency, to formulate some sort of spatial framework to coordinate and integrate these policies. In reality, however, there was no chance of influencing EU policy within the highly fragmented structure of the directorates-general of the European Commission (Faludi and Waterhout 2002).

At this point, it is important to explain that in the early 1990s not all member states insisted on horizontal coordination. It was mainly those whose planning systems had been ranked by the EU compendium of spatial planning systems under the so-called comprehensive integrated approach that did so (CEC 1997a). The main characteristic of this approach is inter-sectoral coordination among policies through a spatial planning framework and additional institutional support systems, but also vertical coordination among administrative levels.

Only a few EU member states actually share this tradition. Famous examples are Denmark and the Netherlands, but the German and Flemish systems fit into this category as well. The French system of *aménagement du territoire*, which used to be identified with a different regional economic approach, recently began to move in this direction (Faludi 2004). Of the new member states, Slovenia is known to take a similar approach to planning. However, inspired by the ESDP and the *Guiding Principles for Sustainable Spatial Development of the European Continent* (CEMAT 2000), many countries (old and new member states) now draft spatial planning frameworks, a key element of the comprehensive integrated approach (see Zonneveld, Meijers, and Waterhout 2005). Furthermore, it is expected that, because of the intensification of EU policies, each country will experience situations in which, seen from a spatial perspective, EU policies are in conflict with each other, not to mention with domestic spatial policy objectives (see Robert et al. 2001; Ravesteyn and Evers 2004).

However, without a formal competency, and because of the EU's current sectoral organization, planners find it almost impossible to gain influence, and so their strategy is to gather evidence that demonstrates the malfunctioning of EU policies from a territorial perspective. For example, the Directorate General for Regional Policy (DG Regio) financed a study to demonstrate the conflicting spatial impacts of EU sector policies. The report by Robert et al. (2001) carried the appropriate title *Spatial Impacts of Community Policies and the Costs of Non-coordination*. The study is well known among planners, but less so with sectoral policy makers at EU and national levels.

Also, as part of the consultation round of the first official draft of the ESDP in 1998, DG Regio organized an interservice consultation within the Commission administration (CEC 1997b). The exercise has been described as positive and stimulating (Faludi and Waterhout 2002), but because of the lack of spatial concern in current EU policies it has not led to further results. Persistence is the only option left, and currently member states and DG Regio are supporting research under ESPON that is assessing the territorial impacts of certain EU sector policies. Meanwhile, spurred by alarming headlines in newspapers, the Netherlands Institute of Spatial

Research has also carried out a study of the impact of EU policies called *Unseen Europe* (Ravesteyn and Evers 2004). Among the policies with a spatial impact are the EU's regional policy, the common agricultural policy, the Trans-European Network for Transport (TEN-T) policy, the environmental directives such as the habitat and birds directives and recently the air quality directive, and the water framework directive. Some EU policies, such as the policy on competition and state aid, affect the spatial planning systems of countries.

Territorial cohesion policy that addresses the issue of enhanced policy coordination seems to be quite a distant prospect; it simply does not fit the administrative culture of the European Commission. It is probably because European spatial planners sense this situation that the document "Territorial State and Perspectives of the European Union" includes the somewhat mysterious statement that "spatial development is more than territorial cohesion" (Ministers for Spatial Development and European Commission 2005, 5). Apparently, policy coherence is deemed too large an issue for territorial cohesion.

Although the issue of policy coherence is typically a theme for spatial planners, other parties share their concerns. The European Commission, in its white paper on European governance drafted by the Secretariat-General, states that "the territorial impact of EU policies in areas such as transport, energy or environment should be addressed. These policies should form part of a coherent whole as stated in the EU's second cohesion report; there is a need to avoid a logic which is too sector specific. In the same way, decisions taken at the regional and local levels should be coherent with a broader set of principles that would underpin more sustainable and balanced territorial development within the Union" (CEC 2001b, 13).

Unfortunately, the Commission has refrained from pursuing this objective. In a 2003 report on the consultations on the white paper, there is almost nothing related to this aspect of governance. The only instruments being mentioned in relation to coordinating the territorial impacts of EU policies are tripartite contracts and agreements and so-called territorial impact assessments (CEC 2003), which obviously reduces the scope for integrated territorial cohesion policy. Nevertheless, with the recent support of the European Parliament and Committee of the Regions for the use of spatial frameworks, there might still be some political scope in territorial cohesion policy so that a storyline such as "Coherent European Policy" would survive.

"Competitive Europe"

The storyline "Competitive Europe" is directed at the global competitiveness of Europe as a whole, as well as at the competitiveness of individual regions. It is aiming for a well-structured territory and to develop Europe's territory in all its diversity, but in contrast to "Europe in Balance" redistribution is not an issue, so that the ball is in the court of the regions themselves. The focus is not exclusively on cities as motors of the economy, but rather on regions and their unique territorial capital. Although initially the issue of competitiveness was the concern of only some member states involved in the ESDP process, recently support for this storyline has increased, fueled by the Lisbon Agenda and the relatively weak performance of cohesion policy, as emphasized by the Sapir Report.

The ESDP process: Introducing competitiveness and potential

During the ESDP process, EU member states in northwestern Europe brought attention to the need to keep economic core regions in good shape, stressing their importance for Europe's competitiveness. A country strongly associated with this idea is the Netherlands. In 1991 it used its EU presidency to introduce the concept of urban networks in order to combine Dutch ideas with the high interest expressed at earlier meetings in lagging regions. As Zonneveld (2000) describes, transposing domestic ideas onto a European scale, the Dutch designed a new map of the EU in which all major European cities were represented as part of one and the same urban network covering the whole territory (Ministry of Housing, Physical Planning and the Environment 1991; Zonneveld 2000; Waterhout 2002). Suddenly, Europe appeared integrated, as opposed to the center-periphery model that until then had framed the thinking of European spatial planners. Also during the ESDP process, Europe's global position was considered for the first time.

Zonneveld (2000) describes the long and twisting road of the ESDP process and what happened to the "stories" of the Dutch (also see chapter 10 by Zonneveld in this volume). In 1997, when the Dutch once again held the presidency of the EU, one of the greatest shifts in the ESDP process took place: the first official draft of the ESDP lists Europe's global competitiveness among its objectives (CEC 1997b). However, in the ESDP, after a Spanish intervention, this objective is reduced to balanced competitiveness, and thus the emphasis remains on cohesion (CEC 1999). Nevertheless, albeit reluctantly and less prominently than in the first official draft, the ESDP recognizes the strong "locomotives" of the economy as an official policy category (Schön 1997). So-called gateway cities linking Europe to the rest of the world are identified as being important for the national and European economies, along with the need for good accessibility. The clearest example, though, of competitiveness being taken into account is the concept of global economic integration zones. The polycentric development strategy calls for several such zones to be promoted based on their endogenous potential in order to create counterweights to the pentagon area forming the economic core of the EU and in due turn a more balanced territory (CEC 1999). Here polycentric development includes goals of both cohesion and competitiveness. However, as described in a previous section, over time the concept of polycentricity ceased to be related to competitiveness.

DG Regio: Widening its scope

After publication of the ESDP, European competitiveness disappeared as a planning issue. With the abolition of the Committee on Spatial Development, member states were no longer in a position to inject their storylines into the European discourse. When in the driver's seat, DG Regio had never shown much interest in competitiveness, and so the second cohesion report focuses on reducing disparities between regions and invokes polycentricity for this purpose and this purpose alone. In it, Europe is viewed as a "very centralised territory," a situation that polycentrism should rectify (CEC 2001d, 29).

However, the third cohesion report, published in 2004, frames cohesion in terms of development and competitiveness. It signals that territorial disparities such as "serious difficulties in outermost and peripheral areas or problems of congestion in certain central areas . . . affect the overall competitiveness of the EU economy" and "cannot be ignored" (CEC 2004a, 28). Further down, it identifies "urban systems [as] the engines of regional development," and it is because of "their geographical distribution across the EU that an imbalance between the core and periphery is most evident." This statement represents a more refined stance toward conceptualizing the European territory. An important new and related element is that of the urban hierarchy, indicating the relative importance of cities and regions for Europe. The third cohesion report distinguishes between "growth metropolises of European importance," mainly located in northwestern Europe and thus forming a core area, and cities outside of this area, which, according to four different indicators, have various degrees of development potential. Obviously, invoking such terms would have been impossible without the evidence provided by ESPON. In general, then, the third cohesion report breathes a development-oriented spirit. The term *competitiveness* is omnipresent, in contrast to its almost total absence in the second cohesion report.

Unmistakably, in putting forward a territorial cohesion agenda, DG Regio is increasingly adopting the competitiveness storyline, which can be explained by the strong emphasis that both the former president of the Commission, Romano Prodi, and the current president, Manuel Barroso, put on the Lisbon Agenda. Over the last few years, this agenda has, together with the constitutional treaty, become the dominant discourse in EU politics. Policy is increasingly being framed in terms of growth and jobs, the key themes of the revised Lisbon Agenda (CEC 2005). An important example relevant to territorial cohesion is the recent non-paper *Cohesion Policy in Support of Growth and Jobs* by DG Regio and DG Employment (2005), which includes a short chapter on territorial cohesion and cooperation. Other than the third cohesion report, the non-paper does not present new perspectives on competitiveness. Interestingly, though, it explains "the contribution of cities to growth and jobs" (DG Regio and DG Environment 2005, 19).

A new concept takes over: Territorial capital

More interesting in terms of producing discourse are the documents tabled at the informal ministerial meetings in Rotterdam in 2004 and Luxembourg in 2005, forming between them the launching pad of the so-called Agenda 2007 process. Again, with the help of others, it was the Dutch who used their EU presidency to promote the competitiveness discourse on territorial cohesion. Inspired by a report by the Organisation for Economic Co-operation and Development (OECD 2001), they introduced the concept of territorial capital, arguing that each region has its own specific territorial capital, thereby making investments in one region more effective than in another. Some factors that play a part in territorial capital are geographic location, geographical size of the region, climate, natural resources, quality of life, and economies of scale. Other factors are related to local and regional traditions and customs and the quality of governance, including issues such as mutual trust and informal rules. Finally, there is an intangible factor—that is, something in the air or the quality of the milieu (MINVROM 2004; Zonneveld and Waterhout 2005).

The concept of territorial capital has been further elaborated in the "Territorial State and Perspectives of the Union," a document discussed in Luxembourg. Framed in terms of the Lisbon Agenda, the document carries the subtitle "Towards a Stronger European Territorial Cohesion in the Light of the Lisbon and Gothenburg Ambitions" (Ministers for Spatial Development and European Union 2005). In this document, territorial capital is the key concept, and within this storyline it is thus the successor of the ESDP concept of polycentricity. Yet the meaning of territorial capital, like some other politically successful concepts, is not fully explained. Never-theless, policy makers are encouraged to design policies so that regions can develop their territorial capital, thereby maximizing their competitive advantage.

The concept of territorial capital means a change of paradigm. The emphasis is no longer restricted to strongly urbanized areas, like cities and metropolitan areas, and keeping them in good shape. By paying attention to factors such as size of the region, quality of life, and natural resources, the paradigm has widened the focus to include virtually all sorts of European regions, including rural and peripheral ones, as long as these regions find ways to exploit their unique territorial capital so that it contributes to Europe's competitiveness. This storyline may therefore appeal to a large audience.

In conclusion, the storyline "Competitive Europe" is mainly advanced by member states in northwestern Europe. However, inspired by the Lisbon discourse, DG Regio also has become more receptive to and uses the vocabulary of this storyline for territorial cohesion purposes. The Guellec resolution is less clear on this storyline, but it acknowledges that the territorial dimension should be considered a major element of the Lisbon Strategy (European Parliament 2005).

"Green and Clean Europe"

This final storyline, "Green and Clean Europe," is related to sustainable development and sound management of the environment. It links the European environmental discourse with that of European spatial planning. This storyline has influenced the ESDP process and now looms in the background of territorial cohesion policy. Although the main advocates of this storyline from the beginning have been the Nordic countries as well as Germany and Ireland, the discourse coalition around this storyline has gradually widened.

Sustainable development and spatial planning were first brought closely together in 1992 when Denmark held the EU presidency. In a document tabled at a meeting of the Committee on Spatial Development, Denmark introduced the concept of spatial balance. The concept amounted to a decentralized urban system based on three principles: (1) urban spread; (2) the development of corridors; and (3) the appropriate use of energy and transport. However, with its connotation of uncontrolled urban growth, the concept of urban spread was a poor choice. What the Danes had in mind was something more in line with polycentric development, based on compact cities in order to avoid the development of megacities (Faludi and Waterhout 2002). Later, in 1994, the so-called Leipzig Principles referred to sustainable development in its original meaning in the Brundtland Report, published by the World Commission on Environment and Development (WCED) in 1987, and noted that "this fundamental concept implies not only economic development which respects the environment, but also balanced spatial development" (BMBau 1995, 43). This definition reflected the Danish concept of spatial balance.

It was no coincidence that the Danes introduced an environmental agenda into the ESDP process. As Böhme (2002) explains, Danish planning covers regional development as well as environmental protection. Business development and transport have to pay attention to environmental concerns as well. In fact, environmental concerns are omnipresent in Danish policy. According to Böhme (2002, 97) "the spatial planning system in general and also the planning act illustrate an increasing environmental orientation." The Brundtland Report was significant in providing a rationale for the policy goals pursued.

In 1992 Denmark's spatial planning agency moved to the Ministry of Environment and Energy, and Denmark in its 1997 national planning report "Denmark and European Spatial Planning Policy" presents itself as "a green room in the European House" (Böhme 2002, 91). Moreover, when the Danes in the early 1990s decided to play a more active role in EU politics, their priority was to inject Danish green policies into the agenda. It is therefore no coincidence that the European Environmental Agency is located in Copenhagen and that Dane Ritt Bjerregard was the EU's environmental commissioner from 1994 to 1999.

What goes for the Danish attitude toward the environment is also valid for other Nordic countries such as Sweden and Finland, as well as non-EU member Norway. Böhme and Faludi (2000) argue that an emphasis on environmental issues is common to Nordic countries (see also Böhme 2002). Not only do these countries give priority to environmental protection, but they have also made progress in embracing a wider concept of sustainable development. Rifkin (2004), too, finds a stronger environmental discourse in Nordic countries than elsewhere in Europe and probably in the world.

Be that as it may, the sustainability discourse does not go unchallenged. Schön (1997, 290) reports that, in contrast to the Leipzig Principles, in the first official draft of the ESDP "the emphasis on competitiveness had come, in part, at the expense of the sustainability concept." Under the influence of, among others, the U.K. and German EU presidencies and the consultation process, where mainly actors from member states in northwestern Europe pleaded for a stronger emphasis on environmental protection, this problem was "repaired" in the final ESDP (see Faludi and Waterhout 2002). This "repair" is also evident in the differences between the subtitles of the first draft of the ESDP and the final version—the first subtitle does not refer to sustainable development, but the second does.

Without a doubt, then, the sustainability discourse has successfully penetrated the ESDP. There is great concern about ecologically sensitive areas, which in the densely populated EU are often being threatened by urban development. Reducing urban sprawl has therefore become a central concern of European planners. The EU Natura 2000 program requiring member states to designate habitat areas and the EU water framework directive offer planners many possibilities for pursuing the policy options of the ESDP, in particular those concerning the use of integrated territorial development strategies.

In the years since approval of the ESDP in 1999, the argument that planners can help to achieve sustainable development in Europe by formulating integrated territorial development strategies has been reiterated many times. For example, a document produced by the Spatial and Urban Development Subcommittee (2003) argues for an integrated space-based approach, something that was repeated while referring to the Gothenburg aims[3] in the documents discussed at the informal ministerial meetings in

---

[3] "Gothenburg aims" refer to the European Council of 2001 in Gothenburg where a sustainable development agenda for Europe was adopted as a counterweight to the Lisbon agenda that was developed in 2000 and exclusively focuses on economic development. Since then the Lisbon agenda is often referred to as the Lisbon and Gothenburg agenda.

Rotterdam and Luxembourg (MINVROM 2004; Ministers for Spatial Development and European Commission 2005). In fact, the Rotterdam and Luxembourg documents fully recognize the importance of good environmental quality as part of a region's territorial capital. The Bristol Accord, approved in December 2005 by ministers of the member states explores how to develop sustainable communities and contributes to this line of thinking (ODPM 2005).

Interestingly the concept of sustainable communities also relates to the concept of territorial capital, and planners concerned with territorial cohesion point to the Stockholm-Kista region as an example where sustainability and competitiveness have come together (Heijde and Houtsma 2006). This region, it is claimed, is one of the most innovative in the world. It is home to a thriving large city that offers all the relevant services and yet is located in a natural green fjord area in which strict environmental regulations apply. Planners are seeking spatial strategies that would integrate the Lisbon and Gothenburg aims by focusing on innovative urban networks, and apparently such networks may include a large dose of greenness and cleanness. The sustainability and environmental discourse may thus become part and parcel of urban design and development. Planners promote integrated approaches and are not afraid of combining several storylines that may eventually feed into territorial cohesion policy and into the development of the relevant discourse.

The storyline of a "Green and Clean Europe" seems to be supported by a wide discourse coalition consisting of Nordic countries, their neighbors in northwestern Europe, the Alpine countries, and presumably (although there is little evidence for this) some countries in southern, central, and eastern Europe (such as Slovenia). The coalition also includes the European Parliament, which has argued that "the European Sustainable Development Strategy agreed in Gothenburg in 2001 . . . should be more visible . . . in the future Structural Funds and Cohesion Fund interventions" (European Parliament 2004, 8). The chapter on territorial development in the third cohesion report of the European Commission uses exactly the same vocabulary (CEC 2004a). One sign of hope is that new Objective 3 of the Structural Funds aims to stimulate transnational territorial cooperation. Whether integrated strategic projects will be sponsored as well remains to be seen. Finally, as part of a "Green and Clean Europe," DG Regio and DG Employment (2005), in their non-paper on jobs and growth, call attention to the need to redevelop brownfield sites, public spaces, and industrial sites within cities and emphasize the need for an integrated approach especially to rural regions that depend heavily on tourism in order to find in these regions a better balance between their various assets, including natural and environmental ones.

Storylines Compared

Together, the four storylines point out the potential elements of a territorial cohesion policy. As noted, because of the current institutional uncertainty, territorial cohesion will for a while remain subject to a political struggle between these storylines and the discourse coalitions that support them. A comparison of the storylines using four indicators—(1) geographic focus and key concepts; (2) discourse coalition; (3) operationalization and scope; and (4) elements of European models of society—reveals overlaps and where tensions and conflicts might occur (table 3.1).

As for geographic focus, there is quite a bit of divergence among storylines. The storyline "Europe in Balance" is concerned with only part of the EU territory—the weaker and marginal regions—whereas, potentially at least, the other storylines are related to the whole territory of the EU.

In terms of support or the composition of discourse coalitions, a comparison of storylines reveals considerable overlap among them, with the result that actors may support more than one storyline. Moreover, coalitions are not easy to determine. For example, the support for "Europe in Balance" seems quite stable, but "Competitive Europe" is relatively new and may thus soon receive greater support. Support itself can vary from active to passive. Therefore, although stakeholders may not be against a "Green and Clean Europe," their hearts may beat faster for a "Europe in Balance," because they expect, for example, a higher direct return in terms of investments, subsidies, and extra jobs. Assessing potential tension between one storyline or the other may come down to analyzing the priorities of the stakeholders, but because of the strong position of EU cohesion policy and the relatively stable coalitions supporting that policy, it is safe to conclude that "Europe in Balance" will receive the most support. Nevertheless, this storyline is receiving increasingly greater criticism for its methods of operation and lack of effectiveness, while there seems to be growing support for the principles and perspectives of the relatively new storylines of a "Competitive Europe" and a "Green and Clean Europe." It is conceivable that, to counter this trend, "Europe in Balance" will have to gradually incorporate the new storylines in order to sustain its broad support. In fact, the remarkable change of tone and vocabulary in the third cohesion report may be a sign that such discursive adoption is already under way (CEC 2004a).

In terms of operationalization and scope, the four storylines seem to largely agree on the use of strategic territorial frameworks, except that "Europe in Balance" and "Coherent European Policy" would formulate strategies on the scale of the EU as a whole, while the other storylines would focus on lower administrative levels. Another difference is the use of subsidies. Support seems to be growing for a more incentive-based policy. This means that in the case of territorial cohesion regions have to convince investors that they are worthy of investments (the philosophy of "Competitive Europe"). Finally, there is a difference among storylines in scope.

Table 3.1

Storylines Compared

	Geographical Focus and Key Concepts	Discourse Coalition	Operationalization and Scope	Elements of European Models of Society
"Europe in Balance"	Regions performing under EU average Polycentric and balanced development Services of general interest Center-periphery	CEC, EP, CoR Probably all member states with emphasis on member states outside the center CPMR, AER, etc. Stable coalition but growing criticism	Subsidies Territorial strategies or territorial indicators Cooperation Cohesion policy	*Dirigiste* Solidarity Culturally bound A little pessimistic
"Coherent European Policy"	EU territory Good governance Reduce spatial conflicts	Netherlands, Denmark, Germany, France, Belgium DG Regio, Secretariat-General, EP Increasing support	Territorial development frameworks EU policies with spatial impact Territorial impact assessments Tripartite contracts	Moderately *dirigiste* Environmental concerns
"Competitive Europe"	EU territory with emphasis on potentially well-performing regions Territorial capital Territorial main structures Networks Lisbon/Gothenburg Agenda	Netherlands, north-western member states DG Regio, CEC Positive ministerial meetings; support may be growing	Incentives Territorial framework indicating EU main structure Voluntary regional and local spatial positioning reports Cooperation Cross sectoral	Liberal (moderately) Cultural independence Optimistic Environmental concerns
"Green and Clean Europe"	EU territory with emphasis on environmentally sensitive areas Spatial balance	Denmark, Sweden, Finland, Germany, Ireland, U.K., Slovenia CEC, EP, CoR In general, broad, passive support	Environmental directives Local and regional integrated territorial development strategies Cross sectoral	Global responsibility Moderately optimistic

Note: DG Regio = Directorate General for Regional Policy; CEC = Commission of the European Communities; EP = European Parliament; CoR = Committee of the Regions; CPMR = Conference of Peripheral and Maritime Regions of Europe; AER = Assembly of European Regions.

"Europe in Balance" primarily focuses on existing cohesion policies, and all other storylines potentially address all sector policies, with "Coherent European Policy" the prime example. In terms of support and discourse coalitions, this factor also makes "Europe in Balance" a more likely winner, because fewer stakeholders have to be convinced.

How do storylines relate to each other in terms of European models of society? Because there are no easy definitions of such models (see chapter 1 in this volume), analysts must rely on their own interpretations of the models. In this chapter the models are described by using general concepts that are relevant in the context of this chapter. One element of the models often cited is the style of government, be it the liberal Anglo-Saxon style or the French *dirigiste* style. Storylines focusing on weaker regions tend to adopt the French style, while "Competitive Europe" in particular is based on a more liberal attitude.

These storylines also differ in their emphasis on solidarity. Solidarity is not totally absent in the "Competitive Europe" storyline; it is just less important. In a sense, this finding is related to the more relaxed attitude that the "Competitive Europe" storyline seems to have toward cultural identity. By contrast, identity is a key rationale underlying "Europe in Balance," assuming that Europeans are in a sense bound to their place of birth. "Competitive Europe" takes the view that identity is something much more fluid. Indeed, in this respect Reid (2004) describes a Generation E—Europeans in their twenties and thirties who are connected to Europe-wide networks via telecommunication and cheap airlines and who use English as their lingua franca, but who also retain their national, regional, and local identities. Like the storyline "Green and Clean Europe," this Generation E is credited with a perfect sense of what is going on in the world, making this and the "Competitive Europe" storylines more outward looking and globalized than those confined to weaker regions. Taking this argument further, one might pose the hypothesis that the storylines will attract different audiences, in terms of individuals, than "Europe in Balance." "Europe in Balance" might sound more convincing to the proverbial blue-collar workers and their political representatives, whereas "Competitive Europe" and "Green and Clean Europe" would attract the highly educated, white-collar knowledge workers or, in modern European lingo, the Lisbon/Gothenburg professional. Likewise, it could be argued that the two sets of storylines are grounded, respectively, in pessimistic and optimistic outlooks. Rifkin (2004) has touched on this issue in an attempt to pinpoint elementary differences between Europeans and Americans in attitude and perception.

Conclusions

The picture, then, is one in which the "Europe in Balance" storyline seems to be in the best position to remain the leading storyline and to sustain its current strong position as the main source of inspiration for future territorial cohesion policy. However, its foundation seems to have some cracks, and, in fact, the major opposition in terms of discursive power may come from the relative newcomer, "Competitive Europe." This storyline tells a diametrically opposed story and is grounded in a fundamentally different European model of society. It is a more optimistic, more individualistic, and at the same time more globally integrated model. However, as appealing as the story may sound, telling such stories requires political courage, something that is in scarce supply these days. It is most likely that the "Europe in Balance" storyline will become less pessimistic and attractive elements of the other storylines, including "Green and Clean Europe" and "Coherent European Policy," will be added, leading the way toward emergence of a new territorial cohesion discourse.

References

Baudelle, G., and J. Peyrony. 2005. Striving for equity: Polycentric development policies in France. *Built Environment* 31(2):103–111.

BMBau—Bundesministerium für Raumordnung, Bauwesen und Städtebau. 1995. *Principles for a European spatial development policy*. Bonn: Selbstverlag der Bundesforschungsanstalt für Landeskunde und Raumordnung (BfLR).

Böhme, K. 2002. *Nordic echoes of European spatial planning*. Stockholm: Nordregio.

Böhme, K., and A. Faludi. 2000. Nordic planning meets Europe. *Built Environment* 26(1):5–12.

CEC—Commission of the European Communities. 1997a. *The EU compendium of spatial planning systems and policies*. Regional Development Studies 28. Luxembourg: Office for Official Publications of the European Communities.

———. 1997b. *European Spatial Development Perspective: First official draft*. Luxembourg: Office for Official Publications of the European Communities.

———. 1999. *European Spatial Development Perspective: Towards balanced and sustainable development of the territory of the EU*. Luxembourg: Office for Official Publications of the European Communities.

———. 2001a. *Services of general interest in Europe (communication from the Commission)*. OJC 17. Brussels. 19 January.

———. 2001b. *European governance: A white paper (communication from the Commission)*. COM (2001) 428. Brussels: CEC.

———. 2001c. *Report to the Laeken European Council: Services of general interest*. COM (2001) 598. Brussels. 17 October.

———. 2001d. *Unity, solidarity, diversity for Europe, its people and its territory. Second report on economic and social cohesion*. Luxembourg: Office for Official Publications of the European Communities.

———. 2003. *Report from the Commission on European Governance*. Luxembourg: Office for Official Publications of the European Communities.

———. 2004a. *A new partnership for cohesion: Convergence, competitiveness, cooperation. Third report on economic and social cohesion*. Luxembourg: Office for Official Publications of the European Communities.

———. 2004b. *White paper on services of general interest (communication from the Commission to the European Parliament, the Council, the European Economic and Social Committee and the Committee of the Regions)*. COM (2004) 374 final. Brussels: CEC.

———. 2005. *Integrated guidelines for growth and jobs (2005–2008)*. COM (2005) 141 final, 2005/0057 (CNS). Brussels: CEC.

CEMAT—Conférence Européenne des Ministres de l'Aménagement du Territoire. 2000. *Guiding principles for sustainable spatial development of the European continent.* Strasbourg: Council of Europe.

Commission Staff. 2004. *Report on the public consultation on the green paper on services of general interest.* Commission Staff Working Paper. SEC (2004) 326. Brussels.

CoR—Committee of the Regions. 2003. *Opinion of the Committee of the Regions of 10 April 2003 on territorial cohesion.* COTER-012. Brussels. 29 April. Issued to the European Convention. CONV 754/03.

———. 2005. *Opinion of the Committee of the Regions of 23 February 2005 on the white paper on services of general interest.* ECOS/040 – CdR 327/2004 final. 15 March.

Davoudi, S. 2003. Polycentricity in European spatial planning: From analytical tool to a normative agenda. *European Planning Studies* 11(8):979–999.

DG Regio and DG Employment. 2005. *Cohesion policy in support of growth and jobs. Community Strategic Guidelines, 2007–2013.* Non-paper. Brussels: DG Regio.

Dutch Presidency. 2004. *Presidency conclusions.* EU Informal Ministerial Meeting on Territorial Cohesion, Rotterdam, 29 November.

EcoSoc—European Economic and Social Committee. 2005. *Opinion of the European Economic and Social Committee on the white paper on services of general interest.* TEN/196–CESE 121/2005. 9 February.

European Convention. 2003. *Proposed amendments to the text of the articles of the treaty establishing a constitution for Europe.* http://europeanconvention.eu.int/amendments.asp ?content=1&lang=EN.

European Parliament. 2002. *Report on the first progress report from the Commission on economic and social cohesion.* COM (2002) 46–C5-0198/2002–2002/2094(COS). Committee on Regional Policy, Transport and Tourism. Rapporteur: Elisabeth Schroedter.

———. 2003. *European Parliament resolution on the green paper on services of general interest.* COM (2003) 270–2003/2152(INI).

———. 2004. *Report on the third report on economic and social cohesion.* COM (2004) 107–C5-0092/2004–2004/2005(INI). Committee on Regional Policy, Transport and Tourism. Rapporteur: Konstantinos Hatzidakis.

———. 2005. *European Parliament resolution on the role of territorial cohesion in regional development.* 2004/2256(INI), A6-0251/2005. Strasbourg. 28 September.

Faludi, A. 2004. Territorial cohesion: Old (French) wine in new bottles? *Urban Studies* 41(7):1349–1365.

———, ed. 2005. Territorial cohesion. Special issue, *Town Planning Review* 76(1):1–118.

Faludi, A., and B. Waterhout. 2002. *The making of the European Spatial Development Perspective. No master plan!* London: Routledge.

———. 2005. The usual suspects: The Rotterdam Informal Ministerial Meeting on Territorial Cohesion. *Tijdschrift voor Economische en Sociale Geografie* 96(3):338–342.

Guigou, J.-L. 2001. Europe and territorial planning. In *Europe and its states: A geography*, A. Bailly and A. Frémont, eds., 3–4. Paris: La documentation française.

Hajer, M. 1995. *The politics of environmental discourse: Ecological modernization and the policy process.* Oxford: Oxford University Press.

———. 2000. Transnational networks as transnational policy discourse: Some observations on the politics of spatial development in Europe. In *The revival of strategic spatial planning*, W. Salet and A. Faludi, eds., 135–142. Amsterdam: Royal Netherlands Academy of Arts and Sciences.

Heijde, W. van der, and W. H. Houtsma. 2006. Van territoriale cohesie naar innovatieve stedelijke netwerken: Ruimtelijke implicaties van de Lissabon en Gothenburgstrategie. In *Grenzeloze ruimte: Regionale gebiedsgerichte ontwikkelingsplanologie in Europees perspectief*, L. Janssen-Jansen and B. Waterhout, eds., 121–135. The Hague: SDU Uitgevers.

Héritier, A. 1999. *Policy-making and diversity in Europe: Escaping deadlock.* Cambridge: Cambridge University Press.

Husson, C. 2002. *L'Europe sans territoire: Essai sur le concept de cohésion territoire.* La Tour d'Aigues: Éditions de l'Aube.

Kohler-Koch, B. 1999. The evolution and transformation of European governance. In *The transfomation of governance in the European Union* (ECPR Studies in European Policy Science 12), B. Kohler-Koch and R. Eising, eds., 14–35. London: Routledge.

Luxembourg Presidency. 2005. *Presidency conclusions.* EU Informal Ministerial Meeting for Regional Policy and Territorial Cohesion, Luxembourg, 20–21 May.

Ministers for Spatial Development and European Commission. 2005. *Territorial state and perspectives of the European Union: Towards a stronger European territorial cohesion in the light of the Lisbon and Gothenburg ambitions.* Endorsed for further development by the Ministers for Spatial Development and the European Commission at the Informal Ministerial Meeting for Regional Policy and Territorial Cohesion, Luxembourg, 20–21 May.

MINVROM—Netherlands Ministry of Housing, Spatial Planning and the Environment. 1991. *Urban networks in Europe: Contribution to the third meeting of ministers of the EC member states responsible for physical planning and regional policy.* The Hague: National Physical Planning Agency.

———. 2004. Exploiting Europe's territorial diversity for sustainable economic growth. Discussion paper, EU Informal Ministerial Meeting on Territorial Cohesion, Rotterdam, 29 November.

ODPM—Office of the Deputy Prime Minister. 2005. *Bristol Accord: Conclusions of the Ministerial Informal Meeting on Sustainable Communities in Europe, UK Presidency, Bristol, 6–7 December 2005.* London: ODPM.

OECD—Organisation for Economic Co-operation and Development. 2001. *OECD territorial outlook 2001.* Paris: OECD Publications.

Peters, D. 2003. Cohesion, polycentricity, missing links and bottlenecks: Conflicting spatial storylines for Pan-European transport investments. *European Planning Studies* 11(3): 317–339.

Prodi, R. 2002. Services of general interest: A role for Europe. Speech, University Paris IX Dauphine, Paris, 18 October.

———. 2003. Services of general economic interest and the European model of development. Speech, CEEP dinner, Brussels, 5 February.

Ravesteyn, N. van, and D. Evers. 2004. *Unseen Europe. A survey of EU politics and its impact on spatial development in the Netherlands.* The Hague/Rotterdam: Ruimtelijk Planbureau/NAI Uitgevers.

Reid, T. R. 2004. *The United States of Europe. The new superpower and the end of American supremacy.* New York: Penguin.

Rifkin, J. 2004. *The European dream: How Europe's vision of the future is quietly eclipsing the American dream.* Cambridge: Polity Press.

Robert, J., T. Stumm, J. M. de Vet, C. J. Reincke, M. Hollanders, and M. A. Figueiredo. 2001. *Spatial impacts of Community policies and the costs of non-coordination.* Brussels: European Commission.

Sapir, A., P. Aghion, G. Bertola, M. Hellwig, J. Pisani-Ferry, D. Rosati, J. Viñals, and H. Wallace, with M. Butti, M. Nava, and P. M. Smith. 2004. *An agenda for a growing Europe: The Sapir Report.* Oxford: Oxford University Press.

Schön, K. P. 1997. What became of the Leipzig Principles? *Built Environment* 23(4):288–297.

Shaw, D., and O. Sykes. 2004. The concept of polycentricity in European spatial planning: Reflections on its interpretation and application in the practice of spatial planning. *International Planning Studies* 9(4):283–306.

Study Group for European Policies. 2002. *Territorial cohesion in Europe*. Brussels: Committee of the Regions.

SUD—Spatial and Urban Development Subcommittee. 2003. *Managing the territorial dimension of EU policies after enlargement*. Expert document. Brussels: DG Regio.

Tatzberger, G. 2003. The concept of territorial cohesion in Europe: Its genesis and interpretations and link to polycentric development. Paper presented at Joint Conference AESOP/ACSP, Leuven, 9–12 July.

Throgmorton, J. A. 1992. Planning as persuasive storytelling about the future: Negotiating an electric power rate settlement in Illinois. *Journal of Planning Education and Research* 12:17–31.

Waterhout, B. 2002. Polycentric development: What is behind it? In *European Spatial Planning*, A. Faludi, ed., 83–103. Cambridge, MA: Lincoln Institute of Land Policy.

Waterhout, B., W. Zonneveld, and E. Meijers. 2005. Polycentric development policies in Europe: Overview and debate. *Built Environment* 31(2):163–173.

WCED—World Commission on Environment and Development. 1987. *Our common future*. Brundtland Report. Oxford: Oxford University Press.

Zonneveld, W. 2000. Discursive aspects of strategic planning: A deconstruction of the "balanced competitiveness" concept in European spatial planning. In *The revival of strategic spatial planning*, W. Salet and A. Faludi, eds., 267–280. Amsterdam: Royal Netherlands Academy of Arts and Sciences.

Zonneveld, W., E. Meijers, and B. Waterhout, eds. 2005. Polycentric development policies across Europe. *Built Environment* 31(2):93–176.

Zonneveld, W., and B. Waterhout. 2005. Visions on territorial cohesion. *Town Planning Review* 76(1):15–27.

Chapter 4

Territorial Cohesion and the European Model of Society

French Perspectives

JEAN PEYRONY

Territorial cohesion, European Spatial Development Perspective—Europeans now seem to have on hand such common concepts, which can be invoked in territorial development policies of various kinds. France has played a special role in the history of these common concepts, a role that is linked to France's role in the European construction itself, and particularly in cohesion policy. The reasons are probably found in French geography and history, which are those of an old and large country (when compared with its neighbors) characterized by a rather low density and geographic and sociocultural diversity. In France, *aménagement du territoire* (the French name for territorial development policies) is taught in geography classes in secondary schools. All French schoolchildren have learned about the harmony of the French *territoire*; its natural borders are in the shape of a regular hexagon, mixing diversity into a unity guaranteed by the nation-state.

The geographer Jacques Lévy (1997) quotes a French elected member of the Committee of the Regions who said, "Europe is too much history, and not enough geography." To this, Lévy comments: "Although Europeans have had many joint histories (past history), to imagine a present voluntarily built on consensus is another history (story), that is to say inevitably and firstly a space being not only unique but, for the first time, common. The construction of Europe consists of directly modifying . . . the relative disposition of its places: it is a geographic event."

It is difficult, or even impossible, to define Europe by its borders, its physical identity, or its cultural identity. What unites Europe, says Lévy, is a community of problems: those posed by this immense mixing of populations in a space that is mostly open and welcoming to human settlement, and the obligation to respond by integrating these multiple identities within a single identity that incorporates them without abolishing them. For this integration, each one of the present states (state being at present the most successful form of cohesion) developed its own proper method, emanating from its culture, religion, and government tradition. For some, like France, it is the centralism of a 10-centuries-old state; for others, like Germany, it is the federation of a plurality of regions. These methods of integration are varied, but they have converged toward a common European model, that of the democratic nation-state. Since 1950 the European states have tried to take new steps toward unity, this time on a continental level.

From this perspective, this chapter sketches a brief history of the concept of (economic, social, and territorial) cohesion. Then, because this concept seems to have French origins, this chapter tells the story of *aménagement du territoire* in France—in the earliest years implicitly through the building of large infrastructure networks and public services at the heart of the Republican model, and then, after 1950, explicitly through the development of a new policy, aiming at a compromise between efficiency and equity, which may find a philosophical basis in philosopher John Rawls's theory of justice applied to spatial concerns.

This chapter then elaborates on which type of territorial cohesion policy could be defined at the level of the European Union (EU) to implement the common concept. It does so by briefly surveying the perceptions of the concept in different member states, thereby reflecting their historical and geographical diversity, and concludes by returning to France to see how *aménagement du territoire* could in the future be more articulated with EU policies.

Cohesion Since the Early Beginnings

In *La cohésion sociale et territoriale en Europe*, Donzel (2002) sketches a brief history of cohesion throughout the centuries. In ancient Greece, social cohesion was linked to the political government of the city. Later, Christianity and modern progressives drew a distinction between society and the state. Philosophers of the Enlightenment tried to base the notion of political sovereignty on that of citizenship. The nascent social sciences reinforced the distinction between the political sphere and society, whereas for classical economics the market was where cohesion developed. At the same time, the idea of European integration appeared. Napoleon I had already pursued his desire to *cohésionner l'Europe* (make Europe cohesive), but obviously by the force of arms. In the declaration of 9 May 1950 launching the European construction, Robert Schuman, whose origin was genuinely European (his father was from Lorraine, a French region that was German at the time of Schuman's birth, and his mother was from Luxembourg), drew lessons from the failure of previous attempts to impose unity by force and proposed that European countries join together by developing "concrete solidarities" from two complementary perspectives: (1) economic development through a single market allowing free movement of people and goods; and (2) the development of a new social and political community through cooperation—not domination.

For Jacques Delors, who as president of the European Commission from 1985 to 1995 explicitly introduced the notion of cohesion into the Treaties, cohesion is part of the European model of society. This model is composed of four elements: (1) the market; (2) the state, which gives overall directions for development and correcting market failures; (3) social bargaining, which is used to implement objectives; and (4) the welfare state, which guarantees minimum rights to citizens.[1]

It is important to bear in mind that, from the beginning, the European construction has entailed a specific process that is neither purely economic (the European Union is not simply a free trade area) nor purely political (it is not a new superstate either). Territorial cohesion appeared within this logic in 1997 in the Amsterdam Treaty in an article legitimating public intervention when the market does not ensure public services in certain areas. The constitutional treaty, if ratified, will give more weight to this notion, often presented, particularly by French politicians, as having its origins in French *aménagement du territoire*, a term that is better left untranslated to avoid any misunderstanding. For this reason, it seems useful to have a look at the history of this policy in France.

Territorial Cohesion and Public Services

In *Les grands textes de l'aménagement du territoire et de la décentralisation*, Alvergne and Musso (2003) show that historically there have been two French policies of *aménagement du territoire*—the first one implicit, centralized, and Colbertist (after the finance minister of Louis XIV, Jean-Baptiste Colbert) and the second explicit, decentralized, and anti-Colbertist, and developed only after 1950. The French Revolution revealed these two logics of *aménagement du territoire* and the organization of public authorities through the struggle between the Girondins (after the province of Gironde in southwestern of France) and the Jacobins. The Girondins favored decentralization, whereas the victorious Jacobins favored—and received—a centralized French Republic.

Between the seventeenth and the twentieth centuries, all the important communication networks in France (roads, railways, post offices, telephone lines) were organized from Paris in a "hub and spokes" framework. The symbol of this centralization is the *étoile de Legrand*—Legrand is the French engineer (a polytechnician and Saint-Simonian, as described later in this

---

[1] In the early 1970s, Jacques Delors served as an adviser to the Gaullist prime minister Jacques Chaban-Delmas, promoting "the new society." From 1981 to 1984, he served as Socialist finance minister under President François Mitterrand.

chapter) who designed the national railway plan with Paris in its center (Guigou 1993).

Significant players in this history during the seventeenth century were Colbert and Vauban, a military engineer who compared society to the human body: "One may say that the capital city is for its state what the heart is for the body." Likewise, he went on to observe that communications allow trade, thereby ensuring that the "provinces can communicate their needs without satisfying them elsewhere." Communications "facilitate circulation and the movement of money, as necessary to the political body as blood to the human body. . . . It is for sure that all the provinces of this kingdom need each other, because all abound with certain goods and lack others" (quoted by Alvergne and Musso 2003). Thus, the existence of the state and the market are the twin conditions for national wealth.

At the beginning of the nineteenth century, a major figure was Claude Henri de Saint-Simon (Boltanski and Thévenot 1991; Musso 1999). Earlier, Saint-Simon, together with the Marquis de Lafayette, had taken part in the American War of Independence, altogether spending four years in America, where Saint-Simon observed the new society. For him, America was a model of society. Young America was industrial, based on firms, whereas old Europe was feudal, based on warrior states. Once back in Europe, Saint-Simon studied hydraulics in the Netherlands and made plans for waterways in Spain. In 1790 he waived his noble title of comte and became an entrepreneur. Then from 1798 on, he devoted himself to philosophy, studying physics at the Ecole Polytechnique (created during the French Revolution to educate military and civil engineers) and physiology at the Ecole de Médecine.

The analogy is clear. Engineers develop artificial networks for the circulation of trade, money, and knowledge in the "social body," whereas physicians cure networks for the circulation of blood in the human body (see chapter 10 in this volume, which describes the importance of spatial images or concepts as "frames" allowing people to construct problems). For Saint-Simon, who wanted to found a rational religion, a "new Christianity," the aim was to promote not only industry, but also the "universal association" of men called upon to become brothers.

Just before the Congress of Vienna in 1814, Saint-Simon published *De la réorganisation de la société européenne*, in which he theorized a united Europe in the form of a confederation as the first step toward a "universal association." In Saint-Simon's view, the American Revolution should have helped to conclude the French one. Saint-Simon was in search of a new social system that he called the "industrial system" as opposed to the previous "feudal-military" system. Communication networks were supposed to facilitate the development of this new system through the circulation of ideas and wealth. The new society would be egalitarian with the division of labor replacing social divisions.

As the teacher of philosopher Auguste Comte (who for a while was his secretary), Saint-Simon was considered by fellow philosopher Emile Durkheim to be the father of sociology (Musso 1999). Saint-Simon had a deep influence on socialism (including Pierre-Joseph Proudhon and Karl Marx himself) as well as on Napoleon III. The many industrialists, bankers, and engineers who have been influenced by Saint-Simon as well have contributed significantly to establishing the French railway network, water companies, and other elements of France's infrastructure. The Suez waterway, too, is a Saint-Simonian idea. In *Le système de la Méditerranée*, Michel Chevalier, polytechnician, economic adviser to Napoleon III, and follower of Saint-Simon, put forward a development plan for the Mediterranean Basin based on communication networks. He hoped to transform this area of conflict between East and West into the "wedding bed" of their union. Chevalier's last activity was to study a project aimed at building a tunnel under the English Channel.

Thus in the French context, the delivery of *services publics* in the form of networks such as roads, railways, and telecommunications clearly appears to be an important condition for the generation of wealth as well as for social and territorial cohesion. The major operators of these networks are engineers, members of the elite *corps d'État*, who are educated in state-run institutions established specifically for this purpose. For example, the Ecole des Ponts et Chaussées, created by Louis XV, continues to educate the engineers in charge of developing transport networks, thus structuring the territory.

In an issue of *Informations sociales* devoted to "Borders of Public Service," Hastings (2003, 26) profiles the French public service. He reveals that the history of the public service is inextricably linked to the history of the Republic itself. The legitimacy of the state is rooted in the maintenance of a social contract based on solidarity and equality. In the nineteenth century, the Industrial Revolution seemed to endanger the internal cohesion of society. The state was progressively assimilated to the existing set of public services. The French Republican model links the social and the political. In 1927 the legal theorist Léon Duguit said, "Public authority cannot be legitimated by its origin, but only by the services it delivers according to the law; thus the modern State appears more and more as a group of individuals working under the control of governments to provide for material and moral needs of participants; so the notion of public authority is replaced by public service; the state is no longer a ruling power, but a working group" (quoted by Hastings 2003, 30). This viewpoint is a very clear example of what Boltanski and Thévenot (1991) call the "civic-industrial compromise"—that is, civic values based on equality and industrial values based on efficiency, with the most representative of industrial values being those proposed by Saint-Simon himself.

Throughout the twentieth century, social policies became an essential part of the national identity of France (the two world wars even reinforce this observation). Today, the state is becoming the guarantor of universal social welfare. "Solidarism" is a general theory of social links under which the Republic supports social progress in an intermediate way between liberalism and socialism. Public service supports citizenship and equality. Yet the "great debate" launched in 1993 by Gaullist minister Charles Pasqua to elaborate a new policy of *aménagement du territoire* exposes the risk of "territorial fracture" (the exact antonym of "territorial cohesion") in legitimating this new policy.

Meanwhile, the French vision of public service is being threatened by growing unemployment and precariousness, the decline of social authorities, technological changes, globalization, deregulation, and the growing importance of EU norms and regulations. According to Hélène Thomas (quoted by Hastings 2003, 36), "equity is substituted for equality, social justice for solidarity, individual dignity for citizen rights as principles of public action." The French Republican model seems to be endangered. However, others such as Bauby (2003) think that this model may survive through a European version of the "social market economy" and by means of "services of general interest" promoting social and territorial cohesion. In a paper published in *Le Figaro* on October 7, 1996, and quoted by Husson (2002, 122), the Gaullist Michel Barnier, at that time French minister of European affairs (and since then European commissioner in charge of regional policy), comments on the introduction of territorial cohesion into the Amsterdam Treaty in these terms: "Public services, or services of general economic interest in the communautarian jargon, are an essential element of social and territorial cohesion in Europe. Equality of treatment and access for all citizens to essential services, quality and continuity of service, harmonious planning without territories lagging behind, preservation of long term interests; all these dimensions are to be taken into account in fields like transport, energy, water, telecommunications, or postal communications." Another representative of this French determination to preserve public services by building a common European vision is Philippe Herzog, polytechnician, economist, and a former member of the Communist Party, who as member of the European Parliament was the author of a major report about services of general economic interest (Herzog 2004).

The Birth of *Aménagement du territoire* as a Compromise Between Efficiency and Equity

After World War II, France faced reconstruction. The Commissariat général du Plan was created in 1946 to plan the modernization of the country, which then was still mostly rural. The first *commissaire* was Jean Monnet, who later instilled the idea of European construction into Schuman. At first, the approach of the French plan was mostly sectoral, but in 1962 it was "regionalized," and DATAR (Délégation à l'aménagement du territoire et à l'action régionale) was created by President Charles de Gaulle in 1963. DATAR, an interministerial administration, under the direct responsibility of the Prime Minister at that time, is in charge of coordinating sector policies at national level, as well as policies performed by national and local authorities, in the field of territorial development; its name was changed on 1 January 2006 to DIACT (for Délégation interministérielle pour l'aménagement et la compétitivité des territoires, that is to say, interministerial delegation for territorial planning and competitiveness). In parallel, a process of decentralization was launched, leading to the laws of 1982, which, in particular, created the regions as local authorities.

In their analysis "L'État et l'aménagement du territoire," Gérard-Varet and Mougeot (2001) paint a clear picture of the state of the art of economics as applied to *aménagement du territoire*. They recall that in France *aménagement du territoire* was developed after 1950 as a deliberate policy for the geographic distribution of activities. The reasoning was that the market must be corrected for reasons of efficiency (so that market forces would not force activities into undesirable locations) and equity (*aménagement* is the territorial component of national solidarity). Thus, *aménagement* is an alternative to human mobility (the preference in the Anglo-Saxon approach). According to Gérard-Varet and Mougeot, however, globalization presents a challenge to this approach, because the attractiveness of local areas now plays a role at the global level and not just at the national level.

Economic analysis provides consistent reasons for concentrating production (lower transportation costs, economies of scale, positive externalities) and consumption (diversified labor and service markets). These centripetal forces are opposed to centrifugal forces associated with property prices and negative externalities (pollution, congestion). The combination of these antagonistic forces leads to polycentric structures. Because concentration factors are also growth factors, any attempt to offset them may have a negative impact on growth. Nevertheless, Gérard-Varet and Mougeot admit that polarization is also guided by prices that do not take into account negative externalities and that, in terms of efficiency, choices about spatial planning require more rigorous cost-benefit analyses.

Territorial equity should be examined with caution because of its close association with a lack of mobility and the resulting inefficiencies, and because interpersonal redistribution mechanisms have implicitly a strong territorial effect and limit regional disparities (Davezies 2001). However, *aménagement du territoire* may be legitimate for reasons such as

- the costs associated with territorial mobility (such as the costs of managing deserted areas) or the social costs (for example, a joint localization may be necessary to maintain social links with families or neighborhoods, particularly for poor or elderly people);

- the principle of equal opportunity, which legitimates a territorially equitable production of collective goods (for example, for education or health); or

- the need to mutualize the asymmetrical risks faced by regions.

All this highlights the fact that *aménagement du territoire* always implies choosing between equity and efficiency.

In terms of instruments, Gérard-Varet and Mougeot (2003) emphasize

- the need to better understand and take into consideration the social and territorial impact of public policies;

- the need for price policies in order to improve the quality of signals guiding locational choices;

- the role of public services as positive locational factors; and

- the importance of decentralization in a more efficient public service, but also the role of the state in containing competition and encouraging cooperation between local authorities (that is, between municipalities at the agglomeration or metropolitan scale, between regions within each country, but also in a transnational context, although Gérard-Varet and Mougeot do not mention this aspect).

Davezies (2001) develops similar ideas, and both Davezies and Gérard-Varet and Mougeot explicitly refer to Rawls.

In his book *A Theory of Justice*, the American philosopher John Rawls (1971) puts forth the theory that democratic societies should be based on *freedom* and *equity*—compatible with the existence of genuine inequalities between individuals, provided that equal opportunity is ensured—and the principle of *difference*, whereby genuine inequalities are justified only if they benefit the most underprivileged. In other words, one must strive to obtain the greatest equality compatible with efficiency (in the sense of Pareto's optimum). It is understood, however, that beyond a certain level of redistribution even the most underprivileged will lose. Rawls's theory thus constitutes the most successful attempt to rethink justice and to justify affirmative action in concrete terms.

Rawls later extended his principle of equity to future generations. Sustainable development thus appears to be an optimum balance between economy (efficiency), society (intragenerational equity), and conservation of the environment (transgenerational equity). According to Rawls, this balance is not only a question of compromise among various antagonistic aims, but also a means of defining the very principles of the *social contract* binding the different parts of the society on a shared objective.

Set in the American context in which the geographical mobility of individuals is greater and the space is more "neutral" than in Europe, Rawls's theory lacks a territorial dimension (see chapters 1 and 2 in this volume). But as Lévy (2003, 531) has demonstrated, it is possible from this perspective to develop a concept of *spatial justice*, extending and applying the Rawlsian principle of equity to territorial development (for more on spatial justice, see chapter 5). The territorial policy concept that lies behind all this is polycentricity (Baudelle and Peyrony 2005).

In fact, the equity aspect of *aménagement du territoire* was there from the beginning. In 1964, while he was the head of the Commissariat général du Plan, Pierre Massé, *Ingénieur des Ponts et Chaussées*, wrote a paper entitled "L'aménagement du territoire: Projection géographique de la société de l'avenir" (The *aménagement du territoire*: Geographical Projection of the Society of the Future). What follows is a lengthy excerpt from this paper (translated by this author), which was republished in 1990 in *Le Plan ou l'anti-hasard* with a foreword by Jacques Delors:

> The policy of *aménagement du territoire* . . . is not and cannot be an aim in itself; it can only be an element in the overall policy aiming at the best organization of the economic activities of the nation. . . . The development of a nation is a totality. Between its political, economic, social, cultural and geographic aspects there is such a very strong interdependence that to consider one of them separately would be like mutilating a face by isolating one of its features. Claudius-Petit [minister of reconstruction and urbanism between 1948 and 1952], inventor of the expression and apostle of the idea, said one day: "*Aménagement du territoire* is in fact '*aménagement*' of our society." . . .
>
> One cannot accept the optimistic thesis of natural harmony, according to which the maximum development of each region would ensure the maximum development of the whole. . . . One may apply to this problem the traditional but nevertheless enlightening approach of Pareto's optimum. It results in an elimination of all inefficient situations, i.e. marked by waste of resources, in which it is possible to improve the position of a region without impeding the position of any other. Once this elimination has been carried out, one is in the presence of a series of Pareto-optimal situations, A, B, C . . . , the passage from A to B improving the position of one or more regions and worsening that of one or more others. There is no criterion of rationality that allows establishing a choice between A, B and C. A thesis sometimes advanced consists of choosing the situation corresponding to the maximum growth rate of the economy. One may say in its favor that strong growth is necessary to allow simultaneously the improvement of living conditions and realization of broad aims. But pushed to its limits, this thesis endangers a quality of development which, beyond economic values, is related to ethics. The persistence of too marked regional disparities and the massive migrations which would be the consequence would run up against the idea that we have of an equitable and humane society, even if it were shown that by accepting them we would support overall growth. One could bet on a maximum expansion of strong regions, under the condition of the transfer of a share of the profit to the weak regions. But, in addition to the concrete difficulties facing this redistribution, the very principle of assistance raises serious objections. The human problem that is posed to us is not only to implement national solidarity. It

is also to involve the weak regions in a development path based on their own characteristics.

If the efficiency point-of-view cannot be accepted without qualification, it would be a much more serious error to go to the other extreme and, for example, take as a selection criterion the minimum of migratory movements. The attachment to territory is a respectable feeling, but growth implies mobility. One cannot have at one and the same time the advantages of rapid expansion and those of traditional roots. One needs a political compromise, which economic analysis may enlighten without dictating it, while emphasizing the cost of nonmobility in terms of growth and, in addition, in terms of competitiveness. We should never forget that, in adhering to the Treaty of Rome, and more generally taking part in freer and broader exchanges, we accepted a new rule of the game. A vigorous policy must be courageously implemented, but it finds its limit in the weight of the load that the economy may support without hampering its competitiveness. If not, it would endanger all, including the destiny of weak regions.

Massé's approach appears to be Rawlsian *avant la lettre*. All the elements that underlie the present questions about territorial cohesion are clearly expressed in his paper: the necessary compromise between efficiency and equity and the new European dimension of the question stemming from European integration. At this point, then, territorial cohesion, as originating in the French notion of *aménagement du territoire* based on efficiency and equity complemented by the environment, can be defined as the territorial dimension of sustainable development. This definition is in line what Camagni proposes in chapter 7 of this volume.

■ EU Cohesion Policy: Toward Territorial Cohesion

If one assumes a Rawlsian interpretation of *aménagement du territoire* and territorial cohesion, how can such a policy be thought of at the EU level? The conceptual difficulty relates not so much to the trade-off between utilitarian and equitable approaches (Rawls gives a clear foundation for this), but to the question about at what territorial level this policy may apply (for this Rawls holds no message, because he does not take space into consideration). It is clear that today the nation-state is the preferred place for discussing and implementing social justice, based on the idea of a social contract, mainly through public transfers. If territorial cohesion is to become an EU objective, it remains to be determined (1) to what entities it applies; and (2) what kind of EU support will be given, with what financial intensity, and with what objectives defined by whom.

At this point, a conceptual (not historical) approach to this question might be useful. In the European treaties, economic and social cohesion policies have been introduced to balance the Single Market and European integration. The underlying European model, in contrast to a purely liberal model in which cohesion is obtained by the social division of labor and the market, assumes that the market alone cannot ensure welfare, and that public authorities are justified in implementing policies intended to produce a better balance between individuals or communities. However, placing economic and social on a par does not translate into a purely redistributive policy, but also action directed at the capacity of individuals or communities to participate more successfully in the economy.

Because of the financial means at the EU level, cohesion defined in this way is still broadly, and will remain, the responsibility of EU's member states (Davezies 2001, 2002). The solidarity of Europe with regard to the poorest states (the "cohesion countries"), so that they can participate in the Single Market, is accepted by all. By contrast, the need for European intervention aimed at regions (and in particular at those of the rich states) is disputed by some in the name of the principle of subsidiarity. The question of territorial cohesion arises here implicitly, because the notion of region in the treaties has no precise political or administrative meaning; the internal organization of member states is not a competence of the European Union. This notion is generally understood in the implementation of the cohesion policy as the statistical NUTS 2 level (NUTS refers to Nomenclature of Territorial Units of Statistics), but it is, in fact, already equivalent to that of territory (see Article 158 of the Treaty establishing the European Community) referring to regions, but also islands and rural areas), even before the constitutional treaty might confirm this "territorial" approach.

The points yet to be examined are (1) the extent to which "territorial" is not fully included in "economic and social"; and (2) the extent to which this question is one of European interest. On the first point, the states agreed on the extent to which "territorial" is not fully included in "economic and social" by approving the European Spatial Development Perspective, or ESDP (CEC 1999). In a way, the ESDP affirms a European model in which space is not neutral toward the logic of the market. In a society in which space is neutral, people would be mobile like goods, and only social, not territorial, issues would be involved. By contrast, European countries share a view in which territories (states, regions, cities) are factors of production (place of identity, place of collective purpose) and of solidarity, which is the basis for the existence of different political levels and territorially differentiated policies. This notion is related to the notion of "territorial capital" (see Lévy 2003, who speaks of the equivalent concept of *capital spatial*, and chapters 3, 7, and 10 in this volume). In other words, places contribute to efficiency, based on local (natural or human) assets, and also on accessibility to the networks provided by "public services," thereby contributing to the territorial structure (see chapter 10). In this sense, the notion of territorial cohesion combines coherence (territorial integration) and solidarity (territorial equity).

In the ESDP, the European states have identified methods for dealing with this territorial complexity. The first principle is that of *horizontal cooperation* (between policies and between public and private players) *at each level.* For example, no one in Europe doubts that public regulation is necessary at the local level through spatial planning. A second principle, less obvious, is that of *vertical cooperation between levels.* Invoking the principle of subsidiarity, the management of a given territory should be the concern of one political entity and that entity alone. However, the free movement of persons, goods, and capital, and the interdependence of levels, both of which are accelerating with globalization, mean that no territorial level can on its own deal with all the issues related to space, and that spatial regulation is becoming a problem shared between several levels. In France, DATAR can be viewed as the operator of horizontal and vertical territorial cooperation.

As for the second point—what European intervention is required?—the first case of EU intervention is represented by the Structural Funds, which aim at convergence. As noted earlier, it is agreed that the Single Market has to benefit all member states, and that, where necessary, the EU has to support convergence among them (for example, with tools such as the Cohesion Fund). European society is composed of national societies, which minimally implies a first level of polycentricity—that is, between the EU level and the member state level.

But the question is really more about whether the EU should support *regional* development (through Objectives 1 and 2 of the Structural Funds). Before the negotiation of the EU budget 2007–2013, two different positions were possible. The first was that of the macroeconomists of the Sapir Report (Sapir et al. 2004). They argued that the EU must concentrate its limited financial means on a policy of convergence in favor of the poorest states (with no regional focus) and direct the remainder toward policies of European interest (transport, research, safety, defense). The states are responsible for (and the only ones financially capable of) ensuring (social and territorial) cohesion. It was the starting position being taken by the Netherlands and the U.K. in the negotiations. Thus, the U.K. in its green paper on regional policy admitted the benefits of EU programs for cooperation and experience sharing. It even proposed European coordination of regional policies implemented by each state, but without an EU budget except for the poorest countries.

The second position, which consists in preserving EU support for *regional* development through Objectives 1 and 2, was that of the European Commission in its initial proposal (CEC 2004), and was finally agreed by the European Council in December 2005. To justify it, the Commission, used political arguments, not just economic ones. This position holds that the extension of strategic guidance from the EU to local actors (under the Lisbon/Gothenburg Strategy), along with effective implementation of sectoral EU policies (such as transport, environment, research), require European intervention within a regional, not just a national, framework. France made a clear-cut decision in favor of the architecture proposed by the Commission, while asking that the budget of the EU be reined in. This request is in keeping with French practice under which DATAR, to perform its mission of horizontal and vertical coordination, disposes of its own financial means (Fonds national d'aménagement et de développement du territoire—National Fund for Territorial Development), which is incontestably one of the conditions of its effectiveness.

A second case of EU intervention is when European territories (such as urban or rural areas in difficulty, mountainous areas, sparsely populated areas, islands) suffering from common problems find it useful to share experiences (this is the logic behind the URBAN, Leader, and Interreg IIIC programs) or to be recognized by EU regulations (possibility to allocate more money to territories with a geographical handicap or for these handicaps to be taken into account in other EU policies). The emblematic policy here relates to services of general interest. The constitutional treaty emphasizes this "handicap" approach, adding northern regions, cross-border regions, and mountainous regions to the previous list.

A third case of EU intervention is where the problems or the opportunities are transnational—that is, in the language of economists, where the discrepancy between the administrative frontiers of the states and the economic and social reality generates "externalities" that can justify an intervention by the higher level. Examples are the Trans-European Networks (TENs); cross-border cooperation where the persistence of linguistic, legal, or cultural barriers hampers the development of cross-border conurbations; transnational cooperation promoting on a larger scale networks of cities or development corridors (which the French sometimes call "little Europes"— see Peyrony 2006); and sustainable development of transnational sea and river basins or mountain ranges. Cross-border and transnational cooperation, as Zonneveld points out in chapter 10 of this volume, allows the construction of new common "visions" of European space as well as "strategic projects" that contribute to "trans-European structuring elements" (see also Peyrony 2003). In chapter 9, Tatzberger gives a convincing example of such cooperation.

The Perception of Territorial Cohesion in Various National Contexts

If the hypothesis is put forward that the shared reference to territorial cohesion means an attempt to combine efficiency and equity in the field of territorial development (pursuing spatial equity or justice) and that polycentrism is its physical translation, one might presume that how the various states conceive of this political aim is strongly related to their own territorial realities and to their positions in European space.

Now let us test this hypothesis. In Germany, beyond the federal remit, territorial development is a competence of the *Länder* (states); anyway, before 1989, Germany was polycentric in its urban morphology and organization, and did not have major problems with unbalanced territorial development at national level, unlike the case in France. It was the reunification of Germany—with its consequences in terms of East-West disparities, and the eccentric character of Berlin as viewed from the vantage point of the "pentagon" (London-Paris-Milan-Munich-Hamburg)—that revived in Germany the question of a federal, or even European, policy of territorial development (Ministère fédéral 1993). As for the rest of Europe, the Benelux countries are conducting a policy debate about the relationship between their capital cities and other large cities with the remainder of their territories, but the scale in question here is more meso than macro. For these countries, the macro scale is European. The European North West Metropolitan Area is authentically polycentric, and territorial development at this scale is more a question of cooperation (in which these countries have a long tradition) than of planning. France and the U.K. are both large, old states, each with a "global city," but also peripheral territories. Thus, these two countries have, more than one might think, things in common, in particular a history of national intervention in the territorial balance, even if the results diverge according to the different roles played by the respective states. The majority of other European countries are totally or partially "peripheral," and so they naturally approve the objectives of territorial cohesion and European polycentrism. For the richer northern states, cohesion and polycentrism must mainly grow out of intra- and transnational (Baltic space) cooperation, but Finland and Sweden also claim recognition of the northern peripheries' specificities. For the poorer southern and eastern states, territorial cohesion and polycentrism support the quest for European solidarity and for correcting imbalances, which is the logic of Objective 1 of cohesion policy.

Even the core countries have approved the European Spatial Development Perspective with its principle of polycentrism (CEC 1999), and now territorial cohesion within the constitutional treaty, if and when it is ratified. Whatever has been their position during the negotiation on the future cohesion policy 2007–2013, primarily determined by their contribution to the EU budget, they see the emergence of territorial development policy as a cooperative game. The Netherlands, home to the transport hub Rotterdam, but also transit countries such as France and Germany may wish that their territories were being recognized as being of benefit to all Europeans, and that, for example, congestion—not just poor territorial accessibility—could be invoked as a criterion for European funding of transport infrastructures. These countries might then achieve a win-win situation between the core and the periphery, a new presentation of the rhetoric of the head and the body, just like the Paris region has done with respect to the Paris Basin and the national territory. In addition to its own national tradition, the intermediate character of France—at one and the same time central and peripheral in Europe and a net contributor to the EU budget, though less intensely than the Netherlands or Germany—is surely one reason for the central role it has played in the invention of European regional policy and the ESDP process (Faludi and Peyrony 2001; Faludi 2004). In the 1990s, DATAR, often through the agency of the same actors, simultaneously participated in the actualization of French policy (for example, as a laboratory in the planning of the Paris Basin) and made a significant contribution to the elaboration of the ESDP.

After this test, the EU seems to some extent to have gained legitimation in dealing with territorial cohesion. Yet because of the nature of social welfare mechanisms (which remain more national than European) and because of the diversity of national configurations and of ways of implementing national cohesion and territorial development, an EU territorial cohesion policy addressing regions or infraregional entities (such as cities and rural areas) should perhaps rely more on an "open method of coordination" (CEC 2001) than on a centralized approach—that is, a polycentric approach, according to Faludi (2005).

What Future for *Aménagement du territoire* in Combination with EU Policies?

What will the French policy of *aménagement du territoire*, conceived more explicitly from the point of view of the ESDP (polycentric development) and territorial cohesion, look like in the future? It likely will be based on a compromise between efficiency and territorial equity and will be the result of a collective process, indicated by the ESDP, of horizontal and vertical coordination (Peyrony 2002). This process leaves the initiative to the actors on the ground, but with the support of the higher levels. For example, the process in which DATAR issues a "call for metropolitan co-operation" in implementation of its projects meets this criterion (DATAR 2004). The toolbox of "multilevel governance," as the European Commission calls it, can then be mobilized (CEC 2001 and 2004):

- *Tools for strategic territorial planning.* These tools are needed at the level of each agglomeration. However, such tools may be needed at the regional or even interregional and national levels as well, although at these levels such tools must be more flexible (they are not master plans), and their relation to planning documents conceived at a lower level is more a question of compatibility than conformity. At the European level, the regulations for 2007–2013 (published in July 2006) propose a new strategic framework: "community strategic guidelines" for cohesion shall be adopted by the European Council and then "national strategic frameworks" shall be presented by the member states. A regular discussion on cohesion shall take place within the Council, allowing a strategic follow-up of this policy (see chapter 6 in this volume). This process will help to solidify the fact that the EU's sustainable development strategy (Lisbon plus Gothenburg) has a regional (territorial?) strand, implemented in particular through cohesion policy. The big, vertical sectoral policies (such as those on research and transport) should be encouraged to take territorial diversity into account through the spatial strategies on which regional programs should be based. The new regulations clearly envisage such a matricial logic (vertical sectoral themes, such as transport accessibility, crossing the horizontal territorial dimension through spatial themes, such as urban, rural, or handicapped territories).

- *Tools for contracting.* Programming "contracts" allow a dialogue among regions, states, and European institutions (Objectives 1 and 2 programs, combined in France with *contrats de plan Etat-région*).

- *Tools of "shared intelligence" of territories (foresight, observation, assessment of policies).* The Observatory of Territories set up by DATAR[2] is important in two senses: in its function of observation and in the recognition, new in France, of its political nature. Under this arrangement, every third year the government will submit to the parliament a report on the territorial state of France. The Observatory will assess not only the competitiveness of the national territory and of its components (regions, cities, and so forth), but also the inequalities among individuals in their territorial dimension. If one takes the Rawlsian interpretation of *aménagement du territoire* seriously, then any policy that does not reduce inequalities should be amended—even if they maximize the total growth of a country. At the EU level, as decided by the EU ministers in Luxembourg on 20–21 May 2005, coming presidencies shall elaborate a "Territorial State and Perspectives of the Union" (Luxembourg Presidency 2005). The European Spatial Planning Observation Network (ESPON) could, in the same way, enlighten the Council of the European Union. Such an understanding of territorial cohesion makes it possible to counter the argument, often advanced against it, that the invocation of general objectives such as cohesion or polycentrism may be indicative of a lack of political determination.

Last but not least, if one takes seriously the "European construction" without limiting it to a large market regulated from Brussels by means of laws and subsidies, European "territorial cooperation" could prove to be a powerful way to develop territorial capital by implementing territorial cohesion and polycentrism through the concerted development of cross-border agglomerations, of transnational clusters of cities or large-scale networks, and of transnational development corridors. In fact, Europe may be only at the beginning of a new way of building itself through its territories.

Conclusions

In a study commissioned by DATAR, Bieber, Massot, and Orfeuil (1993), analyzed different models of daily mobility, whose significance may be extended to spatial planning in general. They propose consideration of three ideal types: (1) the California model, based on individual housing and transportation, dispersed urban pattern, and individualism; (2) the Saint-Simon model, based on strong public intervention in housing and transport,

[2] See http://www.territoires.gouv.fr for more information.

polarization of big cities, and industrial values; and (3) the Rhenish model, based on subsidiarity, compact cities and polycentricity, and ecological values. The Rhenish model is obviously preferred by the authors.

After a review of the history of French *aménagement du territoire*, it seems clear that the French model is less unique than one might think at first glance, and that many French thinkers or politicians have been inspired by ideas from elsewhere: Saint-Simon from America; Schuman from Germany; and French planners inspired by the Rhenish model in the 1990s (Baudelle and Peyrony 2005). What remains is a specifically French territorial approach, part of a specific vision of social linkages. However, the French people lack an understanding of a free trade economy, and sometimes appear to be stuck in an out-of-date collectivist dream, wavering between its realization at the national or the global level. Lévy (1997, 209–210), in a premonition of the French no to the constitutional referendum, characterizes the French communist attitude, which is also somewhat representative of the opinions held in the no camp, as

> opposed to the European utopia, a "utopianism" with internationalist pretensions but nevertheless using nationalism as a bridge to the reality of today. . . . Ranged against the Europe of elites (capitalist, Christian, and dominated by Germany or controlled from a distance by the USA) we find, on the one hand, a nation supposed to bridge, provisionally and partially, the gap between oppressors and oppressed and, on the other hand, a "humanity" larger than Europe. . . . Here one may discern the dual method . . . that Europeans have often used to contest the center: to become themselves the center . . . or to oppose it radically. . . . The problem with Europe is that it is a moving centrality launched by preexisting centers: this presents a mortal danger, of forming a detour, or even the illusion of a solution in this world on the way to salvation. (Translated by the author)

But there is a real need to formulate critical views of the prevalent liberal approach. In fact, as the French geographer Pierre Beckouche (2001) reveals in *Le royaume des frères: Aux sources de l'État-nation* (The Kingdom of Brothers: At the Source of the Nation-State), the global market and the nation-states now constitute a system, which requires comprehensive analysis and critique. The articulation between individuals and the collectivity, as structured by this system, is problematic: within nation-states—individualism, fewer social links, rights but no duties, solidarity largely maintained by the state; between nation-states—overinvestment in borders, which now constitute the only remaining form of transcendence, this time "horizontal." To overcome the nation-state, Beckouche rejects the idea of a European Union that would duplicate the nation-state model at the continental level, and he pleads simultaneously for the rehabilitation of a "symbolic register," based on common values, and for the progressive constitution of a global government, the EU being only a first step in this direction.

In his diary (January 1877), Dostoyevski talks about "great ideas borne by great peoples." He gives the examples of France inheriting from Rome the "Catholic idea," which then became the "Socialist idea," and of Germany developing in reaction Protestantism and freedom of thought. Dostoyevski proposes the Russian idea as the promotion of universality through diversity. According to him, all European thinkers, while cooperating in the building and development of a European civilization, have always thought that their own nation was the most advanced. Let us hope that this book will contribute to contradicting this statement.

References

Alvergne, C., and P. Musso. 2003. *Les grands textes de l'aménagement du territoire et de la décentralisation*. Paris: La documentation française.

Bauby, P. 2003. Les cultures du service public en Europe: Par delà les diversités. In *Les frontières du service public*, special issue, no. 109: 52–63.

Baudelle, G., and J. Peyrony. 2005. Striving for equity, polycentric development in France. *Built Environment* 31(2):103–111.

Beckouche, P. 2001. *Le royaume des frères: Aux sources de l'État nation*. Paris: Grasset.

Bieber, A., M. H. Massot, and J. P. Orfeuil. 1993. *Questions vives pour une prospective de la mobilité quotidienne*. Rapport de convention d'étude, INRETS-DATAR.

Boltanski, L., and L. Thévenot. 1991. *De la justification: Les économies de la grandeur*. Paris: Gallimard.

CEC—Commission of the European Communities. 1999. *European Spatial Development Perspective: Towards balanced and sustainable development of the territory of the EU*. Luxembourg: Office for Official Publications of the European Communities.

———. 2001. *La gouvernance européenne: Un livre blanc (communication de la Commission)*. Luxembourg: Office for Official Publications of the European Communities.

———. 2004. *Un nouveau partenariat pour la cohésion: 3e rapport sur la cohésion économique et sociale*. Luxembourg: Office for Official Publications of the European Communities.

DATAR. 2004. Pour un rayonnement européen des métropoles françaises: Eléments de diagnostic et d'orientation. Comité interministériel de l'aménagement et du développement du territoire (CIADT), 18 December 2003, supplement to La lettre de la DATAR, 2004, 179.

Davezies, L. 2001. Policies for social development. In *OECD territorial outlook 2001*. Paris: OECD Publications.

———. 2002. Notes de lecture du 2e rapport sur la cohésion. In *Territoires 2020*, no. 5. Paris: La documentation française.

Donzel, A. 2002. *La cohésion sociale et territoriale en Europe*. Étude réalisée pour la DATAR, Laboratoire Méditerranéen de Sociologie, Université de Provence–CNRS, Aix-en-Provence.

Faludi, A. 2004. Territorial cohesion: Old (French) wine in new bottles? *Urban Studies* 41(7):1349–1365.

———, ed. 2005. Territorial cohesion. Special issue, *Town Planning Review* 76(1):1–118.

Faludi, A., and J. Peyrony. 2001. The French pioneering role. In Regulatory competition and cooperation in European spatial planning, A. Faludi, ed., special issue, *Built Environment* 27(4):253–262.

Gérard-Varet, L. A., and M. Mougeot. 2001. L'État et l'aménagement du territoire. In *Aménagement du territoire*. Rapport du Conseil d'Analyse économique, no. 31. Paris: La documentation française.

Guigou, J. -L. 1993. *France 2015: Recomposition du territoire national*. La Tour d'Aigues: Éditions de l'Aube.

Hastings, M. 2003. La carte d'identité du service public français. In *Les frontières du service public*, special issue, *Informations sociales*, no. 109: 26–36.

Herzog, P. 2004. *Report on the green paper from the Commission about the future of services of general interest in Europe*. Strasbourg: European Parliament.

Husson, C. 2002. *L'Europe sans territoire*. La Tour d'Aigues: Éditions de l'Aube.

Lévy, J. 1997. *L'Europe, une géographie*. Paris: Hachette.

———. 2003. Aménagement du territoire, capital spatial, justice spatiale. In *Dictionnaire de la géographie et de l'espace des société*, J. Lévy and M. Lussault (dir.), eds. Paris: Belin.

Luxembourg Presidency. 2005. *Scoping document and summary of political messages for an assessment of "The territorial state and perspectives of the European Union: Towards a stronger European territorial cohesion in the light of the Lisbon and Gothenburg ambitions."* Endorsed for further development by the Ministers for Spatial Development and the European Commission at the Informal Ministerial Meeting for Regional Policy and Territorial Cohesion, Luxembourg, 20–21 May.

Massé, P. 1964. L'aménagement du territoire: Projection géographique de la société de l'avenir. *Revue d'économie politique*. Reprinted in *Le plan ou l'anti-hasard*, 105–143. Paris: Gallimard, 1965, 1990.

Ministère fédéral de l'aménagement du territoire de la construction et de l'urbanisme de RFA. 1993. *Guide de l'aménagement du territoire: Orientations pour le développement territorial en République fédérale d'Allemagne*. Bonn.

Musso, P. 1999. *Saint-Simon et le saint-simonisme*. Paris: PUF.

Peyrony, J. 2002. *Le schéma de développement de l'espace communautaire*. Paris: La documentation française (collection Territoires en movement).

———. 2003. Une démarche de prospective territoriale: la vision spatiale de l'Europe du Nord Ouest. In *Territoires 2020*, no. 7. Paris: La documentation française.

———. 2006. De nouveaux territoires européens: Les petites Europes. In *Territoires institutionnels, territoires fonctionnels*. Mâcon: Institut de recherche de Val de Saône-Mâconnais.

Rawls, J. 1971. *A theory of justice*. Oxford: Oxford University Press.

Sapir, A., P. Aghion, G. Bertola, M. Hellwig, J. Pisani-Ferry, D. Rosati, J. Viñals, and H. Wallace, with M. Butti, M. Nava, and P. M. Smith. 2004. *An agenda for a growing Europe: The Sapir Report*. Oxford: Oxford University Press.

Chapter 5

Territorial Cohesion, the European Social Model, and Spatial Policy Research

SIMIN DAVOUDI

A growing body of literature is now devoted to tracing the origins and defining the ambiguous notion of territorial cohesion (Davoudi 2004; Faludi 2004; *Town Planning Review* 2005; Davoudi 2005a). Particular attention has been given to the definitions offered by an increasing number of European Union (EU) publications, notably the European Commission's second and third cohesion reports (CEC 2001, 2004) and the emerging progress reports of the European Spatial Planning Observation Network (ESPON 2004a, 2005b). Most important, the concept has also appeared in Articles I-3 and II-96 of the proposed EU constitution, which, prior to the recent no votes in the Netherlands and France, seemed to be a sign that territorial cohesion would play a significant role in future EU policies. It was hoped that the reshuffling of the terminology might help to overcome the lack of an EU competency in spatial planning.

If the territorial cohesion agenda enables such developments at the EU level, its spatial translation can be interpreted as the victory of two influential planning traditions in Europe that have already left a visible mark on the EU spatial policy.[1] The first tradition is based on the French principle of *aménagement du territoire*, which has been described as the regional economic approach to planning (CEC 1997; see also chapter 4 in this volume). The other is based on the German tradition of the integrated comprehensive approach. As Faludi (2004, 1355) points out, the French tradition focuses on "the location of economic development and what government can do about it," whereas the German tradition "is more about

[1] EU spatial policy refers to any EU policy that is spatially specific or is, in effect, spatial in practice (Williams 1996, 7).

balancing development claims against the carrying capacity of the land." In other words, one concentrates on reducing territorial disparities, and the other emphasizes integrating sectoral policies. It can be argued that the French planning tradition is a manifestation of the French egalitarian tradition and its concerns with equity; while the German planning tradition reflects Germany's long-time preference for the "holistic approach," as reflected in Martin Heidegger's philosophical affiliation with nature. The territorial cohesion agenda clearly draws on both of these conceptions of space and spatial policy, which themselves are rooted in the European social model.

The aim of this chapter is twofold. First, it examines the place of the concept of territorial cohesion within the European model of society, suggesting that the concept is not just rooted in the European model (see chapter 1 in this volume), but also extends the European model's affiliation with *social* protection to incorporate concerns about *spatial* protection. As a result, the concept of territorial cohesion has reconceptualized European spatial policy by adding to it a spatial justice dimension. Second, by drawing on this conviction, the chapter explores the ways in which the discourse of territorial cohesion has shaped both the process and the content of the emerging European spatial policy research and, in particular, the ESPON program. It is suggested that ESPON, through its program of research and process of networking, has provided a forum in which some underlying assumptions of the technical rational model, which has dominated European research, are unraveled and challenged.

Territorial Cohesion: Spatializing the European Social Model

The general term *social model* refers to "ideal types," which, according to the German sociologist Max Weber, are designed to capture the underlying similarities and differences of complex social phenomena (Martin and Ross 2004). Social models conceptualize the ways in which societies construct social interdependence. In market democratic social models, a combination of public policies, market mechanisms, and kinship relations are drawn upon to "distribute obligations amongst interdependent members [who are] differently and unequally located in the division of labour and economically related to each other primarily by market transactions regulated by politically constructed institutions" (Martin and Ross 2004, 11). Social models shape people's access to resources through income from work and welfare state provisions.

However, if one moves away from "ideal types" to reality, one will observe as many European social models as there are European countries.[2]

---

[2] Modifying Esping-Andersen's "three worlds of welfare state," Martin and Ross (2004, 13) group the continental cases into three categories—Bismarckian conservative or corporatist, Nordic social democratic or universalist, and southern dual or familist—all of which stand in contrast to the Anglo-American liberal or residual model.

In spite of these variations, the European social model refers to the systems of welfare state and employment relations, with the exception of Britain's, that share enough commonality to be distinguished from the American and Anglo-Saxon model. While the European social model relies on public institutions and collective choice, the American and Anglo-Saxon model is dependent on markets and individual choice. Thus, the European model offers greater protection against economic insecurity and inequality. At the heart of both models lie centuries-old debates about the relations among the state, market, and civic society, between individual liberty and social responsibility, between economic efficiency and social equity, and between the state as provider and interventionist and the state as facilitator and enabler. In short, the debates have raised significant political and normative issues.

The concept of territorial cohesion brings a new dimension to these debates by extending the application of the principles of social models beyond individuals and social groups to places and territories. This new dimension suggests that different social models not only "decisively shape the structure of social stratification and the ways individuals are socialised and recruited into different social roles" (Martin and Ross 2004, 12), but also reconfigure the structure of territorial stratification and the ways in which territories are developed and perform different functions. Within the context of the European social model, territorial cohesion both brings the model's embedded political tensions to the fore and gives them a spatial dimension.

Among the myriad of definitions of territorial cohesion offered by various EU publications, none territorializes the European model more clearly than the third cohesion report. It draws on a simple, yet powerful rationale to convey the meaning of territorial cohesion, stating that "people should not be disadvantaged by wherever they happen to live or work in the Union" (CEC 2004, 27). This rationale adds a radical new dimension to the debate about social models. Based on this rational, the concept of territorial cohesion suggests that an individual's life chances are shaped not only by social models that "affect how and to what extent individuals are subjected to and protected from typical biographical risks (unemployment, disability, poverty, illness, old age) throughout their life course" (Martin and Ross 2004, 12), but also by where an individual lives and works—in other words, by the location and quality of places and territories. Territorial cohesion further suggests that the quality of places where people live and work can influence their access to economic and social opportunities and the quality of their lives. Thus, the concept of territorial cohesion *spatializes* the biographical risks that people face throughout their life course. From this, it can be concluded that social models not only "conceptualise the ways in which different types of societies construct *social* interdependence" (Martin and Ross 2004, 11, emphasis added), but also construct the ways in which they structure *territorial* interdependence. Thus, territorial development trajectories depend as much on the type of social models as on the life chances of individuals.

Although the term *social model* is not itself political or value-laden, terms such as *economic cohesion*, *social cohesion*, and *territorial cohesion* convey a strong normative dimension. They call for a specific social model that puts the emphasis on reducing disparities, inequalities, and injustices—objectives that are arguably embedded in the European model of society. For example, Janin Rivolin (2005, 95) suggests that "the cohesion principle expresses nothing but a concern for rebalancing the uncertain distributive effects of an internal market without borders and, in so doing, avoiding the pernicious risk of Europe disintegrating." Therefore, when the EU agreed to adopt the cohesion principle, the implementation of EU policy on territorial and urban issues became indispensable.

It is within this context that the territorial cohesion debate is closely linked to the wider debate about the European social model (see chapter 1 in this volume). That debate calls for extending the underlying principles of the European model from individuals to places and territories. It also calls for solidarity, not only among European citizens but also among European territories. And it extends the call for work-based social protection to place-based territorial protection. In the words of the third cohesion report, "the concept of territorial cohesion extends beyond the notion of economic and social cohesion by both adding to this and reinforcing it. In policy terms, the objective is to help achieve a more balanced development by reducing existing disparities, preventing territorial imbalances and by making both sectoral policies which have a spatial impact and regional policy more coherent" (CEC 2004, 27).

Thus, the concept of territorial cohesion has not only replaced the notion of spatial planning within the EU arena, but also reconceptualized it by emphasizing a new rationality for organizing European space. The discourse of territorial cohesion has added a spatial justice dimension to European spatial policy. In addition, and closer to the focus of this chapter, this perspective has begun to challenge the conventional European spatial policy research and its dominant technical-rational approach, as discussed in the sections that follow.

ESDP and the Evidence Base

Although it is now widely acknowledged that issuance of the European Spatial Development Perspective (ESDP) marked a new era in the European spatial policy field, its contribution to the emerging European spatial policy research has been largely unnoticed and hardly analyzed (CEC 1999; Davoudi 1999; Faludi and Waterhout 2002). This section explores the link between the ESDP and the emergence of this new research agenda. It examines the ways in which the underlying assumptions of the dominant technical-rational approach to European research have begun to be unraveled and challenged by this process and its substantive focus on territorial cohesion. Emphasis is placed on the role of one of the key spin-offs from the ESDP—the European Spatial Planning Observation Network, a major European research program that is funded jointly by the EU and its member states.

Acknowledging the need for improving the evidence base of EU spatial policy goes back to the late 1980s when the European Commission embarked on a series of studies that resulted in reports such as *Europe 2000* and *Europe 2000+* (CEC 1991, 1994; see also Gestel and Faludi 2005; Davoudi 2005b). Although these reports represented an important step in providing pan-EU spatial analysis,[3] their scope was confined to data collection, at a limited level, and description of spatial development trends. Thus, during the developmental stages of the ESDP, it became clear that improvements were needed in the evidence base of the ESDP's policy framework and, in particular, in its concern with territorial differentiation (Davoudi 2005b). The policy vocabulary of the ESDP was presenting difficult challenges of definition and policy application. While concepts such as polycentricity, cohesion, integration, territorial impact, and partnership were (and still are) understood broadly, their precise meanings had remained elusive (Davoudi 2003). Furthermore, because the spatial dimension in public policy had been neglected for many years, developing these ideas into analytical propositions and indicators for policy options was proving to be difficult, particularly where trans-European comparisons were to be made. It was therefore evident that a well-established, integrated conceptual base and a coherent body of research at the European level to further develop the ESDP's policy concerns were lacking. This lack was reflected in the first official draft of the ESDP, which pointed to the need to undertake "longer term research on relevant spatial issues as a part of continuing updating process of the ESDP. . . . The European Observatory should concentrate on the technical and the scientific aspects of the drawing up and the periodic updating of the ESDP" (CSD 1997, 90).

Before exploring the formation of such an observatory, it is important to highlight two characteristics of the upsurge in the European Commission's interests in evidence-based spatial policy. First, as is clear from the statement in the ESDP, the desire to improve the evidence base was, and still is, coupled with a utilitarian view of research. The idea was to "set up of a network of study and research centres to gather data needed for spatial planning at the Community level" (ESPON 2004b, 13). The danger of such an emphasis on "research for policy's sake" (Weiss 1977) is that it often leads to a highly selective construction of knowledge, leaving behind areas perceived as not having immediate policy relevance. A striking example of such neglect is the limited research, and even data, on the social, and to a lesser extent environmental, dimension of the territorial cohesion agenda, a point

[3] At that time, the EU had 15 member states.

to which the chapter later returns. Second, contrary to what the rhetoric of evidence-based policy suggests, the interface between evidence and policy is far from unproblematic, linear, and direct (Davoudi 2006a).

Such complications, along with political unease about entering into an unknown and potentially contested terrain, may well explain why the journey from recognition of a need for "a solid analytical base" for the future development of the ESDP to the actual establishment of a research program took so long and was by no means swift and seamless. Another reason was the EU's labyrinthine financial procedures and the requirement for all 15 member states to sign up to the program, despite the initial reluctance of some countries such as Spain. However, a major breakthrough came with the Commission's decision to support a one-year Study Programme on European Spatial Planning (SPESP) in December 1998. This program laid the foundation for the forthcoming ESPON by, first, clarifying the main areas of debate, the scope for future research questions, and the data availability at the pan-European level, and, second, by bringing together a network of spatial planning researchers to carry out the work.

The SPESP was viewed as a pilot project for testing the feasibility and desirability of setting up a network that could, through collaborative work, enrich existing spatial analyses and widen their scope to cover the European territory as a whole. The SPESP experience also revealed the extremity of the utilitarian view of research, which was reflected in an explicit demand for researchers to come up with "punchy policy messages," in spite of fragile analytical grounds. Such demands, although contested, continued to overshadow the process and timetable of the first round of ESPON projects. In order to incorporate input from ESPON into the forthcoming third cohesion report, the deadline for the final research outcomes was brought forward from 2004 to 2003. Furthermore, these outcomes had to be "designed in such a way that they [could] feed into discussions on EU policies" (Zonneveld and Waterhout 2005, 20).

Three years after publication of the SPESP report (BBR 2001), ESPON found itself expanding its focus from providing an analytical basis for revising and updating the ESDP to improving the evidence base for EU spatial policy. Meanwhile, territorial cohesion became its emerging rationale for organizing European space. More important, ESPON began to evolve from a mere umbrella arrangement and a set of bureaucratic procedures for a research schema into a process of collective learning with the potential to question the relevance and effectiveness of the technical-rational approach to research.

◼ European Spatial Policy Research and Technical Rationality

European research on spatial policy has been criticized for its technical nature and its overreliance on quantitative data and indicators (Zonneveld and Waterhout 2005). It is argued that research on EU spatial issues has remained "relatively descriptive in its analysis of European policy-making, or focuses on spatial development trends," which, in turn, is thought to be the cause of the limited "understanding of the many ways in which new spatial focus is emerging across EU policy sectors" (Böhme et al. 2004, 1178). It is also argued that too little attention has been paid to the ways in which the emerging European spatial policy is shaping and conditioning national policy making.

At some risk of simplification, such shortcomings can be attributed to the fact that the research in this area is largely grounded in the technical-rational tradition. Its footprint can be traced in a myriad of studies related to evaluation of the Structural Funds or under the banner of spatial/territorial policy (including the work for *Europe 2000* and *Europe 2000+*). The technical-rational approach is based on the assumption that objective assessment and scientific advice, underpinned by positivist epistemology, will lead directly and unproblematically to better decisions. The technocratic nature of EU policies with their emphasis on quantitative and relatively easy to measure indicators has helped to reinforce the use of the technical-rational model. Schön (1999, 31) describes technical rationality as "the heritage of Positivism . . . [as] the Positivist epistemology of practice."

Despite the extensive critique, as Owens, Rayner, and Bina (2004) point out, the technical-rational model has had significant leverage in legislation, policy rhetoric, and evaluation techniques. The resilience, and indeed popularity, of this model at both the national and EU levels can be attributed to the fact that "policy makers, social groups and researchers still implicitly cherish the classic concept of objective and value-free knowledge" (In't Veld 2000, 7). For policy makers, its emphasis on scientific, technical, and objectivity provides policy rationality and legitimization. It is a "pragmatic resolution of the controversies in which they are embroiled" (Schön and Rein 1994, 37). For professionals, it gives the impression of being sheltered from what Gandy (1999, 63) calls the "intrusion of the messy ambiguities of political debate."

The technical-rational model is distinguished from the postpositivist approaches—notably the deliberative processes of decision making—by its assumption that a clear dividing line exists between knowledge and power, experts and policy makers, technical and social dimensions, and objective and subjective knowledge. Within the ESPON, too, such perceptions are shared among many participants, as clearly portrayed in a post-ESPON reflection by one of ESPON's leading researchers. Drawing implicitly on the dualism embedded in technical rationality, Bengs (2004, 2) distinguishes between "the two worlds of politics and science" and argues that any intrusion from one to the other would be "an uneasy fusion because the two worlds [of policy and research] are very different from each other. Indeed they are perhaps even contradictory in many respects."

Yet despite the existence, and maybe even the dominance, of such views in ESPON, this chapter is based on the conviction that ESPON, as a program of research and a process of networking, has created an environment, most likely by default rather than by design, for social learning in which some of these assumptions are being unraveled and contested. Indeed, instead of searching for a utopia where a neat dividing line exists between the world of policy and the world of research and where one straightforwardly feeds into the other and thus leads to better decisions, it is more constructive to acknowledge the existence of a world in which these relations are closely interlocked. Furthermore, it is more useful to acknowledge that conflicts and tensions are inevitable in such a world—that is, in the real world (Davoudi 2006a). However, the issue is not how to eradicate such conflicts and tensions, but how to treat them by being engaged in what Blackler (1995, 1034) calls "the process of knowing." Despite its shortcomings, the ESPON process, with its relatively long time span, has created a window of opportunity for both policy makers and researchers to become increasingly engaged in this collective learning. The next two sections elaborate on this proposition, taking process and content in turn.

ESPON as a Process of Networking

One of the distinct features of the ESPON is its institutional architecture, which incorporates two important dimensions: the network approach to research and the interface with policy community. The following sections elaborate on these features in the context of the technical-rational model's approach to the interrelationships between experts and policy makers, knowledge and power, and technical issues and sociopolitical issues.

Experts and Policy Makers

The technical-rational conceptualization of the knowledge-policy interface assumes a separation of roles and powers between the value-free expert advisers and the value-driven decision makers. In this model, expert professionals are not supposed to be concerned about power and politics (Booher and Innes 2002), and politicians are not supposed to intervene in science and research. The postpositivist critique of technical rationality, however, rejects the concept of neutral, objective science and its disregard for uncodified, nontechnical forms of knowledge. This critique argues that, in practice, the technical processes are padded with hidden normative presuppositions and that there is an intricate interweaving of facts and values (Owens and Cowell 2002; Davoudi 2006b). On the one hand, the ESPON experience has demonstrated the existence of these interrelationships. On the other hand, it has been instrumental in reinforcing them, despite the persistent desire to keep them apart. ESPON's relatively unique institutional architecture, described later in this chapter, has created an environment that has enabled, and indeed encouraged, both researchers and policy makers to cross these elusive lines. Although this development has not gone uncontested and complaints about the perceived confusion of roles and powers have been rife (Bengs 2004), the resulting tensions and the need to manage them have led to a social learning process that has begun to question the separation of powers and roles between the users and producers of knowledge.

An illustrative example of this learning process is researchers' continuing pursuit of what is clearly a political role: pushing the spatial policy agenda higher in the European Commission's order of priorities. Zonneveld and Waterhout (2005, 21), for example, argue that "ESPON is used as a tool, by invoking 'hard' evidence, to convince politicians of the importance of the territorial dimension of sectoral policies." However, this role of researchers could be viewed not as an act of political expediency, but as the pursuit of an underlying value shared by most participants in ESPON, politicians and researchers alike. Such a role for researchers also reveals the blurring of the boundaries between science and policy and the manifestation of a dialectic relationship between power and knowledge, a point to which this chapter returns later.

Indeed, researchers began to enter into the sphere of politics, although not self-consciously, during the course of the SPESP (ESPON's predecessor) when it became clear that uncertainties and political unease about the need for ESPON were widespread. Although spatial planning was high on the agenda of the Committee on Spatial Development (CSD) and had the backing of the Directorate General for Regional Policy (DG Regio), other parts of the Commission had doubts about the relevance and usefulness of a focus on territorial planning. Thus, the participating researchers in the program were not only engaged in scientific research, but also found themselves in the quasi-lobbying position of promoting the spatiality of EU policies. In other words, they were clearly crossing the perceived dividing line between knowledge producers and knowledge users—that is, the dividing line between policy and science.

As mentioned earlier, the institutional architecture of ESPON has much to do with creating the space for interaction between researchers and policy makers and an opportunity to challenge the deep-seated technical-rational model. In 2002 ESPON was created by bringing together policy makers and researchers from across Europe. The policy-making communities are represented on the Monitoring Committee of ESPON, which consists of two delegates from ministries responsible for spatial planning in each member state and two representatives from the European Commission (DG Regio). The research community is a network of over 600 researchers from a range of disciplinary backgrounds, who cluster around the Transnational Project Groups (TPGs). These groups consist of voluntary partnerships between researchers from several EU countries, who are commissioned by the Monitoring Committee through a process of competitive tendering to undertake specific projects.

Like the ESDP, then, ESPON is not only a program of research, but also a process of networking. The networking nature of ESPON, which is now one of its constituent and novel features, was contested initially. As Gestel and Faludi (2005) point out, at a ministerial meeting in Lisbon in 1992 questions were raised about whether the EU's territorial research program should be carried out by a single European planning research institute or by a network of existing research institutes in Europe. The single research institute would have given the Commission a stronger voice and kept intact the formal hierarchical procedures of EU institutions, which perpetuate the illusive separation of powers and roles. Some have even speculated that the Commission's intention to use the SPESP as a test phase for ESPON was based on an unspoken agenda to "show that networked research does not work, thus making the case for creating an institution analogous to the European Environment Agency" (Williams 1999, 7).

Despite this speculation, the network approach was adopted, and indeed it became pertinent to the creation of a dynamic forum that has continued to recruit new researchers to the program. This forum, plus the fact that all project reports are posted on ESPON's Web site and are available for public scrutiny, has reduced the risk of building up an unhealthy, closed, cozy relationship between researchers and policy makers within what is known as the ESPON family. The TPG networks are complemented with another network of professionals from each member state, called the ESPON Contact Points, who link the Luxembourg-based Coordination Unit with the national planning communities.

Knowledge and Power

The interfaces between policy and evidence and between experts and policy makers are also reflected in the interplay between knowledge and power. Francis Bacon's widely rehearsed dictum that "knowledge is power" is a key tenet of Enlightenment (Bacon 2000). However, because power relations are often unequal, knowledge can be used strategically to pursue a specific policy direction. As discussed earlier, the outcomes of ESPON research, and particularly its maps, whose visual power has a strong and enduring impact, have been drawn upon for various EU documents (see, for example, CEC 2004) in order to influence the wider policy community, drive the spatial policy agenda, and help restructure the distribution of EU funds. In other words, the EU has called upon ESPON's power of rationality to rationalize the emerging EU spatial policy.

ESPON's demonstration of another dimension of the knowledge-power relationship has been captured in Flyvbjerg's dictum that "power is knowledge." He argues that power "determines what counts as knowledge, what kind of interpretation attains authority as the dominant interpretation" (Flyvbjerg 1998, 226). The strategic use of the rationality of power in ESPON is manifested in the powerful coalitions within the EU that sustain the hegemony of economic discourse and the supremacy of economic indicators in measuring EU policy outcomes. The Monitoring Committee has often used its powers to challenge research findings, to pursue certain directions for research, and to insist on the types of evidence needed. As Zonneveld and Waterhout (2005, 19) point out, "Based on earlier experience, these policy makers have a good idea of what evidence is needed." ESPON processes are an example of the ways in which power contextualizes the interface between evidence and policy and determines the extent to which evidence can influence policy or change behavior. Researchers' appreciation of what counts as important is an integral part of knowledge creation and a necessary step toward overcoming what Weiss (1975) calls the problem of "little effects"—that is, the large amount of research that is never used in policy making.

Technical Issues and Sociopolitical Issues

Another tenet of technical rationality is its separation of technical issues from social and political issues. Conventional European spatial policy research is littered with such assumed separations. Within this context, technical discussions among experts are often temporally sequenced and spatially segregated from sociopolitical discussions among policy makers. From this perspective, any intervention by policy makers is considered an intrusion of "political powers" into the "scientific authority." For example, the fact that the Monitoring Committee tried to influence which indicators would be used to map the "Typology of Functional Urban Areas" is considered an act of expediency rather than a political input into the process of constructing such indicators (Zonneveld and Waterhout 2005, 21). After all, the indicators are not necessarily technical; nor are they necessarily scientific or objective. As Faludi (2005, 5) points out, "Territorial cohesion is a political concept whose function is to generate consensus. Razor-sharp criteria are not always helpful in achieving agreement."

Indeed, the real problem is not that the policy makers intervene in the discussions, but that they do not do so sufficiently and in a more inclusive, transparent, and explicit manner. The ESPON experience demonstrates confirmation of the postpositivist view that the relationship between science and policy and between the technical and the sociopolitical forms a continuum in which it is difficult to identify where and when one finishes and the other starts. In the context of ESPON, opportunities for integrating the discussions are provided at various levels. For example, the ESPON process of evaluating project proposals and issuing interim and final reports closely involves members of the Monitoring Committee, which meets regularly.

Of particular significance in integrating the technical and the sociopolitical debates are ESPON's biannual seminars at which the outcomes of research projects are presented, debated, contested, and defended by the participants. These encounters between researchers and policy makers have helped, over time, to create a social learning process in which different types of knowledge are harnessed to pursue the central objective of understanding, measuring, and operationalizing the concept of territorial cohesion. This is not to suggest that the participants share a common understanding of what constitutes territorial cohesion and how best to implement it. Rather, it is to suggest that the opportunity exists, albeit still to a limited degree, for discursive dialogue and reciprocal learning among the participants, whose frames of reference may be wide apart.

One practical advantage of an integrated approach is that it raises the potential for policy makers to buy into, or develop a sense of ownership in, the research outcomes. Within ESPON, however, both researchers and policy makers may encounter some bumpy terrain, particularly when research produces politically uncomfortable results such as pointing out the perverse impacts of EU policies. A potent example is the seemingly adverse impact of the common agricultural policy (CAP) on achieving territorial cohesion (ESPON 2004a).

It is therefore not surprising that the Monitoring Committee insists that an official disclaimer be placed on all ESPON maps.[4] And yet the shared aspiration to push spatial planning on the EU policy agenda has already created a common platform from which a negotiated consensus between researchers and policy makers may emerge. Although it is true that there are institutional and political barriers to knowledge transfer, more attention needs to be paid to the potential of penetrating such barriers by conceiving the scientific and technical as part of a social world. Knowledge transfer may become easier if the social and political are acknowledged as frameworks from the outset (Nutley, Percy-Smith, and Solesbury 2003).

■ ESPON as a Program of Research

ESPON was established in 2002 as an ambitious four-year program of research. Since its inception, it has grown to include 33 research projects, engaging a wide range of researchers from across Europe. Its research priorities are driven by the ESDP's central goal of achieving a more "balanced European territory" and improving the knowledge base of EU territorial cohesion policy. This substantive emphasis and its associated spatial justice perspective have reconceptualized the EU spatial policy and reframed its research agenda. By doing so, ESPON has begun to unravel the inadequacies of the technical-rational approach to the construction of knowledge.

ESPON was created with the objective of developing "a *technical* framework through which to understand and monitor territorial development in the EU" (Zonneveld and Waterhout 2005, 20, emphasis added). A utilitarian, and in some instances opportunistic, view of research has also prevailed, which insists that ESPON has to produce "databases, quantifiable territorial indicators, evaluation models to assess the relationships between the EU policies and territorial development and . . . techniques for making sound

---

[4] The disclaimer states: "This map does not necessarily reflect the opinion of the ESPON Monitoring Committee."

and reliable maps" (Zonneveld and Waterhout 2005, 20). Furthermore, the scope of the program was determined by the conviction that devising spatial policy at the EU level requires pan-European analyses and interpretation. Thus, ESPON had to widen its scale of analysis to cover for the first time what is now known as the ESPON Study Area, consisting of 29 European countries.[5] Although the outcome represents an admirable achievement in providing new knowledge and valuable analysis on a pan-ESPON scale, it has had its drawbacks. Among these, the most notable is that the nature and scope of analyses have been almost totally dictated by the availability of harmonized, comparable data for the whole of Europe. This drawback has inevitably led to a selective approach to the development of indicators, criteria, models, and typologies, using those that can be quantified by pan-European data. It can therefore be argued that the deepening of knowledge about spatial development processes had to give way to the desire for widening the analysis. A longer-term concern is that the limitation of techniques and data availability will condition, if not determine, the relevance and legitimacy of certain forms of knowledge over others. For example, it is likely that what would count as legitimate knowledge might be a set of data and "relationships among selected variables or facts in isolation or abstracted from their social context" (Innes 1990, 232).

Nevertheless, ESPON's underlying goals of providing a better understanding of the concept of territorial cohesion, as defined in the first part of this chapter, and of finding ways to operationalize it have already confronted the program with the challenge of searching for new ways of conceptualizing and measuring peripherality and imbalances. As mentioned earlier, the notion of territorial cohesion extends the European social model's concern with social protection to a focus on spatial protection. This expansion implies that territorial cohesion is about targeting places rather than sectors as the focus of policy and measuring policy performance by the ways in which the ensemble of sectoral policies are affecting places and the life chances of people who live and work there. The concept puts the spatial dimension of economic, social, and environmental development at the heart of the EU policy agenda. It also calls for better integration of public policy and better coordination within and between governmental and nongovernmental bodies.

The implication of this policy discourse for ESPON research has been twofold. First, researchers and policy makers have had to revisit some of the traditional indicators used for spatial and regional policy, such as the gross domestic product (GDP) and unemployment, which do not necessarily capture the spatial disparities associated with structural imbalances. Factors such as demography, population density, accessibility, urban-rural relations, access to basic services, and quality of life are viewed as critical in

---

[5] The 29 countries are the 25 EU members, two EU candidate countries (Romania and Bulgaria), and two nonmember states (Norway and Switzerland).

understanding territorial differentiation. Second, quantifiable, pan-European indicators have had to be complemented by qualitative, in-depth case studies. The addition of case studies to the research methods is a clear outcome of the collective learning process in which researchers have succeeded in convincing policy makers of the need for and the value of case study research methods in achieving a better understanding of the fine-grained trajectory of spatial development.

A notable example of the ways in which ESPON projects have begun to challenge the traditional assumptions about the evidence-policy interface is the project on scenario building (ESPON 2005c). Its methodology, discussed in the next section, sits uncomfortably with the technical-rational supposition about what constitutes knowledge.

Subjective and Objective Knowledge

One of the principal doctrines of positivism, as laid down by Auguste Comte, considers "empirical science as not just a form of knowledge but the only source of positive knowledge of the world" (Schön 1999, 32). From a technical-rational perspective, reliable knowledge is knowledge that is objectively proven, scientific, and based on positivist epistemology (Chalmers 1982). By subscribing to the view that "facts are facts," it underplays the ways in which facts are interpreted and given meaning by the underlying conceptions and frames of reference (De Magalhaes, Healey, and Madanipour 2002, 55).

Meanwhile, a sharp division is deemed to exist between knowledge that is scientific, objective, systematic, and explicit and knowledge that is experiential, subjective, implicit, and tacit. Within the positivist tradition, propositions that are neither analytically nor empirically testable are often held to have no meaning at all; "they are dismissed as 'emotive utterance'" (Schön 1999, 32). The unacceptability of such a conception of knowledge may be widespread (see Star 1992), but it still figures strongly in research and policy alike. The ESPON process is no exception. The supremacy of scientific research is so powerful that the term is often used not in an epistemological sense, but as justification for the validity and legitimacy of research outcomes.

The scenario project, however, offers a different approach (ESPON 2005c). Instead of insisting on the rhetoric of "scientific" knowledge, it attempts to use deliberative processes to build up a discourse that incorporates not only objective and systematic knowledge, but also subjective and experiential knowledge in order to draw a picture of possible and probable futures for territorial trends in Europe. It implicitly draws on the Aristotelian concept of *phronesis*,[6] which refers to practical knowledge or wisdom and suggests that "subjectivity is not an intrusion to be minimised but an

---

[6] As opposed to *episteme*, related to theoretical know-why, and *techne*, denoting technical know-how (Owens, Rayner, and Bina 2004, drawing on Flyvbjerg 2001).

essential constituent of practical rationality, in which intuition and appreciation of context are regarded as intellectual virtues" (Owens, Rayner, and Bina 2004, drawing on Flyvbjerg 2001). For example, the framing and reframing of scenarios, including the selection of key trends and themes and the criteria for the final choice of integrated scenarios, have been achieved through a process of deliberation between researchers and policy makers that has drawn on various forms of knowledge.

The scenarios themselves are developed not to predict the future but to raise awareness. They are pedagogical and aim to raise the alarm among politicians about the consequences of doing nothing or choosing the wrong course of action. The idea is to portray an explicit, and to some extent extreme, picture of the way in which strategic policy choices for the future of Europe can be conditioned not only by social and economic trends but also by territorial structures of localities. The goal is to illustrate how such policy choices can lead to differentiated impacts on various territories, reconfiguring the balance of winners and losers. The emphasis is placed on provoking a political debate based on justifiable and defensible, though not necessarily scientific, knowledge. Overall, the process of scenario building has enlarged the space for dialogue and collective learning. It has facilitated testing and adapting expert-based knowledge in practice through "tinkering," which bonds explicit and tacit knowledge and contributes to knowledge creation (Hargreaves 1999). As Huberman (1993) asserts, such processes of social interactions can lead to the development of shared meaning over time.

Economic and Social Indicators

A key contribution of ESPON to the debates about indicators has begun to emerge from the ongoing attempt to develop a European Territorial Cohesion Index (ETCI). The index was to be used by the Commission for identifying areas in need of aid; in other words, for allocating Structural and Cohesion Funds. But over the course of the project such intentions were rejected, or made less explicit, by the researchers, and the emphasis was put on developing a synthetic indicator to evaluate the territorial scenarios (ESPON 2005c). The idea is to identify and develop criteria that reflect three key features of territorial cohesion: holistic, territorial, and dynamic (ESPON 2005c, 518–527).

The holistic nature of territorial cohesion stems from its link with the German tradition of an integrated comprehensive approach to planning. This approach covers not only economic concerns, but also social and environmental considerations. In addition, it includes the demographic dimension, which, because of the rising cost of an aging Europe, now appears to be a threat to the stability of the European model of society.

The emphasis on territorial lies at the heart of the way in which the concept of territorial cohesion spatializes the European model's concerns with social protection issues. The territorial dimension is to be captured through two key elements: multiscalarity and accessibility. Multiscalarity refers to the fact that the degree of "cohesion" can fluctuate according to the scale on which it is applied. Thus, spatial disparities at, for example, the national level may be masqueraded if the analyses are up-scaled to the EU level or down-scaled to the regional level. More specifically, it is becoming evident that in some countries, such as Ireland (see Davoudi and Wishardt 2005), the pursuit of polycentrism at the European level has led to monocentrism at the national level. Such monocentric trends are represented in an overconcentration of population and economic activity, often in the capital cities or major urban centers. The Irish experience is likely to be replicated in the new member states that will soon be the main recipients of EU funds (Davoudi in press). The second element of territoriality is *accessibility*, or parity of access as the ESDP puts it. Here the notion of accessibility applies to both services of general economic interest, as mentioned in the Amsterdam Treaty, and access to social and environmental services, resources, and opportunities. These are shaped not only by work-based social protection measures, but also by place-based qualities.

Finally, the term *dynamic* points to the time dimension and the evolving nature of territorial cohesion. It emphasizes that the degree of cohesion and disparities not only changes across the geographic scale but also ebbs and flows across the temporal scale, indicating that territorial cohesion cannot be captured in a snapshot.

The multifaceted nature of the concept and the problems of developing an index that can effectively capture complexity have presented ESPON with not just a technical challenge, but also a highly political one. Building the index requires combining various dimensions into one measurable indicator. This feat inevitably involves skillful use of techniques as well as hard political choices about the selection of criteria, the weighing of variables, and the demarcation of thresholds. Although the process is of immense significance for collective learning and the outcome is crucial for placing territorial cohesion at the core of EU spatial policy, the indicators are bound to be criticized for their limitations. Such composite and data-hungry indicators tend to become crude and restricted. However, as the experience of the United Nations in developing the Human Development Index (HDI) has shown, one can only effectively displace a crude yet convenient indicator such as gross national product (GNP) by using another convenient, albeit crude, indicator (ESPON 2005c). Amartya Sen (1999, 23) points out that while the HDI has been criticized for its limitations, it has been praised for complementing the "overused and oversold" GNP.

A strong parallel can be drawn with the current domination of GDP per capita in European regional policy (Grasland 2004). Indeed, the EU spatial policy field has been heavily influenced and largely handicapped by the "regime of Structural Funds," in which the "region," expressed in statistical representation of NUTS 2 (Nomenclature of Territorial Units of Statistics), has become the dominant unit of analysis, and economic achievement, represented largely by the GDP, has become the dominant indicator. This situation has even led to the reconfiguration of the administrative boundaries in some of the key beneficiaries of the Structural Funds such as Ireland (Davoudi and Wishardt 2005) and, more recently, new member states. They have had to adjust their administrative tiers to fit the regulations governing the Structural Funds, despite the potentially adverse impact of such adjustments on governance relations and public access to decision makers (Mercier 2005, 61).

Thus, in the same way that the HDI has put human development on the world agenda, crossed disciplinary boundaries, and brought together technical-methodological concerns with sociopolitical ones, the ongoing discussions in ESPON about the ETCI have the potential to place territorial cohesion on the EU agenda and provide a space for articulating the intricate interconnections between technical and political choices. These discussions, underpinned by the work of Claude Grasland and his team (ESPON 2004b, 2005c), have challenged technical rationality in two important ways. First, they have revealed how "techniques that claim to be purely technical often have an in-built tendency to support particular outcomes" (Owens, Rayner, and Bina 2004). Indeed, comparing two hypothetical indices of European territorial cohesion, one driven by the Lisbon Strategy's objectives and the other by the ESDP's objectives,[7] they have demonstrated how the Lisbon Strategy–based indices would result in concentration of the Structural Funds in the new member states, whereas the ESDP-based indices would shift the Funds to the southern Mediterranean regions. The value of a hypothetical exercise such as this lies in its ability to illustrate the way in which implicit political choices—that is, the selection of indicators—can be wrapped up in technical judgments to achieve certain aims.

Second, the discussions have highlighted how political choices to invest in collecting certain data and neglect others have influenced the focus of research. The extensive work undertaken by various ESPON projects has revealed the hegemony of economic indicators within the EU databases—hegemony that is sustained over time by the institutional power of, for example, the Statistical Office of the European Commission, known as EUROSTAT. Although environmental indicators are making their way into the EU policy discourses, they are heavily driven by data availability rather than policy goals, and are being developed in a separate institution, the European Environment Agency (EEA), which has less clout when it comes to EU regional policy. Most striking are the limited attempts being made to construct social indicators at the EU level. Of the 103 indicators developed so far within ESPON projects, only four can be considered social (ESPON 2005c, 524). The lack of Europe-wide comparable regional data has led to

---

[7] The objectives of the Lisbon Strategy are knowledge-based economic growth; those of the ESDP are economic competitiveness, social cohesion, and environmental sustainability.

the exclusion of such indicators and thus inhibited the construction of knowledge on an important dimension of territorial cohesion. Similar short-comings exist in relation to quality of life indicators and issues of accessibility to basic services.

The dominance of economic indicators, coupled with a lack of social, and to lesser extent environmental, indicators in ESPON, and more important EUROSTAT, has led to a vicious circle. The research focused on what is available tends to be economically driven, which feeds, in turn, into a policy emphasis on the economic dimension of territorial cohesion, which then requires further investment in research based on economic indicators. This cycle reveals how the institutional setting and the economic policy discourse within the European spatial development research community perpetuate this vicious circle and maintain the policy emphasis on the economic dimension of territorial cohesion. The conclusion so far is that "in the current statistical situation of the EU . . . it is impossible to build any relevant index of territorial cohesion at [the] regional level which could combine the three dimensions of the ESDP" (ESPON 2005c, 525).

As stressed throughout the ESPON process, breaking this cycle will require a political commitment and long-term investment in data collection and harmonization. However, because of the intrinsic link between the concept of territorial cohesion and the European social model, such a commitment will depend largely on the future of the European model, or more precisely on the balance of interplay between its economic competitiveness, social cohesion, and environmental sustainability agenda. This observation returns this discussion to where it started. It places the debate on the future of territorial cohesion and its research agenda at the heart of what can be called the dilemma of the European model.

■ The Dilemma of the European Social Model: A Concluding Remark

The European social model and all its variances are the construct of decades of social negotiations and compromises over the balance of relationship among the state, the market, and the civil society. As a result, the interplay between economic efficiency and social equity has fluctuated over time and in different countries. Despite the general resilience of the European model, it has not been immune to both exogenous pressures, such as globalization, and indigenous challenges, such as the shift from manufacturing to services and the slowdown in productivity and economic growth that has made it difficult for welfare systems to meet the growing demand arising from the changing demographic patterns and family structures (Pierson 2001). These pressures have triggered, and will do so more forcefully in the future, conflicts over the distribution of resources along what Martin and Ross (2004, 15) call "new cleavage lines."

Among the exogenous factors, the most relevant and more powerfully exerted is the political decoupling of European economic integration and social protection issues, which, as Scharpf (2002, 646) points out, "has characterised the real process of European integration from Rome to Maastricht." Such decoupling would not have happened if the French Socialist prime minister Guy Mollet had had his way in the Treaty of Rome and established the harmonization of social regulations as a precondition for the integration of the industrial market. However, if in 1957 such harmonization was difficult to achieve among six countries with more or less similar social models, it is now increasingly impossible when 25 divergent countries are involved (Scharpf 2002).

This decoupling has created an inherent and persistent tension between the EU economic competitiveness and cohesion policies. The conflict reached new heights after publication of the Lisbon Strategy, which was damned by some political constellations as a move too far toward Anglo-American "ultraliberalism." Similar sentiments have now engulfed the discussions about the proposed constitution, with parts of the French and Dutch no camps arguing that it is too Anglo-Saxon–oriented. However, this economic emphasis, which is seen in some quarters as a new step toward the erosion of the European social model, is not new. Similar debates emerged after the introduction of the Single European Act, which, among other things, liberalized hitherto protected, highly regulated, and often state-owned public services, including transport, telecommunication infrastructure, and energy. All this is a continuation of the hegemony of the economic policy discourse that has framed the European agenda mainly in terms of economic integration and liberalization (Scharpf 2002). And, as noted earlier, this hegemony has led to continuing investment in the work on economic data and indicators at the expense of social ones.

The advancement of EU economic integration since the 1950s "has created a fundamental asymmetry between policies promoting market efficiencies and those promoting social protection and equality" (Scharpf 2002, 665). The result is that member states are less able to influence the direction of their economies and to realize self-defined sociopolitical, and by extension spatial, goals. For example, because of European deregulation policies states are unable to use public sector industries as an employment buffer at a time of economic decline. Furthermore, European competition policy largely prevents the use of state aid in reducing regional disparities and increasing territorial cohesion—an issue that is central to the political negotiations on the post-2006 distribution of Structural Funds.

Meanwhile, the asymmetric development of the Europeanization process has led to an increasing demand for re-creating a level playing field and recoupling social protection and economic integration functions at the European level. However, because of the diversity of national systems and the political salience of these differences on which people have based their life plans, it seems almost impossible to reach a common European solution (Scharpf 2002, 652). Similar dilemmas can be observed in the context of the territorial cohesion agenda. There, neither subscription to a European spatial planning directive nor harmonization of national planning systems seems to be a feasible way forward in view of the diversity of such systems and their underlying social philosophies and cultural values.

To get around this dilemma, the EU has proposed a new governing mode called the Open Method of Coordination (OMC), which aims to protect and promote "social Europe." The OMC emphasizes policy learning through exchanging information, benchmarking, peer review, deliberation, voluntary cooperation, and naming and shaming. Although the OMC has been applied mainly to employment policies, it can be, as Faludi (2005) suggests, extended to territorial cohesion and spatial planning. Indeed, the ESDP process and its impact on national strategies demonstrate that the extension of OMC to spatial planning issues may be the way forward (ESPON 2005a).

Within this context, institutions such as ESPON have a major role to play, not only as a program of research for identifying best practices and criteria for benchmarking, but also as a forum for deliberation and social learning among researchers and policy makers. The ESPON experience so far has demonstrated that procedures regarded as technocratic have, in practice, provided a forum for dialogue "within which knowledge can be assembled, arguments can take place, and learning may occur within and between different coalitions" (Owens and Cowell 2002, 71). It has confirmed that even predominantly technical procedures have the potential to provide, as an unintended effect, considerable space for deliberation and learning.

ESPON can thus be considered a step forward in European research. Notwithstanding major shortcomings, ESPON has deepened and widened the Europeanization of spatial policy research; established a new institutional architecture, which has helped to reduce the gap between experts and policy makers; and created a platform from which a more powerful voice for promoting the spatial dimension of EU policies has emerged. More important, despite its continuing preoccupation with technical rationality, it has confronted the policy and research communities with the challenge of moving beyond that to include postpositivist models. As a result, ESPON has advanced understanding of the spatialization of the European social model.

And yet to fulfill its wider role as a forum for knowledge production and knowledge transfer, ESPON must make a concerted effort to widen its research agenda and method of analysis to incorporate qualitative and in-depth inquiries into the diversity of spatial trends across Europe. ESPON also must complement its technical analyses with discursive approaches, particularly when problems are complex and poorly structured, such as the concept of territorial cohesion. Critical research into the differentiated impact of EU spatial policy on national and regional development also should be an integral part of this wider program. Finally, any attempt to shrink the space for interaction between researchers and policy makers should be resisted if the goal is to promote long-term learning processes through which knowledge can inform and even reframe policy problems. Making such critical research possible is vital to finding a negotiated way forward in pursuing the European social model, particularly in the current climate of growing tensions about the future of European integration.

References

Bacon, F. 2000. *The new organon.* Cambridge: Cambridge University Press.

BBR—Bundesamt für Bauwesen und Raumordnung. 2001. *Study Program on European spatial planning* Bonn: BBR.

Bengs, C. 2004. Introduction to a discussion on the third cohesion report: Policy-relevant research and research-relevant policy. *European Journal of Spatial Development.* http://www.nordregio.se/EJSD (online only).

Blackler, F. 1995. Knowledge, knowledge work and organisations: An overview and interpretation. *Organisational Studies* 16(6):1021–1046.

Böhme, K., T. Richardson, G. Dabinett, and O. B. Jensen. 2004. Values in a vacuum? Towards an integrated multi-level analysis of the governance of European space. *European Planning Studies* 12(8):1175–1188.

Booher, D., and J. Innes. 2002. Network power in collaborative planning. *Journal of Planning, Education and Research* 21(3):221–236.

CEC—Commission of the European Communities. 1991. *Europe 2000: Outlook for the development of the Community's territory.* Luxembourg: Office for Official Publications of the European Communities.

———. 1994. *Europe 2000+: Co-operation for European territorial development.* Luxembourg: Office for Official Publications of the European Communities.

———. 1997. *The EU compendium of spatial planning systems and policies.* Regional Development Studies 28. Luxembourg: Office for Official Publications of the European Communities.

———. 1999. *European Spatial Development Perspective: Towards balanced and sustainable development of the territory of the EU.* Luxembourg: Office for Official Publications of the European Communities.

———. 2001. *Unity, solidarity, diversity for Europe, its people and its territory: Second report on economic and social cohesion.* Luxembourg: Office for Official Publications of the European Communities.

———. 2004. *A new partnership for cohesion: Convergence, competitiveness, cooperation. Third report on economic and social cohesion.* COM/2004/107. Luxembourg: Office for Official Publications of the European Communities.

Chalmers, A. F. 1982. *What is this thing called science?* 2d ed. Berkshire, UK: Open University Press.

CSD—Committee on Spatial Development. 1997. *European Spatial Development Perspective, first official draft.* Noordwijk: Committee on Spatial Development.

Davoudi, S. 1999. Making sense of the ESDP. *Town and Country Planning* 68(12):367–369.

———. 2003. Polycentricity in European spatial planning: From an analytical tool to a normative agenda. *European Planning Studies* 11(8):979–999.

———. 2004. Territorial cohesion: An agenda that is gaining momentum. *Town and Country Planning* 73(7/8):224–227.

———. 2005a. Understanding territorial cohesion. *Planning Practice and Research*, 20(4): 433–441.

———. 2005b. ESPON: Past, present and future. *Town and Country Planning* 74(3): 100–102.

———. 2006a. Evidence-based planning: Rhetoric and reality, *DISP*, 165(2):14–25.

————. 2006b. Strategic waste planning: The interface between the "technical" and the "social." *Environment and Planning C* 24(5): 681–700.

————. In press. EU enlargement and the challenges for spatial planning systems in the new member states. In *EU Accession countries and planning*, A. Uwe, S. Guntner, D. Peters, and S. Huning, eds. Berlin: Planungsrundschau Series 12.

Davoudi, S., and M. Wishardt. 2005. Polycentric turn in the Irish spatial strategy. *Built Environment* 31(2):122–132.

De Magalhaes, C., P. Healey, and A. Madanipour. 2002. Assessing institutional capacity for city centre regeneration: Newcastle's Grainger Town. In *Urban governance, institutional capacity and social milieux*, G. Cars, P. Healey, A. Madanipour, and C. De Magalhaes, eds., 45–62. Aldershot, UK: Ashgate.

ESPON—European Spatial Planning Observation Network. 2004a. *ESPON in progress: Preliminary results by autumn 2003.* Luxembourg: ESPON.

————. 2004b. *Integrated tools for European spatial development. Project 3.1, 2002–2004, first interim report.* http://www.espon.eu

————. 2005a. *Application and effects of the ESDP in member states. Project 2.3.1, 2004–2006, second interim report.* http://www.espon.eu.

————. 2005b. *In search of territorial potential: Midterm results by spring 2005.* Luxembourg: ESPON.

————. 2005c. *Spatial scenarios and orientation in relation to the ESDP and EU cohesion policy. Project 3.2, 2004-2006, second interim report.* http://www.espon.eu.

Faludi, A. 2004. Territorial cohesion: Old (French) wine in new bottles? *Urban Studies* 41(7):1349–1365.

————, ed. 2005. Territorial cohesion. Special issue, *Town Planning Review* 76(1):1–118.

Faludi, A., and B. Waterhout. 2002. *The making of the European Spatial Development Perspective: No master plan!* London: Routledge.

Flyvbjerg, B. 1998. *Rationality and power: Democracy in practice.* Chicago: University of Chicago Press.

————. 2001. *Making social science matter.* Cambridge: Cambridge University Press.

Gandy, M. 1999. Rethinking the ecological leviathan: Environmental regulation in an age of risk. *Global Environmental Change* 9:59–69.

Gestel, T. van, and A. Faludi. 2005. Towards a European territorial assessment network: A bright future for ESPON? *Town Planning Review* 76(1):81–93.

Grasland, C. 2004. Les inégalités regionales dans une Europe élargie. In *L'Europe centrale face au grand élargissement*, B. Chavance, ed., 181–214. Paris: L'Harmattan (collection Pays de l'Est).

Hargreaves, D. H. 1999. The knowledge-creating school. *British Journal of Educational Studies* 47:122–144.

Huberman, M. 1993. Linking the practitioner and researchers communities for school improvement. *School Effectiveness and School Improvement* 4:1–16.

Innes, J. 1990. *Knowledge and public policy.* 2d ed. New Brunswick, NJ: Transaction Books.

In't Veld, R. 2000. *Knowingly and willingly: The roles of knowledge about nature and the environment in policy processes.* Utrecht: Lemma Publishers.

Janin Rivolin, U. 2005. Cohesion and subsidiarity: Towards good territorial governance in Europe. *Town Planning Review* 76(1):93–107.

Martin, A., and G. Ross. 2004. Introduction: EMU and the European social model. In *Euros and Europeans: Monetary integration and the European model of society*, A. Martin and G. Ross, eds., 1–19. Cambridge: Cambridge University Press.

Mercier, G. 2005. Which territorial cohesion policy for the new EU members? The example of Slovakia. *Town Planning Review* 76(1):57–69.

Nutley, S., J. Percy-Smith, and W. Solesbury. 2003. *Models of research impact.* London: Learning and Skills Research Centre.

Owens, S., and R. Cowell. 2002. *Land and limits: Interpreting sustainability in the planning process*. London: Routledge.

Owens, S., T. Rayner, and O. Bina. 2004. New agendas for appraisal: Reflection on theory, practice and research. *Environment and Planning A* 36(11):1943–1959.

Pierson, P. 2001. *The new politics of the welfare state*. Oxford: Oxford University Press.

Scharpf, F. 2002. The European social model: Coping with the challenges of diversity. *Journal of Common Market Studies* 40(4):645–670.

Schön, D. 1999. *The reflective practitioner: How professionals think in action*. Aldershot, UK: Ashgate.

Schön D., and M. Rein. 1994. *Frame reflection: Towards the resolution of intractable policy controversies*. New York: Basic Books.

Sen, A. 1999. *Special contribution to the World Report on Human Development*. New York: United Nations.

Star, S. 1992. The Trojan door: Organisations, work, and the "open black box." *Systems Practice* 5:395–410.

Weiss, C. H. 1975. Evaluation research in the political context. In *Handbook of evaluation research*, vol. 1, E. S. Struening and M. Guttentag, eds., 13–25. London: Sage.

———. 1977. Research for policy's sake: The enlightenment function of social research. *Policy Analysis* 3(4):531–545.

Williams, R. H. 1996. *European Union, spatial policy and planning*. London: Paul Chapman Publishing.

———. 1999. Constructing the European Spatial Development Perspective: Consensus without a competence. *Regional Studies* 33:793–797.

Zonneveld, W., and B. Waterhout. 2005. Visions on territorial cohesion. *Town Planning Review* 76(1):15–29.

Chapter 6

Delivering Territorial Cohesion

European Cohesion Policy and the European Model of Society

JOHN BACHTLER AND LAURA POLVERARI

Whether there is a single European model of society is debatable. The definition itself of a "model of society" can be interpreted in different ways. For example, the expression can be used to evoke the differences between the dominant economic development paradigms—for example, between the so-called European models of welfare capitalism and the more liberal Anglo-Saxon formula for capitalism. However, "model of society" can also be used in a wider sense to encompass not just the economic sphere (and the weight attributed to noneconomic factors), but also the whole set of institutional and political interrelations connected to the formation and implementation of policy preferences, the role accorded to society and the individuals within it, and the set of shared values and frames of reference, all of which contribute to rendering the European Union (EU) something more than an open, regulated market space.

It would be tempting to try and define the European model of society by what it is not (in relation to competing models, most notably that of the United States) or by simplification (by invoking evocative visions of Europe, such as the bucolic picture depicted by the American public policy analyst Jeremy Rifkin, as quoted by Faludi in chapter 1), but the explanatory capacity of such approaches is limited. The European Union is a complex reality. It includes at present 25 countries and a population of almost 457 million (more than that of the United States and Japan together) with different national identities, spoken languages, and historical traditions. Further enlargements—with Romania and Bulgaria in 2007 and, potentially, Croatia, Macedonia, and Turkey some time in the future—will enhance this diversity further.

From an institutional and political point of view, the EU is a hybrid reality as well. It is neither a federal super-state nor a simple international organization. Its competencies, policy-making methods, and policies are in a state of flux. In a teleological sense, there is no single process driving toward achievement of a pre-established European model. The EU and its policies are the result of a progressive stratification of ideas and policy decisions, mainly by political elites, toward evolving goals: from the original aim of generating the conditions for an enduring peace across the European continent to the current goal of sustainable growth and employment.

In chapter 1 of this volume, Faludi adopts a pragmatic approach in defining the European model of society.[1] He describes it through analysis of the concrete evolution of European socioeconomic policy from the Delors Commission to the Barroso Commission. This chapter adopts a similar approach. It explores the topic of the European model of society through analysis of a specific European policy sphere: cohesion policy. This policy is particularly relevant for three reasons. First, it is one of the most significant EU policies in financial terms. Second, it has contributed significantly to the Europeanization of domestic policies, as discussed in the copious literature on Europeanization and multilevel governance (see Le Galès, Benz, Börzel, Gualini, and others) contributing to the generation of a European model. And, third, this policy arena epitomizes the differences that exist across member states in relation to the domestic variants of such a model, as the discussion that follows of the different positions on the reform of future European cohesion policy shows.

Also following Faludi's approach, this chapter addresses the topic of territorial cohesion. The first section discusses the evolution of EU cohesion policy up to the informal ministerial meeting that was held in Luxembourg in May 2005. This discussion is followed by a review of the draft Community Strategic Guidelines for the 2007–2013 period, which also touches on the concept of polycentric development.

The chapter then turns to discussing some of the constraints that may hinder the practical achievement of territorial cohesion and reviews the approaches of current EU cohesion policy programs in relation to two central areas for the achievement of territorial cohesion within European cohesion policy: urban development and territorial cooperation (considering all 25 member countries). This last part of the chapter draws on recent research undertaken by the authors in the framework of the ongoing research program of the IQ-Net consortium and draws on country research inputs by researchers at the European Policies Research Centre.[2] The chap-

---

[1] Another extremely insightful conceptualization of the European model of society is provided by Camagni in chapter 7 of this volume. He outlines a hierarchy of "components" of such a model.

[2] The contributions of the following colleagues are acknowledged: Tobias Gross (Austria), Douglas Yuill (Finland), Frederike Gross (France), Sara Davies (Germany), Carlos Mendez (Spain), Nina C. Quiogue (Sweden), Martin Ferry (U.K.), and Vít Novotný (new member states). IQ-Net is one of the two long-running research projects of the European Policies Research Centre (EPRC). It consists of a network of regional and national partners from Structural Funds programs across the European Union for which the EPRC carries out a structured program of applied research.

ter concludes with some final thoughts, including on the evolution of the European model of society.

European Cohesion Policy and Territorial Cohesion: A New Policy Goal

EU cohesion policy is the second largest area of EU expenditure, with an allocation of €212 billion for 2000–2006 (and a further €22 billion in the new member states for 2004–2006) through the EU's Structural and Cohesion Funds. This allocation finances interventions to support the development of lagging regions; the restructuring of industrial, rural, and urban areas; and the promotion of employment, education, and training, as well as cross-border, transnational, and interregional networking.

Cohesion policy is a territorially focused policy—that is, most of the funding is allocated for specific areas. Over two-thirds of the funds are spent on economic and social development in the least prosperous parts of the EU which are home to about 22 percent of the EU population.[3] Some 11 percent of the funding is allocated to regions (covering a further 18 percent of the EU population) affected by specific socioeconomic challenges such as the decline of specific industries, rural decline, peripherality, and urban deprivation. Nonetheless, while discriminating territorially, EU cohesion policy—as defined in the various treaties governing the EU—has essentially been a policy for economic and social development for much of the last 30 years.

Since the late 1990s, however, there has been a trend toward a wider interpretation of the role of regional policy—at the European level and in some member states—that integrates the traditional economic and social policy goals within a broader spatial or territorial framework. This policy approach starts from the premise that spatial differences in living and working conditions result from factors such as access to essential services, basic infrastructure, and knowledge, or are dictated by geographical constraints such as distance, insularity, or topography. Achieving "balanced development" (whether on a local, regional, national, or EU scale) requires a more coherent and integrated approach, not just on the part of regional policy but also on the part of sector policies with spatial impacts.

At the European level, the debate surrounding these issues has been essentially theoretical. The series of studies and concepts undertaken over the past decade culminated in the 1999 European Spatial Development Perspective (ESDP), which sought to analyze and map the territorial imbalances across the EU (see Drevet's contribution in chapter 8 of this volume for an account of the emergence of the European spatial planning agenda since the late 1980s). However, EU member states have resisted giving the EU the competence for policy intervention in the field of spatial develop-

---

[3] The least prosperous regions are those with a gross domestic product (GDP) of less than 75 percent of the EU average.

ment beyond the economic and social remit of the Structural Funds. The exception is the relatively small amounts of funding allocated to cross-border, transnational, and interregional cooperation under the EU's Interreg program.

In recent years, however, several factors have helped to push territorial issues onto the policy agenda. First, in drafting the constitutional treaty currently undergoing ratification the European Convention added territorial cohesion to economic and social cohesion as objectives of EU cohesion policy (Article 3). Second, a major research program, the European Spatial Planning Observation Network (ESPON), was launched by the European Commission to assess the scope of past and future policy action in support of territorial cohesion under EU policies (for more on ESPON, see chapter 5 of this volume). Third, under the Dutch Presidency of the EU (in the second half of 2004) a debate on territorial issues was launched, which has been given impetus under the Austrian, Finnish, and German Presidencies.

The role of the EU in addressing territorial cohesion issues was highlighted in the triennial reports by the Commission first in 2001 and then in 2004 (CEC 2001, 2004b). The third cohesion report, in particular, links territorial cohesion to the issues of balance and harmonious development as a counter to the concentration of human settlement and economic activities that characterize the EU. However, the concept of territorial cohesion, as outlined in the report, is rather vague (Faludi 2005).[4] In fact, that vagueness prompted the Dutch Presidency, in its preparatory document for the Rotterdam Informal Ministerial Meeting on Territorial Cohesion in November 2004, to call for the adoption of "a political agenda for the next 2–3 years with the aim of creating a coherent approach to territorial development in EU policies" and to argue that it was time to "come to a general agreement on what it [territorial cohesion] will mean in terms of implementation" (Dutch Presidency 2004, 2). The preparatory document concludes by advocating a "more coherent approach to the European territory," the foundation of which can be found in the goal of territorial cohesion, and by stating that "in practical terms it [territorial cohesion] could mean the following":

[4] Indeed after publication of the third cohesion report, the Commission (specifically, the Directorate General for Regional Policy) produced an interim territorial cohesion report to track the progress made toward achieving territorial cohesion, defining it as "the balanced distribution of human activities across the Union" which is to be intended as "complementary to economic and social cohesion." In the report, achievement of the territorial dimension of cohesion is related to three spheres: (1) overcoming the territorial imbalances of the EU—that is, the imbalances between the center and the periphery, those related to urban concentration in Europe's 'pentagon'; (London-Paris-Milan-Munich-Hamburg), and the specific geographic handicaps of some regions (islands, mountainous areas, and peripheral, sparsely populated regions); (2) overcoming the imbalances in the distribution of competitiveness factors across the EU, particularly in research and innovation capacity (mostly concentrated in the northern half of Europe); and (3) achieving accessibility conditions throughout the EU in terms of physical transportation (road, rail, airports), telecommunications, and energy access.

- focusing regional and national territorial development policies on better exploiting regional potential and territorial capital. . . .
- better positioning of regions in Europe, both by strengthening their profile and by transnational and interregional cooperation. . . .
- promoting coherence of EU policies with a territorial impact, both horizontally (across sectors) and vertically (between levels of administration). (Dutch Presidency 2004, 12)

The ministers did not reach a general agreement on an operational definition of the concept of territorial cohesion, but they did concur on the need to focus their work "until 2007 on territorial cohesion with the aim of supporting the Lisbon ambitions by better exploiting Europe's diverse potentials," as well as emphasizing structural and cohesion policy. The Dutch Presidency's conclusions identified three areas of further work: (1) the contribution of integrated spatial development approaches to enabling regions and cities to exploit their potentials; (2) the impact of EU policies on national and regional spatial policies and developments; and (3) the key territorial challenges and issues surrounding convergence, competitiveness, and cooperation in the EU in view of the proposals of the EU constitution and the third cohesion report. These research needs were, in practice, translated into a structured work program under the Luxembourg Presidency, and later under the U.K., Austrian, Finnish, and German Presidencies, to assess the "territorial state and development perspectives of the Union . . . [and to contribute to the] identification of a territorial approach for a better integration of the territorial dimension into EU (and national) policies" (Luxembourg Presidency 2005d, 1).

The "scoping document" prepared to inform the discussions at the Informal Ministerial Meeting for Regional Policy and Territorial Cohesion held in Luxembourg 20–21 May 2005 continued along the lines of thinking anticipated by its predecessor. The "Presidency Conclusions" of the meeting stressed that the integration of a territorial dimension in all European policies is a central goal (Luxembourg Presidency 2005c). In particular, the goal of territorial cohesion was cited as being very important for both policy measures implemented under the Lisbon Strategy and the EU cohesion policy. The "Presidency Conclusions" also set out a policy agenda up to 2007, centered on the delivery of a report on the "Territorial State and Perspectives of the European Union" to be adopted by the German Presidency in 2007. Such a document would, among other things, seek to enunciate a "clear policy scope and priorities for strengthening territorial cohesion in the light of the Lisbon aims and address disparities as well as specific territorial conditions in the Member States and their regions" (Luxembourg Presidency 2005c, 2). Finally, referring specifically to EU cohesion policy, the "Presidency Conclusions" stated that it will be important to ensure that *"priorities for the future territorial cohesion*, as identified at the meeting (in particular with regard to the urban dimension, the incorporation of territorial specificities and the transnational dimension of territorial cooperation), *are translated into the new Cohesion Policy* in both the EU and the Member States position documents in accordance with the national context" (Luxembourg Presidency 2005c, 2).

All of the thinking just described is perhaps unambiguous in principle, but in practice it is not clear how a document that should (ideally) be finalized in 2007 will have any effect on the EU cohesion policy strategies that will be adopted at the EU, national, and regional levels. Future Structural Funds programs are scheduled to be launched in 2007, and, even taking into account a probable delay in the start date (which occurred for several countries during the 2000–2006 programming period), the strategies, and priorities of the future programming documents will be well established by 2007.[5]

The Community Strategic Guidelines, 2007–2013

An important factor with a bearing on this debate is how the policy priorities agreed at the Council level translate into practice. Since reform of the Structural Funds in 1988, the implementation of EU cohesion policy has been based on multiannual programs drawn up by member states (at the national or regional levels) and approved or adopted by the Commission. For larger programs, member states prepare Community Support Frameworks (CSFs), which outline the strategic objectives of the funding, and a series of sector-specific or region-specific Operational Programmes (OPs) describing the detailed measures and delivery arrangements for interventions. For smaller programs, these two levels of programming are combined in a Single Programming Document (SPD).

Although the parameters for these documents are outlined in Council regulations, there is considerable scope for interpretation of issues such as the balance of spending, the prioritization of EU policy objectives, and themes and eligible expenditure. Through the process of approval/adoption of programming documents, and, latterly, the requirements for monitoring, reporting, and financial management, the Commission has been able to influence the content and delivery of regional development programs.

For the 2007–2013 programming period, the EU has agreed a new and important form of leverage over the way in which member states spend EU cohesion policy allocations that is of considerable significance for the territorial cohesion agenda. This involves a new planning system with, at the

[5] In this context, it is interesting to note that, under the Austrian Presidency, attention has shifted to the issue of territorial *governance*, rather than strategic objectives. An informal meeting of Member States held in Baden on 8–9 June 2005 discussed how the territorial governance of Cohesion strategies would be taken forward in the next period, with a view to continuing the debate under the Finnish and German Presidencies.

apex, a set of Community Strategic Guidelines agreed by the Council, and National Strategic Reference Frameworks drawn up by the member states governing the delivery of individual operational programs. This arrangement is intended to ensure that overall EU policy objectives are reflected much more clearly in the allocation of resources.

The first draft of the Community Strategic Guidelines was submitted on 11 May 2005 by the Directorates General of Regional Policy (DG Regio) and Employment (2005) to the member states. This draft took into account of some of the policy views expressed at the Rotterdam ministerial meeting, and a chapter was dedicated to the theme of territorial cohesion and cooperation. It set out three clear priorities for cohesion policy: (1) improving the attractiveness of regions and cities; (2) encouraging innovation, entrepreneurship, and the knowledge economy; and (3) creating more and better jobs. Under each priority, the chapter outlined subpriorities and actions, and pointed out that the Convergence and Competitiveness/ Employment Objectives should give prominence, respectively, to growth-enhancing conditions and innovation and job creation. The chapter also explicitly stated that "the overall aim should be to diversify centers of economic activity by working towards a more polycentric model of economic development. This would involve a more concerted approach towards urban and rural development" (DG Regio and DG Employment 2005, 19).

The theme of polycentric development has been featured in debates on spatial development for at least a decade, but it was never before linked so explicitly to EU cohesion policy in formal policy positions. It can be interpreted as a by-product of growth theories centered on cities as engines for growth, in which the role of cities is interpreted in relational terms, advocating the creation of synergies and networking to strengthen the overall competitiveness standing of so-called polycentric regions. This concept was mentioned in the ESDP and has been examined extensively in the research under the framework of the ESPON program.

However, the reference to polycentric development no longer appeared in a subsequent draft of the Community Strategic Guidelines, published by the European Commission in July 2005 (CEC 2005). Nevertheless, the text contained unaltered the three main priorities of cohesion policy and the reference to the fact that in urban areas the focus of cohesion policy should be on "improving competitiveness (through clustering and networking) and achieving a balanced development between the economically strongest cities and the rest of the urban network." These goals should be achieved through rehabilitation of the physical environment; entrepreneurship, local employment, and community economic development; social cohesion and urban regeneration (CEC 2005, 29–30).

The July 2005 version of the guidelines also highlighted territorial cooperation, stressing the need for complementarity of cross-border, transnational, and interregional cooperation with the three priorities identified. Cross-border cooperation was linked to the ultimate goal of integrating "areas divided by national borders that face common problems requiring common solutions," particularly through the development of transport and communications infrastructure, which contributes to the development of integrated border regions.

Transnational cooperation was set to target the integrated development of supranational macro regions (CEC 2005, 31). This goal was to be achieved particularly by means of tangible and intangible actions to increase the interconnection of the territories and actions in the areas of the Trans-European Networks (TENs), natural risk prevention, water management, maritime cooperation, and R&D networking.

Finally, interregional cooperation was linked to the themes of innovation, small and medium enterprises (SMEs) and entrepreneurship, the environment and risk prevention, as well as the exchange of experiences on urban development, the modernization of public services, and cooperation programs. Interestingly, the guidelines pointed out that "interregional cooperation will also be supported within programs for convergence, and regional competitiveness and employment" (CEC 2005, 32). This latter point marks a change from the Commission's initial proposals. These provided for an integration of interregional cooperation within the regional programs, implying that each regional OP or SPD would be expected to devote a proportion of its resources to this type of project. Because of concerns expressed by some member states (such as France) in the consultations over the Community Strategic Guidelines, the Commission slightly amended its positions, and referred to the mainstreaming of interregional cooperation as an option. The view seemed to imply two forms of interregional cooperation activities: first, funding would be set aside within cohesion policy Objectives 1 and 2, possibly with a focus on bilateral forms of interregional cooperation; second, larger partnerships and cooperation projects would be supported under (territorial cooperation) Objective 3 (Ferry and Gross 2005).[6]

■ Practical Constraints: Financial Resources and National Policies

The review just presented reveals that interministerial and Commission policy positions acknowledge the status of territorial cohesion and place this goal high on the agenda of future EU cohesion policy. This said, and to answer the main question put forward in the introduction to this chapter, some practical constraints may hinder that the commitment in principle to territorial cohesion can be translated to more than rhetoric.

[6] The most recent version of the guidelines, published in July 2006, reintroduced a reference to polycentric development but was less prescriptive in obliging member states to promote the territorial dimension of cohesion policy, through, for example, a focus on cities and urban areas (CEC 2006).

Although the Community Strategic Guidelines will inform the shape of future EU cohesion policy intervention in the member states, the actual content of the National Strategic Reference Framework documents and of the subordinate Operational Programmes may not closely align with the territorial objectives described in the Guidelines. Several national delegations at the Informal Ministerial Meeting for Regional Policy and Territorial Cohesion held in Luxembourg 20–21 May 2005 stressed the need to interpret the Community Strategic Guidelines as a flexible tool for supporting the member states in their definition of policy priorities rather than as a set menu to which countries and regions should refer exclusively (Luxembourg Presidency 2005b, 4). A common theme in the discussions was that future cohesion policy should give member states and regions the flexibility needed to choose the most appropriate policy mix, based—as is also acknowledged explicitly in the Guidelines—on their "economic, social, cultural and institutional conditions" (DG Regio and DG Employment 2005, 5). Such views were expressed by, for example, Austria, Denmark, and Slovenia. The translation by member states of the Guidelines into policy priorities, and their coherence with the goal of territorial cohesion, will depend on the financial resources made available for EU cohesion policy in each member state and for each objective and on the content of, and alignment with, domestic regional development policies (which vary from country to country) and the spatial focus of those development policies.

As the Commission brought forward its *Financial Perspectives* for the 2007–2013 period (CEC 2004d), the debate among member states highlighted the difficulty of retaining the proposed ceiling of resources for the EU cohesion policy. The Commission's proposal for the global allocation for cohesion policy changed over time: the draft general regulation earmarked a sum of €336.1 billion, but by January 2005 that amount had fallen by €3.12 billion, to €333 billion. This figure was set to fall even further. For example, although the Commission's proposals referred to a ceiling for its own resources of 1.24 percent of the EU's gross national income (GNI), the "Group of Six" (Austria, France, Germany, the Netherlands, Sweden, and the U.K.) pushed for a reduction to 1 percent, which would leave the cohesion policy with a budget of just €250 billion, or €83 billion less than anticipated by the Commission (Bachtler et al. 2005, 8). In December 2005, the Council of the European Union finally reached agreement on the 2007–2013 EU budget, which allocated to the cohesion policy just over €307.6 billion, or over €28.5 billion less than originally envisaged by the Commission (Council of the European Union 2005, 8).

Not only have the overall financial resources made available to cohesion policy declined over time, but the percentage allocation to the three objectives of the EU cohesion policy—convergence, competitiveness and employment, and territorial cooperation—have also changed throughout the negotiations. The proposed 78, 18, and 4 percent foreseen by the Commission for the three objectives, respectively, in the third cohesion report were gradually adjusted to give more weight, in compensation for the proposed overall reduction in cohesion policy funding, to the regions in the convergence objective (CEC 2004b, xxxviii–xxxix). The percentage allocations to the three objectives changed from the original 78, 18, and 4 percent to 82, 15, and 3 percent in the "negotiating box" of 19 May 2005; 82.3, 15.26, and 2.45 percent in the "negotiating box" of 15 June 2005; and, finally, 81.7, 15.8, and 2.4 percent in the agreement of December 2005, marking, for the territorial cooperation objective, a significant percentage cut (Council of the European Union 2005a, 2005b, 2005c). In absolute terms, the allocations to the new Objective 3 have fallen from €13.2 billion of the draft general regulation (CEC 2004c, 31) to a mere €7.5 billion (Council of the European Union 2005c, 8), a cut of almost €6 billion.

These points lead to two considerations. First, for the nonconvergence objectives, programs will face a significant reduction in resources. This reduction will contribute to a streamlining of the dominant domestic policy priorities, which may imply a lack of spatial focus. Confronting cuts of as much as 40 percent, future programs may choose to focus on a horizontal thematic concentration (for example, related to the development of SMEs, social capital, and innovation) rather than on spatial targeting (for example, on urban development and territorial cooperation). EU cohesion policy has often been criticized for its lack of focus—that is, its aspiration to tackle multiple, not always congruent objectives—and, consequently, for its ambiguous strategies and policy packages. Especially for the regions that will not be eligible for the convergence objective, the inclusion of territorial cohesion–related priorities will depend mainly on the alignment of domestic policies with such aims.

Second, the stress placed on territorial cooperation, first in the third cohesion report and then in the draft Community Strategic Guidelines, is certainly strong in principle, but it has not been matched by financial commitments. Some member states emphasized the importance of territorial cooperation in the debate over the Community Strategic Guidelines (albeit with different foci). However, in the negotiations over the budget of the future cohesion policy, the new Objective 3, territorial cooperation, has effectively been penalized.

The extent to which future Structural Funds programs will deliver territorial cohesion will also depend on the content of domestic development policies in the member states.[7] These policies will probably be reflected in the implementation of European cohesion policy. In some EU member states, such policies are increasingly concerned with growth and overall national development instead of steps to overcome internal disparities. In such countries, a shift has taken place in spatial targeting from selectively

---

[7] Indeed, as argued by Peyrony in chapter 4 in this volume, the very perceptions of territorial cohesion vary in different national contexts. These are emblematically conceptualized in chapter 3 by Waterhout in his "storylines feeding into territorial cohesion."

targeting resources toward designated regions in need to adopting an approach that emphasizes the contribution of all regions to national development and growth—what Yuill has termed the "all-region approach" (Yuill 2004, 21–22).

Perhaps the most striking example of this shift to an "all-region approach" in the domestic regional policies of the member states is found in the 2004 Dutch regional policy white paper. It sets out an economic agenda for six Dutch regions, focusing particularly on large, "ambitious" projects aimed at "the recovery of the growth capacity of the Dutch economy and strengthening the business locations climate" (Ministerie van Economische Zaken 2004, 11). The strategy incorporates two radical innovations: first, the refocusing of "regional economic policy away from the traditional problem regions in the north and towards economic priorities in all Dutch regions; and, second, a move towards a far more selective policy approach, with clear choices being made as to where, in the regions, national policy efforts should be directed" (Yuill 2004, 22).

Similar approaches can be found in the Irish National Spatial Strategy, which aims to provide a framework for the development of an all-island economy (McMaster 2004), as well as in policy documents in the U.K. For example, the *National Planning Framework for Scotland* highlights "the importance of place and identifying priorities for investment in strategic infrastructure to enable each part of the country to play to its strengths in building a Scotland which is competitive, fair and sustainable" (Scottish Executive 2004, 10).

Interestingly, this move to an all-region/national growth approach is not just taking place in those countries in which regional disparities have traditionally been perceived as negligible (such as Austria, Denmark, or the Netherlands), but also in other countries, not least because of the negative economic cycle of recent years and the difficulties met in maintaining sustainable economic growth in even the wealthiest regions. This trend is particularly evident in the new member states where, despite the general rise of regional disparities—caused mainly by the unprecedented accelerated growth, especially in and around the main cities—the policy focus tends to be on reducing the national development gap with the EU average rather than on addressing interregional inequality (Yuill and Quiogue 2005). This said, it should also be acknowledged that some EU10 countries,[8] whose Structural Funds strategies in the 2004–2006 period focused on national development, are considering shifting toward more balanced regional development, but it is too early to say whether this shift will really occur in practice (Davies and Gross 2005, 18).

The policy shift toward national development and all-region approaches

---

[8] EU10 refers to the 10 states that joined the EU in May 2004. This chapter later refers to the EU15, which refers to the 15 member states that made up the EU prior to the 2004 enlargement.

may have both positive and negative effects on the contribution of future Structural Funds programs to the goal of territorial cohesion, if it is understood on a plurality of levels, as illustrated by Robert in chapter 2 of this volume. On the one hand, the emphasis placed on national growth (and catching up) over interregional balance may contribute to the achievement of territorial cohesion on a pan-European level. On the other hand, territorial cohesion may be constrained at the domestic level because of the residual weight attributed to spatial balance across and within regions, which is seen as secondary to overall national growth.

The Current Structural Funds Approaches to Urban Development and Territorial Cooperation

Current experiences with, and approaches to, the implementation of EU cohesion policy— particularly that related to urban development and territorial cooperation, the two key themes identified in the draft Community Strategic Guidelines as associated with territorial cohesion—also have implications for future European cohesion policy. Policy changes are incremental: the evolution of Structural Funds programming over successive periods, from the late 1990s to date, reveals the substantial continuity between subsequent generations of programs. The most significant developments in program strategies over subsequent program periods have two main aspects: first, the progressive broadening of the scope and aims of the programs—for example, to encompass EU-driven priorities such as sustainable development and equal opportunities; and, second, particularly for the current generation of programs, the more explicit linkage of the strategies with stated development models, often based on endogenous growth theories.

Despite new rules and refocused overarching policy objectives (that is, harmonization of strategies with the so-called Lisbon goals), it is likely that current programs will significantly influence their successors. This influence will be particularly true in the new member states, where the 2004–2006 period has been viewed as a preparatory, learning phase for the "real" challenge of the 2007–2013 period.

The sections that follow look at the current strategies in relation to two main themes relevant to territorial cohesion—urban/polycentric development and territorial cooperation—and draw some conclusions on the possible territorial cohesion orientation of future strategies.

Structural Funds Policies for Urban Development

The extent to which urban development interventions are included in the Objectives 1 and 2 programs varies considerably across and within countries, depending on, among other things, the nature of the areas covered by the programs and, in particular, whether they include urban areas. As noted earlier, the approach to territorial cohesion implied by the third cohesion report and in the more recent interministerial policy documents (Rotterdam and Luxembourg) seems to involve a new conception of the role of cities that places emphasis on the full exploitation of their true economic potential. However, in the current generation of programs, even in those in which urban areas feature significantly in the eligible areas (for example, the Western Scotland, Pàis Vasco, and Nordrhein-Westfalen Objective 2 programs), the strategic approaches adopted for the support of urban areas are far from embracing the concept of polycentric development.

Based on the strategic approaches adopted in selected Structural Funds programs, the following categorizations can be made (see table 6.1). First, some programs place special emphasis on the problems and weaknesses of urban areas. This "reactive approach" is found in those programs that include large urban conurbations (such as the Spanish program of the Pàis Vasco, the two U.K. programs of North-East England and Western Scotland, and, to a more limited extent, the two German programs for Nordrhein-Westfalen and Sachsen Anhalt). These programs tend to include large infrastructure projects of urban renewal and regeneration, characterized by a high volume of resources; the participation of local partners, also from the private sector, in the financial package; and the predominance of physical investments (such as buildings, transport infrastructure, and urban development). These measures are often complemented by other types of intervention, such as training initiatives, employment policies, and entrepreneurial support. In such cases, the program intervenes directly to support urban areas with particular socioeconomic problems.

Western Scotland represents a striking example of a comprehensive and integrated treatment of the urban theme, in part because of the nature of the areas covered. It seeks to achieve a balance between social inclusion and urban development as an economic driver. The underlying strategic spatial development principle is the linkage of areas of opportunity and need in line with the domestic policy of the Scottish Executive. The Scottish Executive has developed several categorizations of areas of need, including Social Inclusion Partnerships (mainly brownfield sites), Social Enterprise Zones (aimed at mobilizing local actors and adapting budgets to tackle multiple deprivation), and Urban Regeneration Areas (involving a package of activity that complements or encompasses employment creation, business opportunities, training and related activities, and linkages to exclusion areas). The programming document takes these categories into account when selecting projects.

A second approach, which is evident particularly in the Western Finland Objective 2 program, is more indirect. Urban areas are not targeted in the program per se, but are by default supported as part of a wider economic development strategy that places the spotlight on growth poles and on their specialization. The investments, which are economic in nature (such as

Table 6.1

Strategic Approaches in Selected 2000–2006 Programs Toward Urban Areas

Approach	Rationale	Programs
Reactive Approach	Focus on problems and weaknesses of urban areas	• Pais Vasco (Spain, Obj. 2) • North-East England (U.K., Obj. 2) • Western Scotland (U.K., Obj. 2) • Nordrhein-Westfalen (Germany, Obj. 2) • Sachsen-Anhalt (Germany, Obj. 1)
Proactive Approach	Focus on urban areas as areas of potential	• West of Finland (Finland, Obj. 2)
Urban-Rural Partnership	Creation of more balanced interrelations between main cities and neighboring towns/villages	• Toscana (Italy, Obj. 2) • Niederösterreich (Austria, Obj. 2) • Norra (Sweden, Obj. 2)
No Urban Support	No direct or indirect interventions for towns and cities	• Norra Norrland (Sweden, Obj. 1) • Lombardia (Italy, Obj. 2) • Nordjylland (Denmark, Obj. 2) • Steiermark (Austria, Obj. 2)

Source: Polverari et al. (2005).

business infrastructure, aids to firms and start-ups, training, and R&D), flow naturally toward the main urban centers. The emphasis is on the strengths rather than the weaknesses of the urban centers, which are supported as places of potential. This "proactive approach" is illustrated in more detail later in this chapter.

A third approach, the "urban-rural partnership" (to borrow an expression from the ESDP), is followed by programs that include interventions for urban areas that are smaller in scale (both the urban areas and the interventions). The interventions implemented in urban areas are diversified, ranging from small regeneration projects aimed at the relaunch of local businesses and trade to the rejuvenation of cultural infrastructure such as youth centers, museums, and theaters and social infrastructure such as nurseries. All of these projects aim to improve the standard of living of citizens and the development of communities. Programs that exemplify this approach are Toscana (Italy), Niederösterreich (Austria), and Norra (Sweden).

Finally, there are "nonurban" Structural Funds programs (such as Norra Norrland in Sweden, Lombardia in Italy, Nordjylland in Denmark), which are mainly directed at strengthening settlements and improving standards of living. These goals are often achieved by diversifying economic opportunities and providing essential services to improve the quality of life of local communities. These programs do not contain interventions for urban areas (direct or indirect).

The first three approaches—reactive, proactive, and urban-rural partnership—are not mutually exclusive. Indeed, some programs present a mixed approach. For example, in Nordrhein-Westfalen and Sachsen Anhalt, physical regeneration interventions go hand in hand with social and cultural investments in urban areas. This said, the analysis shows that the types of interventions implemented in the current generation of programs are mainly reactive in nature—that is, the focus is on the problems and weaknesses of urban areas rather than on their potential as engines for growth, with the notable exception of Finland.

Structural Funds approaches in Germany and Finland

The approach adopted in the Structural Funds programs is often a function of domestic policies. Because urban development policies vary across member states, the way in which urban development is reflected in the Structural Funds programs (when these include urban development as a policy goal) varies as well. The degree of variation of urban policies in the member states is illustrated by the two extreme cases of Germany and Finland. In Germany, policies for urban development are mainly regeneration policies related to infrastructure investments and implemented through a range of instruments at both the federal and *Land* level. In Finland, polycentric development strategies are in place to ensure a balanced development across the national territory. These approaches are reflected in the programs implemented under the European cohesion policy.

In Germany, the main instruments at the federal level are the "Stadtteile mit besonderem Entwicklungsbedarf—die soziale Stadt" (Parts of Towns with Particular Development Needs—The Social Town), which is managed by the Federal Ministry for Transport, Construction and Housing; the Stadtumbau Ost (Town Reconstruction in the East); and its twin for the west, Stadtumbau West. The program "Stadtteile mit besonderem Entwicklungsbedarf—die soziale Stadt," which was established by the *Bund* (federal level) and the *Länder* in 1999 to reduce social polarization in urban areas, takes an integrated approach to urban development—that is, it links physical regeneration with funding from other funding programs. From 1999 to 2004, the program funded over 363 measures in 252 communities.

The Stadtumbau Ost program finances urban regeneration in the eastern *Länder* for the renovation and upgrading of urban infrastructure and for the modernization of housing, including rental accommodation. Stadtumbau West, a similar program more recently set up for urban areas in the western *Länder*, provides funding for two towns in Nordrhein-Westfalen (Essen and Gelsekirchen); in 2004 that funding amounted to €40 million from the federal budget. Of the other federal programs in Germany for urban development (for example, to renovate buildings that are perceived to have a certain historical value), some are channeled through and cofinanced by the *Länder* or local authorities, which also may have additional policies for towns and cities.

The initiatives implemented under these domestic programs are included in both of the German Structural Funds programs analyzed, even though they lack an explicit focus on urban development. In both programs, EU cofinancing for urban interventions is channeled into the federal, *Land*, or local authority budget lines such as those for the soziale Stadt or the Stadtumbau Ost or West programs.[9]

In Finland, by contrast, urban and regional policies are closely intertwined. According to the Regional Development Act 602/2002, regional policy aims at creating the "preconditions for economic growth, industrial and business development and a higher employment rate," and one of the secondary objectives linked to this overarching goal is to "promote balanced development among the regions." In a subsequent government decision of January 2004, this goal was specified further in three objectives: (1) to reinforce regional competitiveness; (2) to safeguard the service structure throughout the country; and (3) to achieve a balanced regional structure. For the latter policy goal, urban development comes into play. Emphasis is placed on developing regional centers and urban policy (in particular, through the Regional Centre Development Program); intensifying cooperation within the Helsinki metropolitan area in order to enhance its overall competitiveness; and promoting innovation and competitiveness measures to improve the international competitiveness of nine urban centers (Helsinki, Tampere, Turku, Oulu, Jyväskylä, Kuopio, Lahti, Lappeenranta-Imatra, and Vaasa).[10] It is clear that the main regional policy goal of promoting balanced development across the country is very closely linked to the polycentric development concept noted earlier. Four national special programs support this goal: the Regional Centre Development Program; the Centre of Expertise Program; the Rural Program; and the Islands Program. The first two programs, described here, are particularly significant for the development of urban areas.

The aim of the Regional Centre Development Program is to develop a balanced network of regional centers defined as a natural area of labor markets, service groupings, and municipal collaboration that is larger than any single municipality and that has an economic impact that extends beyond any particular subregion and nearby municipalities—that is, all of Finland (Helsinki is excluded, because it is covered by a separate initiative).

---

[9] Another important initiative in Germany is the International Building Exhibition (Internationale Bauausstellung, or IBA). Under this program, an area is designated for a period of 10 years (often crossing local authority boundaries), and a range of policies is introduced for physical regeneration, housing, local economic development, and social policy, among other things. In 1989–1999, Nordrhein-Westfalen had an IBA for the Emscher Park. The Internationale Bauausstellung (IBA) in Sachsen-Anhalt began in 2003 and is ongoing until 2010.

[10] A fourth emphasis is on promoting rural and island policies, which had been a traditional element of economic development policy in Finland.

The program is seeking to strengthen the competitiveness of regional centers of different sizes and types all over the country by intensifying cooperation and operational partnerships between the municipalities and the public and private sectors in any given region. In doing so, it is seeking to enhance regional dynamism by intensifying joint business and service policies, promoting their coherence, and encouraging networking. The program, which began in November 2000, supports 34 regional centers, plus one other area on a pilot basis. Funding in 2003 amounted to €8.3 million from the central government, and the same amount was provided at the regional level.

The Centre of Expertise Program is directed mainly at the regional competitiveness objective, although it also contributes to the goal of polycentric development. It has the overarching goal of encouraging the development of regional networks among key research providers and users in different sectors. Regions are responsible for different centers of expertise, chosen by competitive tender. Currently, there are 22 centers for 45 fields of knowledge. The basic central government funding for 2004 was some €8.9 million, and the same amount was being provided regionally. Under both this program and the Regional Centre Development Program support is differentiated in favor of the nine internationally competitive urban centers listed earlier. These objectives and national strategies are reflected in the Western Finland Objective 2 program, insofar as the assisted areas are also eligible for the Centre of Expertise and Regional Centre Development programs.

Structural Funds policies for urban development in the EU10

The strategies for urban development of the new member states are different from those of the EU15 countries, reflecting the new states' differing territorial needs and development priorities. Although these countries' spatial problems are significant, by themselves they do not necessarily translate into problems for cities. On the contrary, an "urban advantage" in relation to rural areas rather than an urban problem seems to be the general pattern. Business activities, educational centers, and knowledge networks are concentrated in cities. As a result, cities display relatively stronger economic development than rural areas. In Latvia, for example, real personal incomes in urban areas grew by 32.4 percent between 1996 and 2002, while those in rural areas grew only by 7.5 percent. Migration from rural areas to cities is perceived to be an important issue in Cyprus, Poland, and Slovakia. In Estonia, Latvia, and Malta, the trend has been the opposite, with people leaving cities for towns and villages. In the Czech Republic, Hungary, and Lithuania, people have been leaving the largest cities, but moving into medium-size ones. This trend appears to be mitigated, however, by the fact that young, economically active people are continuing to move to urban areas (Yuill and Quiogue 2005; CEC 2004a, 91).

The problem for cities is that the "urban advantage" has not translated into balanced development of all their areas. Some large cities combine wealthy and prosperous areas with areas in decline. Inner parts of the Cypriot capital of Nicosia, which is divided by the cease-fire line, have suffered because of the political situation and the decline of tourism. In Malta, the extremely high density of the population has created severe environmental pressures. Czech, Hungarian, Polish, and Slovak cities have been affected by dilapidated housing estates, the insufficient capacity of roads, heavy pollution, poverty, and social exclusion in some districts.

The new member states have a more monocentric structure than those making up the rest of the EU. Only Poland, the Czech Republic, Slovakia, and Cyprus are not characterized by the dominance of the nation's capital (CEC 2004a, 20). The polycentric structure of these countries, however, does not necessarily translate into more balanced development. For example, in both the Czech Republic and Slovakia the two capitals significantly outperform the rest of the country in terms of the gross domestic product (GDP), despite the relative polycentrism in terms of population.

A review of the interventions implemented in the new member states for urban development under the Structural Funds programs would be premature, because the programs only began in 2004. An analysis of the overall strategies, however, suggests that although both reactive and proactive approaches to urban development can be found in the EU10 countries, the reactive approach is being underplayed, because these countries are tending to concentrate resources on the areas of potential rather than on those in need.

The programming documents of several new member states present a growth pole strategy of national economic development. This strategy recognizes that urban centers can act as engines of economic growth if high-potential industries within those centers are supported; in other words, support for urban development is considered a means of developing wider areas rather than a goal in itself. Such a strategy is mentioned in the programming documents of those new member states that have over two million inhabitants—that is, Latvia (whose document encourages the development of five economic growth centers), Lithuania, Slovakia, Hungary, the Czech Republic, and Poland. It seems that the more populous countries of the EU10 adopt a growth pole strategy because the population is spread across a relatively large territory and thus the capital cannot act as the single driver of national development. Other growth centers therefore receive support—a point mentioned specifically in the Czech Community Support Framework. In the 2004–2006 programming documents, growth pole strategies are only tentatively developed. They appear to support the long-term national goals of strengthening polycentrism where it exists and developing it where it is weak. Examples of proactive approaches can be found in the Czech Republic, Poland, and Slovakia. Regeneration initiatives also can be found in the new member states, often as complementary to the growth pole strategy. They are featured particularly in Cyprus and the Prague and

Bratislava regions (Czech Republic and Slovakia), but also in Hungary and Poland. In the Czech Republic, two ad hoc Single Programming Documents operate in the Prague region, coextensive with the municipality of Prague. Similarly, in Slovakia, the Bratislava region, which covers the city of Bratislava and three additional districts, is supported by two dedicated programming documents.

By contrast, in Hungary, urban regeneration interventions are included in the Operational Programme for regional development. The development of marginalized areas is part of the combined approach to urban development in Hungary. The country's Community Support Framework, which acknowledges the importance of thriving cities as centers of economic growth, emphasizes urban development, including reactive measures to address poverty and urban decline, as preconditions of the success of the growth pole strategy. Similarly, the Local Development Priority of the Polish Integrated Regional Operational Program aims to support, among other things, marginalized urban areas.

Future support for urban development

Looking to the future, in the "older" EU15 member states (that is, before the 2004 enlargement) views are still unclear about what role cities will play in future economic development. Early feedback from some German regions—which are among the most advanced in discussions of future strategies—seems to indicate a likely shift (now that the major infrastructure deficits have been dealt with) from reactive approaches to proactive, often innovation-oriented measures. Overall, however, the views across countries and regions seem to be mixed on whether urban areas should and will be assisted in future programs, and on the likely content of the support to urban areas. Both will depend on the clarification of fundamental issues such as the level of funding available and the types of eligible activities.

The debate over the Community Strategic Guidelines in Luxembourg exemplifies this variation in views. Although some delegations, such as Hungary, expressed satisfaction about the emphasis placed on urban areas in the guidelines, others, such as Denmark, stressed that cohesion policy should focus on the drivers of economic growth (that is, innovation, information and communication technologies, entrepreneurship, and human resources) and that themes such as "environment, equality and regional balance, including development of areas facing structural difficulties and urban themes" should be treated as "cross-cutting issues in one or more priorities" of future programs (Luxembourg Presidency 2005b, 6).

Despite this diversity of views, three common themes emerge across countries about the role of urban support in future cohesion policy. First, urban support should not be equated with urban regeneration. This point is particularly close to the hearts of the Italian and German authorities. If urban regeneration projects continue to be implemented under the cohesion policy umbrella, efforts should be made to ensure that the quality and coherence of the projects are consistent with the socioeconomic goals of the cohesion policy programs. In other words, the main, overarching goals of cohesion policy should not be forgotten.

Second, support should not be based on the "urban" localization of the initiatives per se, but on the quality of the strategic project design expressed by local actors and the nature of the projects. Views along these lines have been gathered from Italy, Germany, and France.

Last, and perhaps most important, the member states should receive some flexibility in the selection of the areas to be supported, the definition of what an urban areas is, and the choice to include or exclude urban support from the programs. Most member states agree on this point, because they are aware, for example, that the definitions of an urban area vary widely among member states, depending on national administrative and constitutional traditions.

As for the new member states in particular, it appears that the emphasis on areas of potential and on growth poles will continue, at least in some countries. In Poland, for example, current policy thinking is oriented toward the further strengthening of metropolitan areas and the funding of transport infrastructure between the main regional centers (Davies and Gross 2005, 18). Early informal exchanges with representatives of some EU10 countries also suggest that, from a thematic point of view, these countries will stress the infrastructure endowment of the regions, and, in some cases, the strengthening of social and human capital.

Territorial Cooperation

Territorial cooperation is the second main avenue for achieving territorial cohesion in future Structural Funds programs. The current experiences with territorial cooperation are very diverse across regions and countries, depending primarily on geographical situation and institutional context. Generally, territorial cooperation is perceived to be valuable. According to those who have engaged in territorial cooperation, the main benefits are the possibilities it offers to establish long-lasting networks, to overcome borders, to make European integration more visible, and to exchange experiences and information with actors in other regions and countries of Europe. Territorial cooperation is also believed to contribute to raising the role of the regional actor in the management and implementation of Structural Funds programs. It is not the purpose of this chapter to review in detail the main benefits and constraints of cooperation projects; other studies have dealt extensively with this topic (see, for example, Taylor, Olejniczak, and Bachtler 2004; Böhme et al. 2003). Nevertheless, it is useful to look to the future and draw some conclusions about how territorial cooperation might contribute to greater territorial cohesion.

There is broad agreement across the European Union that territorial cooperation presents added value and that it should be retained in the future, even though the policy emphasis placed on different types of territorial cooperation varies across countries. For example, Hungary stresses the importance of cross-border cooperation, particularly with external borders, and France supports the idea of developing long-lasting transnational spaces and the involvement of its eastern and southern neighbors in European territorial cooperation (Luxembourg Presidency 2005b, 11 and 9). Territorial cooperation continues to figure prominently in the policy agenda of the European Commission and of the member states, and yet despite commitments in principle, the current regulations and strategic guidelines do not seem to solve the constraints that typically have hindered the effectiveness of territorial cooperation in the current programming period, like the intangible nature of the outcomes of cooperation and the difficulty in quantifying the money value of cooperation projects. On a more operational level, the complexity, vagueness, and lack of proportionality of the bureaucratic requirements associated with cooperation projects is often a constraint, making it difficult, especially for smaller organizations, to be active partners. Communication between partners also tends to be problematic, not just because of the different languages spoken, but also because of the different domestic institutional settings and traditions. Finally, the future Objective 3 of European cohesion policy risks continuing to be a multipurpose and yet relatively low-budget priority. This problem, accompanied by the complexity of delivery, raises serious concerns about the real impact of this type of intervention on territorial cohesion.

Conclusions

The concept of territorial cohesion encapsulates several of the main characteristics of the European model of society, as outlined in chapter 1 by Faludi. It supposes an EU that is an evolving community of values, incorporating the principles of equal opportunity and of economic, environmental, and social sustainability; the valorization of cultural, social, environmental, and natural resources; a multilateralist interpretation of international relations; and the fundamental belief that wealth and opportunities should be spread across the EU and its inhabitants.

Since the creation of the European Regional Development Fund in 1985, EU cohesion policy has arguably made a substantive, practical contribution to the European model. In particular, over the past 15 years EU cohesion policy has moved beyond its original remit of reducing economic disparities to a broader agenda of economic and social cohesion, driven by the political objectives of the Delors presidencies, when two major fundamental reforms of the Structural Funds were passed, in 1988 and 1993.

The contribution of EU cohesion policy is evident not just in the spending objectives and fields of intervention of the Structural and Cohesion Funds, but also in their impacts on the national policies of the member states by means of their *content*—for example, by introducing into national policies the goal of sustainable development; *governance*—such as by strengthening the role of subnational actors through the subsidiarity principle; and *delivery*—by increasing the involvement of stakeholders in the decision-making process (partnership principle) and providing opportunities to actors across the EU to exchange practices and cooperation (Polverari and Bachtler 2004).

The inclusion of territorial cohesion among the objectives of EU cohesion policy would significantly reinforce the direct role of the Structural and Cohesion Funds in giving concrete expression to the European model of society. However, as this chapter has shown in the context of the urban development and territorial cooperation agendas, the political and policy rhetoric of territorial cohesion is likely to be subject to major constraints.

First, it is clear that member states are uneasy about adopting the European Commission's proposals. The flexibility sought by some member states in implementing the proposed Community Strategic Guidelines suggests that they do not necessarily share the conceptual approach underlying territorial cohesion. Second, the policy priorities of individual countries vary greatly. The discussion of urban policies illustrates fundamental differences in the way urban areas are perceived as part of regional development strategies, ranging from a reactive, regeneration-led policy approach, through proactive promotion of urban areas as drivers of regional economies, to urban-rural partnerships. Third, the scope and capacity of institutional arrangements within member states to address the territorial cohesion agenda vary considerably.

Such differences between the aspirations of political rhetoric and the reality on the ground are at the heart of the profound crisis now affecting the EU. The outcomes of the French and Dutch referendums, the decision at the Brussels ministerial meeting on 17 June in favor of a "reflection pause" in the ratification process of the constitutional treaty, and the difficulties in agreeing on a budget for the 2007–2013 period are clear symptoms of such a crisis. Put simply, there is no agreement on what kind of union the EU should be and what it should do.

EU cohesion policy is central to the debate currently under way in that there are fundamental differences about its objectives, funding, and operation. Although this policy has traditionally been presented as an expression of solidarity among nations, regions, and communities, it is clear that the value and purpose of the Structural and Cohesion Funds are now being questioned. On the one hand, the policy could be bent to support a relatively narrow—predominantly economic—agenda in support of the Lisbon Strategy of growth and competitiveness. On the other hand, it could be broadened to encompass the aspirations of territorial cohesion.

To continue to be an important agent of European integration and an essential tool for the delivery of the European model of society, EU cohesion policy will indeed have to be radically reformed, but the risk is that, in the wave of reform, it will be transformed to such an extent that it puts in jeopardy much of the progress gradually and laboriously built over 50 years.

References

ACT Consultants. 2005. *Contribution des programmes Objectif 1 et Objectif 2 au developpement des territoires prioritaires de la politique de la ville.* Final report, vol. 1. January.

Bachtler, J., C. Méndez, I. McMaster, and F. Wishlade. 2005. Programming with an uncertain future: Review of programme developments Autumn 2004–Spring 2005. IQ-Net Review Paper 16(1). European Policies Research Centre, Glasgow, May.

Böhme K, F. Josserand, P. I. Haraldsson, J. Bachtler, and L. Polverari. 2003. Trans-national Nordic-Scottish co-operation: Lessons for policy and practice. Nordregio Working Paper 2003:3. Stockholm.

CEC—Commission of the European Communities. 2001. *Unity, solidarity, diversity for Europe, its people and its territory. Second report on economic and social cohesion.* Luxembourg: Office for Official Publications of the European Communities.

———. 2004a. DG Regio—*Interim territorial cohesion report (preliminary results of ESPON and EU Commission studies).* Luxembourg: Office for Official Publications of the European Communities.

———. 2004b. *A new partnership for cohesion: Convergence, competitiveness, cooperation. Third report on economic and social cohesion.* Luxembourg: Office for Official Publications of the European Communities.

———. 2004c. *Proposal for a Council regulation laying down the provisions on the European Regional Development Fund, the European Social Fund and the Cohesion Fund (presented by the Commission).* Luxembourg: Office for Official Publications of the European Communities.

———. 2004d. *Building our common future: Policy challenges and budgetary means of the enlarged Union 2007–2013 (communication from the Commission).* COM(2004) 101. Brussels, 10 February.

———. 2005. *Cohesion policy in support of growth and jobs: Community Strategic Guidelines, 2007–2013 (communication from the Commission).* COM (2005) 0299. Brussels, 5 July.

———. 2006. *Proposal for a Council decision on Community strategic guidelines on cohesion (presented by the Commission).* COM (2006) 386. Brussels, 13 June.

Council of the European Union. 2005a. *Financial perspective 2007–2013. Note from the presidency to the European Council.* 9065/05, CADREFIN 108. Brussels, 19 May.

———. 2005b. *Financial perspective 2007–2013. Note from the presidency to the European Council.* 10090/05, CADREFIN 130. Brussels, 15 June.

———. 2005c. *Financial perspective 2007–2013. Note from the presidency to the European Council.* 15915/05, CADREFIN 268. Brussels, 19 December.

Davies, S., and T. Gross. 2005. The challenges of designing cohesion policy strategies. Conference Discussion Paper No. 2. Benchmarking Regional Policy in Europe, Second International Conference, Riga, European Policies Research Centre, 24–26 April.

DG Regio and DG Employment. 2005. *Cohesion policy in support of growth and jobs. Community Strategic Guidelines, 2007–2013.* Non-paper. Brussels: DG Regio.

Dutch Presidency. 2004. Exploiting Europe's territorial diversity for sustainable economic growth. Discussion paper, EU Informal Ministerial Meeting on Territorial Cohesion, Rotterdam, 29 November.

Faludi, A., ed. 2005. Territorial cohesion. Special issue, *Town Planning Review* 76(1):1–118.

Ferry, M., and F. Gross. 2005. The future of territorial cooperation in an enlarged EU. Conference Discussion Paper No. 4. Benchmarking Regional Policy in Europe, Second International Conference, Riga, European Policies Research Centre, 24–26 April.

Government Office for the North East, Office of the Deputy Prime Minister. 2002. *Regional planning guidance for the north east.* RPG1. London: The Stationery Office.

Luxembourg Presidency. 2005a. *Financial perspectives 2007–2013*. Non-paper. Negotiating box. 19 May.

———. 2005b. Interventions by the member states: Malta, Denmark, Hungary and France. Session on Regional Policy, EU Informal Ministerial Meeting for Regional Policy and Territorial Cohesion, Luxembourg, 20–21 May.

———. 2005c. *Presidency conclusions*. EU Informal Ministerial Meeting for Regional Policy and Territorial Cohesion, Luxembourg, 20–21 May.

———. 2005d. *Scoping document and summary of political messages for an assessment of "The territorial state and perspectives of the European Union: Towards a stronger European territorial cohesion in the light of the Lisbon and Gothenburg ambitions."* Endorsed for further development by the Ministers for Spatial Development and the European Commission at the Informal Ministerial Meeting for Regional Policy and Territorial Cohesion, Luxembourg, 20–21 May.

McMaster, I. 2004. Spatial development policy in Ireland: Lessons for the new member states? Paper presented at ECPR Workshop "European Spatial Politics or Spatial Policy for Europe?" Uppsala, Sweden, 13–18 April.

Ministerie van Economishe Zaken. 2004. *Peaks in the Delta: Regional economic perspectives.* The Hague. September.

Polverari, L., and J. Bachtler. 2004. La dimensión territorial de la cohesión económica y social: Política regional y planificación territorial en Europa. In *Ordenación del territorio y desarrollo territorial. El gobierno del territorio en Europa: tradiciones, contextos, culturas y nuevas visiones,* Joan Romero González and Farinós Dasí Joaquín, eds. Gijón, Spain: Ediciones Trea.

Polverari, L., N. C. Quiogue, F. Gross, and V. Novotný. 2005. Territorial cohesion and Structural Funds programmes: Urban development and territorial cooperation. IQ-Net Review Paper 16(2). European Policies Research Centre, Glasgow, May.

Scottish Executive. 2004. *National planning framework for Scotland*. Edinburgh.

Taylor, S., K. Olejniczak, and J. Bachtler. 2004. *A study of the mid-term evaluations of INTERREG programmes for the programming period 2000 until 2006. Report to the INTER-ACT Secretariat.* European Policies Research Centre, Glasgow.

Yuill, D. 2004. Regional policy in the shadow of reform: A comparative overview of recent policy development in the member states and Norway. EoRPA Paper 04/1. European Policies Research Centre, Glasgow, October.

Yuill, D., and N. Quiogue. 2005. Spatial targeting under EU and national regional policies. Conference Discussion Paper No. 5. Benchmarking Regional Policy in Europe, Second International Conference, Riga, European Policies Research Centre, 24–26 April.

Chapter 7

Territorial Development Policies in the European Model of Society

ROBERTO CAMAGNI

This chapter considers the new politicocultural context for structural or cohesion policies that has grown out of the emergence of the concept of territorial cohesion, authoritatively proposed by the European Commission in its third report on cohesion (CEC 2004b) and in the text of the European constitution. The institutional proposal to include territorial cohesion as one of the objectives of the European Union (EU) has not yet been fully assessed at both the scientific and political policy levels. Thus, some risk of confusion persists, despite the incremental changes in its definition since its appearance, and some fuzziness about how it is distinct from the traditional concepts of social and economic cohesion is still apparent. The first goal of this chapter is therefore to propose a clearer definition of territorial cohesion as the territorial dimension of sustainability.

The second goal of this chapter is to clarify the related issue of the relevance and role of territorial development policies in the European model of society. Building on the literature and institutional documents produced recently in association with the adoption in 1999 of the European Spatial Development Perspective (ESDP) and the possible launch of what may amount to a new ESDP in 2007 under the German Presidency, this chapter pinpoints the implicit elements and assumptions that constitute a possibly widely shared philosophy on the territorial dimension of the European model.

■ The Reasons for Territorial Cohesion

Territorial development policies—those focused mainly on development as well as those focused on organizing activities and their "spatial order"—recently received a significant (potential) boost and are receiving greater attention at the European level. The considerable cultural, technical, and political efforts carried out during the second half of the 1990s, which produced documents such as the European Commission's *Framework for Action for Sustainable Urban Development* (CEC 1998) and the Committee on Spatial Development's *European Spatial Development Perspective* (CEC 1999), have reaped a highly significant outcome after a pause for reflection for three to four years. This outcome is the proposed new concept of territorial cohesion (CEC 2004b) and its inclusion among the EU's major objectives in the European constitution approved by the Council of the European Union (also known as the Council of Ministers) in late June 2004: "The Union . . . shall promote economic, social and territorial cohesion" (Article I-3).

The importance of the inclusion of this concept is strengthened by the reference to, in the area of territorial cohesion, the EU's "shared competence" with member states (Article I-14.2). This is an essential step forward. The EU's traditional lack of competence in spatial and planning policies has over time become a significant lacuna in view of the evidence pointing to the increasing importance of territorial balance to competitiveness, collective welfare, and sustainability.

The shared competence of member states, even though it does not apply to territorial "policies" but only to the "area" of territorial cohesion, is an important recognition. On the one hand, it underlines the important role played in the recent past by some EU policies—for example, the Community Initiative URBAN has helped to spread throughout the EU best European practices for integrated policies to revive deprived urban areas. On the other hand, it represents a cautious acceptance of a competence of the EU in the guidance of national and local policies and in the provision of incentives for initiatives connected with territorial balance and cohesion in much wider fields and spatial contexts than purely areas of "multiple deprivation."

The concept of territorial cohesion was first proposed and enhanced by reference to empirical data in the European Commission's Third Report on Cohesion, *A New Partnership for Cohesion* (CEC 2004b). Here it is obvious that there is no intention to just view the concept in terms of correcting disparities in income and living standards, which would not add anything to the traditional objectives of the EU's structural policies. Instead, the document addresses the question of the access of different territorial communities to services of general interest (this right of access is also expressed in the constitution), and it goes on to assess levels of accessibility, differences in levels of education, and the problems arising from insularity, remoteness, and low levels of population density.

This said, a limitation still exists and a challenge emerges. The Commission has not been able to define a new set of quantitative indicators enabling measurement of territorial cohesion, which would have made the new concept a practical reference for adjusting structural policies (on this point see chapter 5 by Davoudi in this volume). Evidently, the differences in territorial conditions between member countries and regions are so great that resorting to a single or a few indicators would have been too narrow and inflexible (for example, a single indicator of accessibility would have favored only the most peripheral and insular areas). Moreover, there was too little time to reach a truly Europe-wide agreement on this issue. Thus, a challenge remains for territorial research.

But the most critical challenge—political and practical—is facing the national and regional authorities responsible for allocating Structural Funds. For the funds to be allocated to the new Objective 2 (for the moment defined as "regional competitiveness and employment"), no criteria have been indicated for allocating funds or for establishing territorial eligibility. There is thus a clear risk, because of the lack of clearly defined territorial priorities and quantitative indicators for individual countries, that regions will fight each other for funding. After all, even the richest will qualify for these funds.

Only the northern and Scandinavian countries have explicitly indicated (during the Convention on the Future of Europe convened to draft the European constitution) that they have a special interest (to them) in being included within the concept of territorial cohesion. Their interest stems from their peripheral, insular, and mountainous areas, or areas of low population density, already covered by a specific "Objective" in the past. The countries of southern Europe have not done the same thing.

How has the territorial approach achieved this success, albeit partial? For one thing, the work carried out by the Committee on Spatial Development,[1] which led to the three different versions of the ESDP between 1997 and 1999, has been receiving greater attention, together with political and cultural support (Faludi 2002). The political support from the Council of the European Union has been particularly significant, especially when it decided in Tampere, Finland, in 1999 to make the Interreg program responsible for implementing the ESDP. And the European Parliament, the Council of Europe, and individual regional authorities are providing additional support. There has also been technical and academic appreciation of the effort to provide a territorial perspective at European level. In fact, the ESDP has soon become a reference both for academics dealing with territorial issues (although they were initially somewhat skeptical, because they are unable by nature to fully appreciate documents with political and

[1] The committee was typically an interministerial body, made up of technical representatives of the ministers responsible for the territorial affairs of the 15 member countries.

diplomatic intent) and for researchers, together with the large European Spatial Planning Observation Network (ESPON) program.[2]

The second reason for the success of the territorial approach is more prosaic but perhaps more relevant. It stems from the problem of allocating the Structural Funds between the EU15 member states and the 10 new members (EU10).[3] It is common knowledge that if the traditional criterion of economic-social cohesion were to be used—a per capita GDP of less than 75 percent of the European average—almost all the regions currently included under Objective 1 (less developed regions) would have no longer been eligible for European support because of a purely statistical effect: the European average has decreased because of the accession of the 10 new countries in Eastern Europe. The agreement on the new distribution of funds for 2007–2013 was reached fairly easily at the political and diplomatic levels; it is split 50–50 between new and old members. But on a technical level, how would it be possible to justify the distribution of funds to regions of the EU15 once the criterion of per capita GDP no longer applies? Thus, the vague concept of territorial cohesion immediately seemed suited for the purpose: the term *cohesion* assures continuity with the traditional approach and evokes the idea of unchallengeable equity, while the term *territorial* indicates a new context for which imbalances can be identified, deserving of European support. Put together, the two terms form a new concept that needs further investigation.

One might be justified in wondering whether the proposals to review the Structural Funds put forward in the Third Report on Cohesion are consistent with all these premises and wondering what might be the effects of a full and consistent adoption of the concept of territorial cohesion. It is certainly true that the report dedicates ample space to territorial cohesion. However, in concluding the analytical and descriptive part with new proposals for methods and procedures, the Commission clearly takes a significant step backward: it does not give the territorial concept the space it deserves in view of the premises. It is understandable that the European Commission found it impossible to identify indicators of territorial cohesion under the present technical and political circumstances, which is likely why no attempt was made to adopt territorial balance as a reference for the allocation of funds. As a consequence, when defining specific objectives apart from those connected to economic and social cohesion (covered under

---

[2] I am pleased to mention this positive political and cultural development because of my personal involvement in the work of the Committee on Spatial Development since 1995 in varying capacities: initially in 1996 as an expert appointed by the Italian Presidency to conduct research on a possible European Urban Agenda; then in 1997–1998 as an Italian institutional representative through my position as head of the Department for Urban Areas of the Italian Presidency of the Council of Ministers in Rome; and then in 1999–2004 as an expert for the Ministry for Community Policies and for the Ministry of Infrastructures (see Camagni and Gibelli 1996).

[3] EU10 refers to the 10 states that joined the EU in May 2004; EU15 refers to the 15 member states that made up the EU prior to the 2004 enlargement.

Objective 1 with the traditional "convergence" label), the Commission preferred to refer to purely socioeconomic objectives for Objective 2: "regional competitiveness and employment." The content of the two objectives is strikingly similar, and they differ only in terms of who will benefit.

What is also understandable is the proposal made by the Commission to delegate to member states the task of presenting their own strategic territorial vision in a National Strategic Reference Framework (on the basis of guidelines presented by the Commission) that will constitute the reference for future Operational Programmes (CEC 2004c). Individual member states have specific responsibilities; in fact, they must indicate their territorial priorities, identify the best indicators, and encourage grassroots feedback on possible projects in order to enable the territorial allocation of funds under the new Objective 2 for the period 2007–2013.

The territorial issue enters into Objective 3, which focuses on "European territorial cooperation." Yet it is less innovative than it may appear, because this objective to a large extent groups together the legacy of existing Community initiatives such as Interreg and in part URBAN.

Incremental Clarification of the Concept

Because the very concept of territorial cohesion still remains fuzzy, it deserves clarification and logical consistency. In the Third Cohesion Report, the Commission refers to territorial cohesion as a synonym for "more balanced development," for "territorial balance," or for "avoiding territorial imbalances" (CEC 2004b, 27)—elements that do not add much in definitional terms. The Commission then declares that "the concern is also to improve territorial integration and encourage cooperation between regions"—an important indication, but one that could be placed in the second tier in terms of priorities for policies.

More telling is the specification of what the new concept encompasses at the different territorial levels: the excessive concentration of economic activity and population in Europe's "pentagon" (London-Paris-Milan-Munich-Hamburg); the imbalance between the main metropolitan areas and the rest of the countries; the growing congestion and pollution and the persistence of social exclusion in the main conurbations; the presence of rural areas suffering from inadequate economic links and peripherality; the sprawling nature of urban growth; and the accumulation of natural and geographical handicaps in outermost areas. These aspects of the concept emerged from the efforts made through the ESDP.

A more thorough presentation of the concept of territorial cohesion is given by the Directorate General for Regional Policy (DG Regio) in its *Interim Territorial Cohesion Report*, which is devoted specifically to the subject, taking advantage of the early results of the ESPON program and of other Commission studies (CEC 2004a). According to the report, territorial cohesion is complementary to economic and social cohesion, meaning "the balanced distribution of human activities across the Union." More important, "it translates the goal of sustainable and balanced development assigned to the Union into territorial terms" (CEC 2004a, 3). The subsequent specification of the fields of application is similar to that in the main cohesion report.

The policy documents and political statements that followed on the subject did not develop the concept any further. "The Presidency Conclusions" of the Informal Ministerial Meeting on Territorial Cohesion held in Rotterdam in November 2004 states in fact that "territorial cohesion adds to the concept of economic and social cohesion by translating the fundamental EU goal of balanced and sustainable development into a territorial setting" (Dutch Presidency 2004, 2). In spite of the persisting fuzziness of the concept, the reference to a "territorial setting" allowed the ministers to begin to engage in a proper identification of "the contribution of integrated spatial development approaches towards enabling regions and cities to exploit their potentials more effectively" (Dutch Presidency 2004, 2). Reference is made to a future document on "the territorial state of the Union," a second ESDP with a stronger policy emphasis, developing the concept of territorial cohesion. The scoping document on this new perspective was presented at the Informal Ministerial Meeting for Regional Policy and Territorial Cohesion, held in Luxembourg in May 2005 (Luxembourg Presidency 2005b). In this document, the definition of territorial cohesion remains the same, but it acquires a new "practical" meaning when it is included in a direct policy frame: "In practical terms territorial cohesion implies: *focusing regional and national territorial development policies* on better exploiting regional potentials and territorial capital—Europe's territorial and cultural diversity; *better positioning of regions in Europe* . . . facilitating their connectivity and territorial integration; and *promoting the coherence of EU policies with a territorial impact*" (Luxembourg Presidency 2005b, 1, emphasis in original).

Relevant innovations appear in this passage. First, traditional "spatial development policies" are called "territorial," using a neologism in the English language that suggests the exploitation of territorial specificities going beyond pure location and distance in space. Second, the concept of territorial capital is used for the first time, implicitly underlining the fact that territory is a resource, potentially generating productivity increases ("higher return for specific kinds of investment") and utility flows to local communities.

A Possible Definition of Territorial Cohesion

At this point, only one more small step forward is needed to arrive at a proper theoretical definition of the concept of territorial cohesion.

If the concept of territorial cohesion has to add to the content of economic and social cohesion, it must necessarily link with the sustainability issue. Thus, territorial cohesion may be seen as *the territorial dimension of sustainability*. And like the concept of sustainability, it bears at the same time a positive and a normative sense (that is, it defines a condition and policy goal) and operates by integrating different dimensions: the economic, the social, and the environmental.

The preceding definition may be explained as follows. Considering both the positive and the normative sides, sustainability conditions (and sustainability goals) refer to and can be reached by operating through four main policy dimensions (Camagni 1998; Camagni, Capello, and Nijkamp 2001):

1. The *technological dimension*, governing production, transportation, and heating processes

2. The *behavioral dimension*, determining lifestyles, consumption habits, and organizational models of production (for example, transport-intensive models such as just-in-time)

3. The *diplomatic dimension*, referring to the international strategies to assure cooperation among countries at different development levels, with different development expectations

4. The *territorial dimension*, residing in an ordered, resource-efficient,[4] environmental-friendly spatial distribution of human activities

Territorial cohesion refers directly to the last dimension.[5]

Taking this reflection further, one can envisage three main components of territorial cohesion:

1. *Territorial quality*: the quality of the living and working environment; comparable living standards across territories; similar access to services of general interest and to knowledge

2. *Territorial efficiency*: resource-efficiency with respect to energy, land, and natural resources; competitiveness of the economic fabric and attractiveness of the local territory; internal and external accessibility

3. *Territorial identity*: presence of "social capital"; capability to develop shared visions of the future; local know-how and specificities, productive "vocations," and competitive advantage of each territory

These objectives could be reached through an integrated approach, securing the virtuous integration and positive coevolution of the three subsystems—the economic, the social, and the physical-natural—in their spatial

---

[4] Land resources, energy resources, and natural and landscape resources.

[5] The sustainability concept also refers to and links the need for ecological equilibria to the needs of the entire society, and therefore it addresses a correct integration or coevolution of the natural, the economic, and the social systems. Here can be found the link with the term *cohesion*.

manifestation or phenomenology (figure 7.1). It requires maximizing the synergies and the positive cross-externalities among the three subsystems and minimizing the negative externalities (Camagni 1998).[6]

The integrated, multidimensional nature of the sustainability concept provides a rationale for an integrated approach to territorial cohesion policies. But two other elements push in the same direction. The first is the fragmentation of decision-making powers in both the public and private spheres, with the diffuse presence of veto powers. This element calls for integration and cooperation, both vertical and horizontal, between the different tiers of the public government structures (usually engaged in different policy fields) and between the different departments of the same administration acting in the territory. The second element is the evidence of growing problems and concerns in specific territorial contexts, which call for complex, multidimensional interventions. Examples of such contexts are metropolitan development, peri-urban settlement structure, coastal development, development through wide industrial corridors, and sensitive environments such as mountainous areas crossed by international mobility corridors. What really matters is the overall result of an equilibrated spatial development process, not the single dimensions (such as infrastructure efficiency, proper land use, or smart development policies) through which such an equilibrium can be reached.

Territorial efficiency, quality, and identity represent objectives and values in themselves; no modern society can do without them, because they are the funding elements of local collective well-being. But they are at the same time preconditions for local competitiveness, and no conflict exists in this sense between the needs of the local population and the needs of the economic fabric, at least not in the long run. This element is conceptually utilized in recent European Commission documents in order to justify compliance with and consistency between cohesion policies and the Lisbon Strategy (Luxembourg Presidency 2005a, 2005b). This argument may be considered a strong political point, but it nevertheless incurs the risk of leaving the quality of life element backstage.

The goal of territorial cohesion applies to all kinds of territories, and therefore also to cities. Thus, the explicit exclusion of cities in the European constitution, in particular in its list of regions to which particular attention will be paid pursuant to the territorial cohesion objective (Article III-220), is striking and surprising. If Europe characterizes itself by its urban specificity and identity, this exclusion could be construed as an unfortunate political, cultural, and juridical accident.

[6] As an example among others: economic development in peripheral areas may be advantageous to the environment if a long-term perspective on the use of local natural resources is taken and if it provides the (public) financial resources that may be channeled toward the betterment of environmental infrastructure. At the same time, it may guarantee the permanence of the local population and the strengthening of its production culture and sense of belonging.

Figure 7.1

The Components of Territorial Cohesion

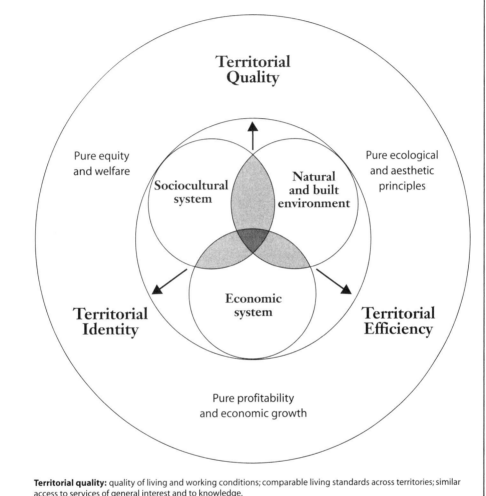

Territorial quality: quality of living and working conditions; comparable living standards across territories; similar access to services of general interest and to knowledge.
Territorial efficiency: resource-efficiency with respect to energy, land, and natural resources; competitiveness and attractiveness; internal and external accessibility.
Territorial identity: presence of "social capital"; capability of developing a shared vision of the future; know-how, specificities, productive "vocations," and competitive advantage of each territory.

Although the first two objectives of territorial cohesion are rather familiar, the third, territorial identity, may seem rather surprising, but it is crucial and will become increasingly central to European policies. Territorial identities incorporated in local culture, know-how, social capital, and landscape are the basic constituents of the territorial realm, because at the same time they represent the ultimate glue holding together local societies; they are linked with the spatial division of labor and often determine its evolution;

and they facilitate processes of collective learning and thus boost the efficiency of the local production fabric.

Identities evolve, but they may be easily destroyed by spatial processes such as those of economic decline and desertification, peripheralization and lack of accessibility, destruction of the natural heritage, and trivialization of territorial landscape through sprawling settlements. For these reasons, they are fundamental constituents of territorial cohesion.

An important step in this sense was taken in the recent scoping document of the Luxembourg Presidency (2005b), in which not just natural but also cultural values are cited as part of the endogenous potential of the different areas and worthy of full exploitation. Furthermore, the ESDP begins and ends with a reference to culture, cultural variety, and cultural heritage as characteristic features of the European identity.

What situations and issues deserve attention from the new territorial policies and possibly from the new European structural policies? They are described in the documents mentioned earlier, particularly in the ESDP, and are summarized in figure 7.2.

Territorial Development Policies and the European Model of Society

In his excellent inspection in chapter 1 of this volume of the possible components of the European model of society, Faludi defines it as a conceptual or even rhetorical device invoked by actors operating in the core area of European integration. Its "shared concerns are equity, competitiveness, sustainability, and good governance." In the same direction, the European model of society refers to achievement of the maximum equity compatible with competitiveness through pursuing good governance and respecting sustainability. Of course, issues related to how large this "maximum" equity should be may persist in the main political interpretations of the model, which could be defined schematically as the British and Franco-German model.

This section tries to disentangle and identify the components of the European model of society in the area of spatial or territorial policy, including cohesion policy. As it is for more general values, the field to be searched lies at the border between ideology and economic theorization in an area called here territorial political economy. The components of the territorial view of the European model of society are mainly implicit ones that can be grasped from the lines of official documents—that is, they are implicit assumptions that may be made clearer through careful analysis. What follows is a list of these components in decreasing order of importance.

- *No trade-off exists between efficiency and equity in the long run.* Cohesion policies are therefore consistent with the present Lisbon Strategy addressing growth and job creation. In fact, cohesion policies (1) activate idle resources and allow full exploitation of regional endogenous potential (see Dutch Presidency 2004 and the introduction to CEC 2005); (2) avoid the need for

Figure 7.2

An Integrated Strategy for Territorial Cohesion: Objectives and Assessment Criteria

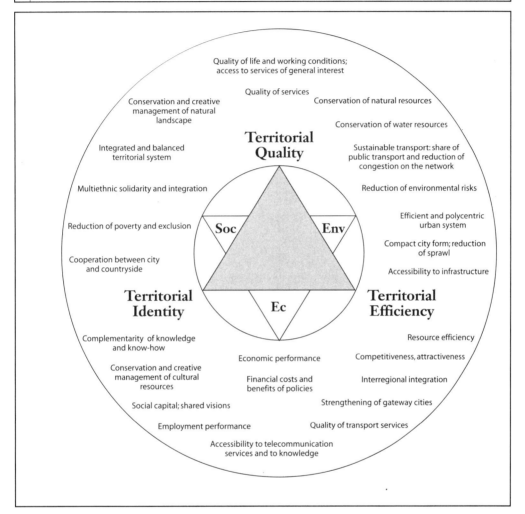

pure welfare intervention in huge localized social crises; (3) limit the inter-regional and international migration of the labor force, thereby preventing overcrowding and housing shortages in stronger areas and, at the same time, desertification and low utilization of local resources in weak areas; and (4) prevent inflationary trends in core areas, which may easily extend to entire countries and quickly reduce price competitiveness,[7] through spatial diffusion of development and a more equilibrated use of territorial resources (Camagni 2001). This argument is widely used at present to

---

[7] This element is very important for the present new member states, in which a few core or border areas are developing quickly.

defend against the criticism that regional and cohesion policies are inefficient, are affected only by equity considerations, and consequently are not apt to cope with present challenges (see Luxembourg Presidency 2005a, in which the new start of the Lisbon Strategy is invoked and the mobilization of all appropriate resources is requested, "including the cohesion policy").

- *The market economy operates as an efficient allocator of resources, but only within the general rules formulated by society and dictated by its ethical values.* According to the path-breaking intuition of Karl Polanyi (1994), these rules refer mainly to the use of production factors—capital (such as rules against usury), labor (such as rules about child labor or working time conditions), natural resources (and international rules to prevent ecological dumping)—but also increasingly to land resources (such as rules to prevent unnecessary urban sprawl), landscape resources, and cultural heritage. As a result, rules governing the sustainable use of territorial resources are necessary, cannot be dictated indirectly by the market and, as long as they avoid in the long run the "tragedy of commons," they have to be regarded as rules governing efficiency, not just morals.

- *From an economic point of view, the territory is an asset, "capital"* (see also chapter 3 by Waterhout) as at the same time it is (1) a system of localized "technological" externalities—that is, an ensemble of material and immaterial factors that, thanks to proximity and the resulting reduction in transaction costs, can also become "pecuniary" externalities (resolving themselves in a price decrease) to the benefit of surrounding economic activities; (2) a system of localized know-how, resulting in historical productive "vocations"; (3) a system of economic and social relations that make up the *relational capital* or the *social capital* of a certain geographic space, resulting in fewer risks and transaction costs, less dynamic uncertainty in innovation processes, and the facilitation of "collective actions" by private actors supplying public goods; and (4) a system of local *governance* that brings together a community, an ensemble of private actors, and a system of local public administration, resulting in easier definition and implementation of local strategies and more efficient bargaining processes with external firms (Camagni 2002).

  Furthermore, some typically territorial processes are intended in part to enhance the efficiency of local production systems: (1) agglomeration economies à la Paul Krugman; (2) city networks, defined as "systems of horizontal linkages and flows among cities of similar size, allowing economies of specialization/division of labor (complementarity networks) or network externalities (synergy networks)" (Camagni 1993); and (3) territorial integration through transport and communication, allowing the EU to take full advantage of the Single European Market for both goods and factors, thereby boosting specialization and economies of scale. By the same token, development may be jeopardized by decreasing returns to urban scale, especially when cities grow in size and form far beyond a manageable limit.

In a recent document, the Luxembourg Presidency (2005b) explicitly underlines the role of "territorial capital" in economic development and competitiveness: "although not explicitly mentioned in the strategy, *the Lisbon aims implicitly incorporate a strong territorial dimension* by strengthening the territorial capital of Europe's cities and regions" (emphasis in the original). The areas of intervention relate to the aspects that are emphasized above: exploitation of endogenous potential, integration and connectivity, and promotion of territorial governance in the form of better consistency among Community policies.

- *For European policies, acting on, or at least considering, the territorial dimension means fulfilling the four main objectives of the treaties establishing the European Union and not just achieving competitiveness.* In fact, especially for the urban dimension, measures dealing with problems facing cities will produce (1) social cohesion, because deprivation and social problems are mainly concentrated in cities; (2) sustainability, because cities are the great polluters of the earth; (3) competitiveness, because cities concentrate excellence nodes of the knowledge society; and (4) democracy and good governance, because decisions may be made more closely in line with citizens' needs (CEC 1998). All these goals were included in the European model of society. *The EU should guarantee equality of opportunity to all its citizens.* The general goal does not extend to "radical" or "sensitive" areas related to distribution of personal wealth (such as taxation of heritage), but to "contextual" conditions related to access to services of general interest (CEC 1999, 2004c) and job opportunities (Luxembourg Presidency 2005b).

- *The European Single Market and European Monetary Union impose on regions and countries a relevant burden in terms of adjustment costs that calls for effective support mechanisms such as cohesion policies.* In particular, with the single currency countries renounce a powerful macroeconomic policy tool, management of the exchange rate, and spontaneous adjustment mechanisms that control differentials in inflation rates or differentials in productivity growth (exchange rate variations).[8] In fact, under a single currency, countries, like cities and regions, compete with each other on the basis of an "absolute" advantage principle, and not on the basis of the Ricardian "comparative" advantage principle, which assures each country a role in the international division of labor, no matter how low its productivity level (Camagni 2002).

- *Because large regional and structural public aid programs may be subject to risk of "government failure" and perverse outcomes, careful countermeasures should be taken in terms of policy design and delivery.* In fact, interventionist strategies may run into the trap of encouraging private parties and public administrators to develop rent-seeking attitudes, of supporting the wrong projects, and

---

[8] Exchange rate flexibility is not a long-term solution to macroeconomic equilibrium, but it does solve many economic and political problems in the short run.

of preventing market forces from fully operating and providing the advantages of resource allocation (within the usual limits of the "market failure" argument).

Policy design and delivery should keep this factor in mind and follow some efficiency rules such as intervening more in context than in firms; imposing a substantial share of private funding; avoiding public guarantees in the event of unsuccessful outcomes (in particular, when supporting project financing schemes) that may easily turn into self-fulfilling prophecies; imposing ex ante assessments at the program and project levels; monitoring the independence of the evaluation teams; fostering partnership, participation, transparency, and public debate.

- *In an integration context, each euro spent on supporting development in weak areas or on integration tools (Trans-European Networks, cooperation) is returned to donor areas* in the form of demand for capital goods and consumption goods, profits on direct investment, and increased efficiency of multilocalized firms.

- *EU support allows best national practices to spread across Europe* (much like the urban regeneration and rehabilitation policies associated with the URBAN initiative) and the strengthening of institutional capacities and governance methods where they are considered to be weak. "The rule of law; its non-discriminatory, predicable and transparent enforcement; the assignment and enforcement of tradable property rights; and a public administration which minimizes the administrative burden for economic agents are . . . the publicly provided backbones for enabling competitive economic activity" (CEC 2005, sec. 32). By the same token, partnership, participation, and consultation are viewed not only as common practices in a modern democracy, but also as tools for the open and transparent construction of regional development strategies and schemes (CEC 2005, sec. 38).

Conclusions

Since the inclusion of the territorial cohesion concept in the draft European Constitution, new opportunities have arisen for the implementation of more robust territorial policies in the EU. The first steps taken in that direction do not seem to have fully met the objective, despite the very encouraging implications of adopting a territorial cohesion perspective. The immediate steps still needed are not a problem; the Commission has done a good job so far. The final steps must be taken by the member states and the regions, because of the fundamental principle of subsidiarity. The European scientific community has a significant responsibility as well as a great opportunity to contribute toward the development of a European planning culture, based on the best national policy traditions and the best scientific theorizations.

The territorial dimension of development policies has an important potential role in the European model of society. European values addressing equity and sustainability and the European specificity—territorial cultural diversity and multiplicity of territorial identities—will probably help to build a very special attitude toward territory and toward using territorial capital wisely, in all its economic, social, environmental, and identitarian dimensions.

Territorial development policies and territorial cohesion policies are already sufficiently well rooted in the European model of society, explicitly or at least implicitly. Their economic justification also looks remarkably sound, even if, recalling Polanyi's intuition, their ultimate legitimacy cannot but derive from the cultural awareness and the ethical values of the European people.

References

Camagni, R. 1993. From city hierarchy to city network: Reflections about an emerging paradigm. In *Structure and change in the space economy: Festschrift in honour of Martin Beckmann*, T. R. Lakshmanan and P. Nijkamp, eds. Berlin: Springer Verlag.

———. 1998. Sustainable urban development: Definition and reasons for a research programme. *International Journal of Environment and Pollution* 1:6–26.

———. 2001. Policies for spatial development. In *OECD territorial outlook 2001*, 147–169. Paris: Organisation for Economic Co-operation and Development.

———. 2002. On the concept of territorial competitiveness: Sound or misleading? *Urban Studies* 13:2395–2412.

Camagni, R., R. Capello, and P. Nijkamp. 2001. Managing sustainable urban environments. In *Handbook of urban studies*, R. Paddison, ed., 124–140. London: Sage.

Camagni, R., and M. C. Gibelli. 1996. Cities in Europe: Globalisation, sustainability and cohesion. In Presidency of the Council of Ministers, *European spatial planning*. Rome: Poligrafico dello Stato.

CEC—Commission of the European Communities. 1998. *Framework for action for sustainable urban development*. Luxembourg: Office for Official Publications of the European Communities.

———. 1999. *European Spatial Development Perspective: Towards balanced and sustainable development of the territory of the EU*. Luxembourg: Office for Official Publications of the European Communities.

———. 2004a. *DG Regio—Interim territorial cohesion report (preliminary results of ESPON and EU Commission studies)*. Luxembourg: Office for Official Publications of the European Communities.

———. 2004b. *A new partnership for cohesion: Convergence, competitiveness, cooperation. Third report on economic and social cohesion*. Luxembourg: Office for Official Publications of the European Communities.

———. 2004c. *Proposal for a Council regulation laying down general provisions on the European Regional Development Fund, the European Social Fund and the Cohesion Fund*. Luxembourg: Office for Official Publications of the European Communities.

———. 2005. *Cohesion policy in support of growth and jobs: Community Strategic Guidelines, 2007–2013 (communication from the Commission)*. COM (2005) 0299. Brussels, 5 July.

Dutch Presidency. 2004. *Presidency conclusions*. EU Informal Ministerial Meeting on Territorial Cohesion, Rotterdam, 29 November.

Faludi, A., ed. 2002. *European spatial planning*. Cambridge, MA: Lincoln Institute of Land Policy.

Luxembourg Presidency. 2005a. *Presidency conclusions*. EU Informal Ministerial Meeting for Regional Policy and Territorial Cohesion, Luxembourg, 20–21 May.

———. 2005b. *Scoping document and summary of political messages for an assessment of "The territorial state and perspectives of the European Union: Towards a stronger European territorial cohesion in the light of the Lisbon and Gothenburg ambitions."* Endorsed for further development by the Ministers for Spatial Development and the European Commission at the Informal Ministerial Meeting for Regional Policy and Territorial Cohesion, Luxembourg, 20–21 May.

Polanyi, K. 1994. *The great transformation*. New York: Holt, Rinehart and Winston.

Chapter 8

Chasing a Moving Target

Territorial Cohesion Policy in a Europe with Uncertain Borders

JEAN-FRANÇOIS DREVET

Since the fall of the Berlin Wall in 1989, the European Union (EU) has been experiencing enormous geographic changes in its size, shape, and prospects. To some extent, these changes can be compared with the development of the American territory in the nineteenth century (see Meining 1998). Like the American West, Central and Eastern Europe appear to be a set of distinct regions striving for full integration into the European Union, but they are still far from achieving this goal. Both are confronted with two needs: to establish new links between isolated units and to manage borders. As for the first, Europe has to forge new "iron bonds" to ensure territorial integration (Meining 1998, 4); in America this forging was achieved through building railroad networks. As for managing borders, a new "frontier" is moving eastward across Europe, just as it moved across the western states of America. Here, the EU has a specific task: ensuring the "canal lock effect" of these borders ("canal lock effect" refers to the specific role of border regions in managing current disparities; see Drevet 2002).

■ American and EU Territories: Similarities and Differences

In the new policies being established by the EU, territorial cohesion appears to be playing a major role as a tool complementing the instruments already in operation within the EU's cohesion policy (better known as its regional policy). Although this policy does not exist in the United States, it is, as the other contributions to this volume demonstrate, a constitutive element of the European model of society.

The views expressed in this article are those of the author and are not necessarily those of the European Commission.

Since its founding, the United States has experienced a continual process of regional and territorial change, but without a deepening of disparities. According to an assessment of the evolution of personal disposable income in the United States since the 1960s, interstate disparities, already lower than in Europe, have been reduced even further. The catching-up process has been fed by the mobility of labor as well as by the equalization effect of some federal spending. Therefore, no regional policy as such has so far been deemed necessary. Put differently, because the process of "people-to-jobs" has been functioning well, the U.S. government has not considered, *up to now*, the option of a "jobs-to-people" policy. Addressing disparities has been achieved through social policies, without consideration of geographical imbalances.

Yet according to Jacques Robert (chapter 2), Jean Peyrony (chapter 4), and other contributors to this volume, different views could emerge from a growing awareness of the impact of disparities, both social and regional, that affect the U.S. territory. Indeed, recent trends, in particular in the major urban areas (for instance, housing costs), point to a widening of income differentials, leading to growing regional, rather than social imbalances.

The socioeconomic disparities among EU member states in terms of gross domestic product (GDP) per capita and unemployment rates are growing as well. North-South as well as East-West disparities can mostly be attributed to history, but the EU enlargement to Central Europe has widened the gap—as a whole, Central Europe's GDP per capita adjusted for purchasing power parity is less than 50 percent of the EU15 average.[1] In addition, Europe lacks the U.S. equalization instruments. Mobility of labor, at least between member states, is very low and not likely to grow because of language and other cultural and administrative obstacles. Moreover, the speed gap between personal and job mobility is growing with the development of "footloose activities." In Europe, contrary to the mostly unskilled workers of the 1960s, the educated labor force of the 1990s faces a number of difficulties to move across the borders: it is very unlikely to get a qualified job without a fluent knowledge of the national language and even more difficult to get another one for his or her partner. The jobs are more and more mobile, but the labor force, with the exception of a small minority of "high flyers," is less "footloose" than before.

The EU budget is about 1 percent of the EU GDP, and its redistributional effect is limited to less than half of this amount: structural policy spending is about 0.4 percent of the EU GDP, with a net transfer rate (wealthier member states to poorer ones) of 38 percent (2000–2006 period). This is the main reason the EU is developing an explicit Community structural and regional policy to which will be allocated around one-third of the EU budget from January 2007(see box 8.1).

---

[1] EU15 refers to the 15 member states that made up the EU prior to the 2004 enlargement to 25 member states (EU25).

Box 8.1
Community Structural and Regional Policy

The European Union's regional policy is based on financial solidarity inasmuch as part of the member states' contributions to the Community budget goes to the less prosperous regions and social groups. For the 2000–2006 period, these transfers will account for one-third of the Community budget, or €213 billion: €195 billion were to be spent by the four Structural Funds (European Regional Development Fund, European Social Fund, Financial Instrument for Fisheries Guidance, and Guidance Section of the European Agricultural Guidance and Guarantee Fund), and the Cohesion Fund will spend €18 billion.

The Structural Funds concentrate on clearly defined priorities, and the funding is divided as follows:

- 70 percent to regions whose development is lagging—regions that are home to 22 percent of the EU population (Objective 1)
- 11.5 percent to assist economic and social conversion in areas experiencing structural difficulties—areas that are home to 18 percent of the EU population (Objective 2)
- 12.3 percent to promote the modernization of training systems and the creation of employment (Objective 3) outside the Objective 1 regions where such measures form part of the strategies for catching up

In addition, four Community initiatives, accounting for 5.35 percent of the Structural Funds, are seeking common solutions to specific problems in the following areas: cross-border, transnational, and interregional cooperation (Interreg III); sustainable development of cities and declining urban areas (URBAN II); rural development through local initiatives (Leader +); and combating inequalities and discrimination in access to the labor market (Equal). A special allocation of funds is made for the adjustment of fisheries structures outside the Objective 1 regions (0.5 percent), and there are also provisions for innovative actions to promote and experiment with new ideas on development (0.51 percent).

Structural Funds also finance multiannual programs, contributing to jointly agreed development strategies between the regions, member states, and European Commission, taking into account guidelines laid down by the Commission that apply throughout the EU. These programs target economic and social structures in an effort to develop infrastructure such as transport and energy; extend telecommunications services; help firms and provide worker training; and disseminate the tools and know-how of the information society.

Development initiatives financed by the Structural Funds must meet specific needs identified by regions or member states. They form part of an approach to development that respects the environment and promotes equal opportunities. Implementation is decentralized, which means it is mainly the responsibility of the national and regional authorities.

The Cohesion Fund provides direct finance for specific projects related to environmental and transport infrastructure in Spain, Greece, Ireland, and Portugal, where this kind of infrastructure is still inadequate. The Instrument for Structural Policies for Pre-Accession (ISPA) has provided assistance along the same lines to the 10 Central and Eastern European countries that joined the EU in 2004.

Whatever the type of assistance provided, these instruments complement but do not replace national efforts.

Similar differences apply to the management of space. Changes in land use seem to meet far less resistance in the United States than in Europe. The rehabilitation operations implemented in the 1980s in the American Northeast demonstrated a flexibility that offered a wider margin of maneuverability than in Europe, where the changes in land use are slower and more expensive (see Osborne 1988). Europe's higher density of population, scarcity of land, concentration trends (headquarters being unable to relocate out of metropolitan areas), and the weight of the cultural heritage have resulted in "spatial surcharges" there. And yet the recent evolution of the U.S. real estate market is witness to the fact that spatial surcharges are not unknown in the United States—for example, in California—and may require specific measures. In parallel, the continuing rise in gasoline prices is likely to affect territorial disparities as well.

This situation is reason enough to streamline spatial planning in general and to promote it at the Community level. After all, territorial cohesion is a tool that can be used to overcome various obstacles to the modernization of the territory. For example, promoting better coherence between transport and environment and giving due consideration to cross-border and transnational issues are likely to improve the management of space and consequently achieve a reduction in the present surcharge on the territorial implications of necessary changes.

The management of moving borders raises problems of a different nature. Since 1989, the eastern limit of the EU has been moving eastward, encompassing Poland, the Czech Republic, Slovakia, and Hungary, as well as the former Soviet Republics of Estonia, Latvia, and Lithuania. Nineteenth-century America experienced a similar advance of the frontier across the continent, as described by Frederick Turner (1996). In Europe, cross-border activities previously located between Austria and Hungary are now likely to be moving to the Hungarian-Romanian border, before settling in 2007, on the Pruth River between Romania and Moldova. Problems such as suitcase trade and a commuting labor force, not to mention illegal immigration and trafficking, are moving as well. Community policies are finding it difficult to master this process.

Like America more than a century ago, Europe has to cope with the impact of the "great divide" between its two parts. The "border problem" relates to the existence of huge income disparities, and yet at the same time it presents some opportunities to reduce their importance. The recent opening of the borders has stimulated various activities in once isolated regions. With new infrastructure, a larger number of border crossings, and the simplification of formalities, these activities are growing steadily. By means of the canal lock effect (see Drevet 2002, 165–167), a kind of osmosis begins to operate, spreading economic development. In the new member states, the western border regions are more developed than the national average of border development (see chapter 9 in this volume). These states' eastern borders are below average, but they are better developed than the western borders of their neighbors, former republics of the Soviet Union.

Thus, the systematic development of cross-border cooperation with Community support operates as a catalyst, contributing to the catching-up process. Nevertheless, there is nothing like a "frontier mentality" in the EU.

On the contrary, many Europeans are afraid of their frontier. By contrast, in the United States the frontier mentality is said to have influenced the outlook of Americans, especially toward land and their territory (see Rifkin 2004).

In summary, the ongoing enlargement of the EU, like that of the United States during the nineteenth century, raises two questions: first, how to manage a moving territory, in particular from the point of view of economic and territorial cohesion; and, second, what to do with the "frontier" (in both the American and European meanings of the word) at the eastern and southern peripheries, Europe not having an eastern limit to stop the process, as did the Pacific rim for the United States and Canada.

As for the first, the EU needs a comprehensive cohesion policy (see box 8.1). To alleviate the risk of a permanent gap with reality, the framework established at the end of the 1980s should be subject to continual policy adaptations and regular changes at the implementation level. Drawing on lessons from various experiences, including the preaccession funds, the delivery mechanism should be improved frequently. Among these adaptations are integrating spatial planning into regional policy and shifting from socioeconomic to territorial cohesion.

As for the second, the EU's final borders, the Commission has been asked more than once to draw a line. However, in Lisbon in 1992 the Commission retorted that "in the absence of a precise definition of Europe, it was neither possible nor advisable to draw the limits of the Union." Now, more than 10 years later, in view of the fact that the 2004 enlargement will not be the last one because of the number of declared and potential candidates queuing at the EU's gate, is another reply possible? And yet would a similar question to President George Washington have received the right answer? The United States was likely to expand, but how far? So far, the Commission has simply begun the difficult process of establishing a "new neighborhood" policy without giving a clear indication of which countries will remain neighbors and which will be allowed to become new members.

Territorial Cohesion and Spatial Planning

Within the framework of defining a European model of society, the territorial implications of EU integration appeared on the EU's agenda in 1987–1988. Since then, although not an established policy per se, "territorial cohesion" has become a major aspect of the formulation of new strategies, taking into account the impact of sector-based policies such as environment and transport, and some interventions of the Structural Funds, at least in an implicit way.

When it issued *Europe 2000* in the early 1990s with a view toward establishing spatial planning at Community level (CEC 1991), the Commission had its eyes set on an evolutionary process:

- Developing awareness of the spatial impact of evolving Community policies such as those on the environment and transport as well as regional or structural policies
- Convincing member states to improve their coordination of spatial policies internally as well as with other member states (and to promote coordination within the Commission itself on similar issues)
- Organizing this coordination in the framework of Commission reference documents elaborated in a consensus-building process

It was assumed that the geographic framework of EU12 (that is, the 12 countries making up the EU until 1995), including the recent entrants Spain and Portugal, was unlikely to change for a while, thereby giving the Community enough time to elaborate and to negotiate such documents and to anticipate major problems that might develop.

The objectives were rather classical, drawn from common views elaborated in particular within the framework of the early cooperation between Dutch and French planning agencies. The objectives took into account, among other aspects, the territorial implications of European integration, in particular for countries and regions with a central position in Europe (France, the Benelux countries, Western Germany, northern Italy); the territorial impacts of Community policies (agriculture, environment, transportation, as well as regional and other structural policies); and the consequences of opening border regions to increased competition. There was a common awareness of the advantages of better cooperation between spatial planning agencies and the hope of bringing more added value to territorial policies that had been somewhat overtaken by the growing speed of economic changes in the late 1980s.

Spatial planning has, however, developed in a rather different way than originally planned. The first meeting of EU regional policy and spatial planning ministers at Nantes in November 1989 coincided with the inception of a far more challenging trajectory: the fall of the Berlin Wall with the extension of the then European Community, now European Union, to a Europe progressively devoid of any real borders.

Instead of having plenty of time to assess a stable European territory and to draw up a strategic document valid for a couple of decades, EU planners urgently needed to develop among member states a common perception of the new territorial challenges—for example, the opening of the eastern borders, the reorganization of Trans-European Networks, and the importance of depolluting transnational catchments areas and inland seas—and to adapt Community instruments to rapid changes in the configuration of a rapidly expanding territory.

After approval of the Commission's documents *Europe 2000* and *Europe 2000+*, the Committee on Spatial Development began to consider establishment of the European Spatial Development Perspective (ESDP), which was adopted at the meeting of ministers in Potsdam in 1999 (CEC 1991, 1994, 1999).

Thus, after many years of negotiations, the Commission and the member states achieved an agreement on a common framework. Its practical implications remain fairly limited, however. Neither the Commission nor other administrations have pursued the level of coordination needed to tackle the contradictions between the territorial implications of their policies such as transport and environment. As long as reference documents lack spatial representations in the form of policy maps, such contradictions remain difficult to overcome. Unfortunately, it appears that the elaboration of a common cartographic document (a "vision" of the EU territory and not at all a master plan) goes beyond the wishes of some member states, as Zonneveld points out in chapter 10 of this volume. Furthermore, such a document runs the risk of being outdated before being published and even approved. Indeed, the territory is becoming increasingly difficult to assess in a process in which the speed of history is greater than that of the elaboration of the studies describing possible futures.

In parallel, the Commission intensified its effort to gain recognition of its right to intervene in the field of spatial planning. Something was achieved, however, through the emergence of the concept of territorial cohesion, mentioned for the first time in the Amsterdam Treaty and more recently in the draft constitution. Rather isolated at the beginning of the negotiations, the Commission gained increasing support, in particular from member states once hostile to the concept, but ready to use it to slow the drift of Structural Funds toward the poorer regions of Central and Eastern Europe.

In a system with explicit geographic priorities, it is very easy to calculate the balance sheets. Therefore, it was quite logical to have a tough debate. In spite of their needs, the Central European countries, disadvantaged by their lack of absorption capacity, did not get as much as expected. On the other hand, the contributing member states, in particular the U.K., had to go beyond their objective to limit the budget to 1 percent of EU GDP, then keeping the cohesion budget higher than their original target. Sadly, the cooperation objective, although an essential contribution to territorial cohesion, has been squeezed, with every member state being obsessed by its own "returns" (see Faludi 2005).

A process of "learning by doing" has developed, however. Through exchanges of experiences and better cooperation, the Commission, the member states, and local and regional authorities have overcome some territorial problems, quite often through both structural and preaccession funding from the EU (see box 8.2). For example, EU insistence has led to enhanced cooperation, greater environment awareness, and promotion of spatial planning, which is explicitly mentioned in the Interreg IIC Community initiative. Furthermore, progress has been made in developing

---

Box 8.2

Some Achievements of EU Structural and Regional Policy

Recent reports on the socioeconomic situation in and development of the EU's regions reveal that the Structural Funds and the Cohesion Fund have already contributed substantially to reducing regional disparities.

The reduction in the gaps in average per capita incomes between regions, and still more between member states, from 1987 to 1997 is particularly encouraging. In the poorest regions, where 10 percent of the EU population lives, the per capita gross domestic product (GDP) rose from 54.2 percent of the Community average in 1987 to 61.1 percent in 1997. At the national level, convergence is still more marked for the least prosperous EU countries (Greece, Portugal, Ireland, and Spain), with average per capita GDP rising from 67.6 percent in 1988 to 78.8 percent in 1998. This progress is all the more noteworthy in that it was achieved in comparison with dynamic regions where growth was naturally faster.

The EU has made a significant contribution to these satisfying results. Several studies have shown that the process of European economic integration and the work of the Structural Funds have largely driven the process of catching up. In the Objective 1 regions, the Funds contributed about 0.5 percent per year to growth between 1989 and 1999. The cumulative effect added about 10 percent to GDP in Greece, Ireland, and Portugal and over 4 percent in Spain. In other words, a third or more of the economic convergence of these countries would not have happened without the Structural Funds. More specifically, it is estimated that from 1989 to 1999 in all the assisted regions of the EU some 2.2 million jobs were maintained or created thanks to the Structural Funds.

Although substantial progress has been made in basic infrastructure, other imbalances remain: in research and technological development, access to skills and the information society, opportunities for education, and ongoing training and the quality of the environment. The Structural Funds and the Cohesion Fund are helping to reduce these imbalances, while creating favorable conditions for growth.

But the achievements of regional policy cannot be summed up merely in statistical terms. The Community-wide scale of certain measures (Community initiatives); the partnership among the various parties involved; the attention paid to the environment and equal opportunities, cooperation, networking, exchange of experiences; and the experimentation with new approaches to development (innovative actions)—all are new assets that help the regions to move forward and make full use of their potential.

Although the economic progress of the least prosperous regions is quite remarkable from a medium-term point of view, the gaps between the richest and the poorest are still considerable and have become even greater since the accession in 2004 of eight new member states from Central Europe. For this reason, the budgetary debate about the future programming period (2007–2013) is especially severe. For the first time, three different positions (instead of the two in the past, net receivers versus net contributors) have been put forward: (1) the "East" wants the highest priority, because it suffers obviously from the most acute problems; (2) the "South" wishes to keep enough funding to tackle the problems not yet solved; and (3) the "North" and the "West," which must foot the bill, refuse to pay for both.

---

territorial indicators for the purpose of diversifying regional policy instruments during the 1990s.

Traditionally, in its efforts to narrow the gap between regions, regional policy has used socioeconomic eligibility criteria: a low GDP per capita (adjusted for purchasing power parity) and a high rate of unemployment. Such policy interventions are supposed to be temporary in nature—that is, as soon as the catching-up process has achieved results, such as GDP per capita over the stipulated 75 percent threshold, Community assistance is phased out. For this reason, the Commission has been reluctant to take into consideration territorial indicators, which are derived from handicaps geographic in nature and are therefore likely to require permanent assistance. Thus, it has often resisted active lobbying by representatives of peripheral, insular, or ultraperipheral regions. Nevertheless, geographic criteria have acquired growing importance in regional policy interventions. Examples of such interventions follow.

Interreg

Interreg (see box 8.3), created in 1990, is the first instrument in which eligibility is based on geography. Allocations for cross-border cooperation are granted to every NUTS 3 unit that has an international land border. (NUTS refers to the Nomenclature of Territorial Units of Statistics; NUTS is the geographic area used for collecting EU statistics.)

Cross-border cooperation has been an important activity of the Council of Europe,[2] which, beginning in the 1960s, developed a common concept and supported various experiments in the most populated areas of Western Europe, in particular the Benelux countries and Switzerland. With the completion of the internal market, the European Commission realized that various centers were losing their customs activities and thus part of their economic base. Rather than offering local or regional compensation measures, it proposed tackling their problem at the Community level.

In 1988 cross-border cooperation was mentioned among the activities eligible for intervention under the European Regional Development Fund (ERDF—see box 8.1), among others. When Interreg was established in 1990 as a Community initiative, the Commission decided to offer financial assistance to all border zones; the allocations were calculated in relation to their eligibility status. Thus, for the first time a geographic criterion was introduced in regional policy: any NUTS 3 unit with an international border was eligible. In addition, on a case-by-case basis, some NUTS 3 units with a maritime border have been included.

Objective 6

Objective 6, established in 1994 in the framework of the EU accession treaty for Austria, Sweden, Finland, and Norway, is based on low population density. Eligibility is granted to those regions with fewer than eight inhabitants per square kilometer.

When negotiating their accession, Sweden, Finland, and Norway realized that the EU regional policy *acquis* was not likely to offer significant

[2] See the minutes of the European Conference of Ministers Responsible for Regional Planning and its *Guiding Principles for Sustainable Spatial Development of the European Continent* (2002), which describe a broad vision of the concept of sustainable spatial development that was adopted on 30 January 2002 (see the Council of Europe Web site, http://www.coe.int).

> **Box 8.3**
>
> The Interreg Initiative

Altogether Europe's states have lengthy borders: 26,300 kilometers for Europe west of the Soviet Union before the break-up of Yugoslavia and Czechoslovakia, compared with 12,000 kilometers for both the United States and Canada. Therefore, the process of integration requires a specific instrument for promoting cooperation, ensuring that border regions avoid the negative effects of free circulation and allowing them to benefit from the new opportunities presented by integration. Interreg III is the Community initiative for trans-European cooperation in the framework of the European Regional Development Fund (ERDF) for the period 2000–2006. Its total budget for that period was €4875 million (1999 prices).

The objective of the new cooperation instrument, which will replace Interreg in 2007, is to strengthen economic and social cohesion in the European Union by promoting cross-border, transnational, and interregional cooperation and balanced development of the EU territory. Actions in relation to the borders and border areas between member states and between the European Union and nonmember countries are, therefore, at the heart of the initiative. Indeed, the external borders of the European Union will receive more attention, particularly in view of enlargement and cooperation with Mediterranean and ex-Soviet neighbors. Specific attention will be given to developing relations between the outermost regions and their Caribbean and African regional environment.

As the former Interreg, the new cooperation initiative will be implemented under three strands:

- Strand A: cross-border cooperation promoting integrated regional development between neighboring border regions, including external borders and certain maritime borders. The objective is to develop cross-border economic and social cooperation through joint strategies and development programs.
- Strand B: transnational cooperation aiming to promote a higher degree of integration across large groupings of European regions, with a view toward achieving sustainable, harmonious, and balanced development in the EU and greater territorial integration, including with candidate and other neighboring countries.
- Strand C: interregional cooperation throughout the territory of the EU (and neighboring countries) to improve regional development and cohesion.

The implementation of joint cross-border transnational strategies and development programs is governed by the following principles:

- A wide partnership between different administrative levels, with socioeconomic and other relevant actors following a bottom-up approach.
- Complementarily with the mainstream programs of the Structural Funds.
- Following a more integrated approach to the implementation of the Community Initiatives. In accordance with the 1999 Structural Funds regulation, Interreg has financed measures for rural development eligible under the European Agricultural Guidance and Guarantee Fund (EAGGF), for the development of human resources eligible under the European Social Fund (ESF), and for the adjustment of fisheries structures eligible under the Financial Instrument for Fisheries Guidance (FIFG).
- Effective coordination between the new cooperation instruments and external EU policy instruments.

European areas eligible for cross-border cooperation (strand A) are those along the internal and external land borders and some maritime areas; for transnational cooperation (strand B), all EU regions under strand B (some are eligible for two, or in some cases even three, cooperation areas); and interregional cooperation (strand C), the whole of the EU territory.

returns. Many of their arctic regions were not in a position to receive Structural Funds because of their high GDP per capita and their low levels of unemployment. This prospect was a very disappointing one for three countries who were likely to be net contributors to the EU budget and who had invested prior to their accession far more than many member states in their rather efficient regional policies, in particular in support of their Arctic zones. Therefore, the Commission went back to the drawing board and created Objective 6 to encompass Arctic regional policies in an EU framework. Although Norway eventually rejected accession altogether, this objective provided the 1.4 million inhabitants of the Arctic regions of Sweden and Finland with €100–€110 per capita annually. This tailor-made eligibility criterion is based on geography: eight inhabitants or fewer per square kilometer at the NUTS 2 level. Thus, a second territorial criterion was added to the toolbox of EU regional policy. As the density of a population in a remote area is not likely to grow significantly, for the first time regional policy would implicitly compensate a permanent handicap, thereby contributing to the territorial cohesion of the EU.

Interreg IIIB

Interreg IIC (1995–1999), followed by Interreg IIIB (2000–2006), was established to support transnational cooperation in large-scale geographic groupings belonging to several member states.

In 1995 the European Commission decided to add another strand to Interreg, complementing cross-border activities, to address the growing issue of transnational cooperation. It specifically mentioned support for spatial planning activities. Member states already participating in rather successful transnational groupings, such as the Baltic Sea or northwestern Europe, managed to convince the Commission that there was a Community interest in cofinancing such activities at the relevant geographic level, midway between the national level (which was too small) and the level of the EU as a whole (which was too big). In this way, the Interreg IIC initiative, and later Interreg IIIB, has provided a very useful framework for stimulating cooperation in tackling, among other common problems of spatial planning, transport (the missing links in the Trans-European Networks) and environment (pollution has no borders). From 1995–1999 to 2000–2006, Interreg allocations were significantly increased. In its proposals for the next programming period, the Commission even upgraded this intervention, thereby raising cooperation to the level of a full-fledged objective of structural policies (see box 8.3), although its original budget has been reduced by the Council.

Ultraperipheral Regions

To a certain extent, remoteness has been recognized as a basis for Community interventions, thereby granting a wide range of advantages to "ultraperipheral" regions. Originally dealt with through CAP allocations, the ultraperipheral problem is increasingly coming under the Regional policy's umbrella. Indeed, the quest to address permanent handicaps is not over. Various lobbies have tried to influence the Commission, asking for compensation for insularity, a mountainous territory, a scarcity of water, or simply remoteness. But up to now, only the ultraperipheral regions,[3] usually depicted in insets in the corners of EU maps, have succeeded in receiving specific advantages, partly inherited from their special positions in their former national context before being included in the EU territory.[4] The European Regional Development Fund is offering these regions rates of funding higher than those offered other regions: up to 85 percent of public expenditure.

Phare, a Preaccession Strategy

During the evolution of Phare (an assistance program for former socialist countries) from technical assistance to institution building and regional development programs, all in preparation for implementation of the instruments under the Structural Funds, growing importance has been attached to territorial interventions, in particular with the creation of Phare CBC (cross-border cooperation), which mirrors Interreg on the candidate countries' side of their EU border.

Since 1994, the Commission has, at the request of the European Parliament, extended the cross-border cooperation instrument beyond the EU in allocating €150 million of Phare funds to candidate countries having a common border with the EU. With the exception of Romania (which does not have such a border), all Central European countries have benefited from this opportunity, anticipating Structural Funds through an instrument of a territorial nature. In some cases, EU allocations to the candidate side of the border turned out to be higher than on the member state side. Although procedural obstacles have at times prevented the smooth operation of the Phare CBC interventions, this first experience has been of exemplary value for border regions separated for more than four decades by the iron curtain.

In summary, these five examples demonstrate the growing importance of addressing new issues by invoking territorial criteria that complement mainstream interventions based on socioeconomic indicators—indicators that do not necessarily embrace territorial problems.

---

[3] The French overseas *départements* of Guadeloupe, Martinique, French Guiana, and Réunion are included in the EU, as well as the Canary islands (Spain), Madeira, and the Azores (Portugal). Their specific status is stated in the new treaties.
[4] Overseas departments enjoy a specific status under French law, and the Canary Islands benefited from a separate customs system when Spain was outside the EU.

Territorial Cohesion and the "Final" EU Borders

Although the EU is legally an economic construction with an unclear political identity (see Biedenkopf, Geremek, and Michalski 2004), it has always been understood from its very beginning that only full-fledged democracies can participate in the EU. In the late 1960s, this dimension was pointed out to the caudillo of Spain's Francisco Franco, with the result that cooperation with Spain was strictly limited to the conclusion of a trade agreement.

In the process of enlarging eastward, the EU has given "political criteria" greater importance to the extent that conditions must to be met before negotiations can start. In Turkey's application for EU membership, the Commission and the member states have made compliance with political criteria a condition for beginning negotiations. To a certain extent Turkey has met the internal requirements, but, like the Central European candidate countries in the 1990s, Ankara has also been asked to improve its relations with its neighbors and it has failed to do so, at least with Cyprus. As the only country in the world to refuse to recognize the Republic of Cyprus, now an EU member state, Turkey runs the risk of having its recent negotiation process frozen for a while.

Since approval of the Amsterdam Treaty in 1997, political criteria have been an explicit part of the *acquis communautaire* (the accumulated body of Community legislation in force at any moment in time) and an increasingly important component of the European model. In this respect, the EU contributes to the improvement of political governance in Europe, not to mention in countries outside the EU, because these criteria have been included in the association or partnership agreements signed by the EU. This inclusion creates permanent pressure for the restoration or the improvement of democracy in many member states—the behavior of their governments is now under the close scrutiny of the Commission and the European Parliament. Therefore, the member states are cautious when tempted into a more "realistic" approach.

It is logical, then, that any European country that has established or restored democracy feels entitled to apply for EU membership. The connection between democracy and accession, established when Greece liberated itself from the colonels in 1974, applied to Central Europe after the fall of the Berlin Wall. Now that the same connection is advocated by Georgia and Ukraine, this question is "Where to go with EU enlargement?" (see Drevet 2004). Up to now, the geographic eastern and southern frontiers of Europe have coincided with the extension of democracy. Is this likely to continue to be the case in the future?

For the European Union, this is not an immediate problem. But taking into account the fact that some former Soviet republics are moving toward democracy and that southern and eastern Mediterranean states with associate status may move in the same direction,[5] a dilemma is lurking under the

[5] Quite often referred to as PSEM (French acronym for *pays du sud et de l'est méditerranéen*).

surface: integration or neighborhood? What does the future hold for the European periphery?

Without a doubt, the development of democracy is a precondition for any future eastern extension of the EU to potential candidate countries. Moreover, Russia would be more inclined to accept such an extension if the candidate countries would move toward democracy. Moldova and Ukraine, and to a lesser extent Georgia and Armenia, feel part of Europe and have already expressed their wish to become members of the EU, if only in the distant future (Russia feels European as well, but it has no intention of joining the EU). Therefore, the eastern limit of the EU is likely to move again, but how far? In the Mediterranean, the situation seems to be more under control, because the southern and eastern rims are supposed to be part of Africa and Asia. But it is the movement of a country toward democracy that will raise the question of a possible accession.

Indeed, far from being the end of history, the 2004 enlargement of the EU will be followed by others. It appears to be a global historical trend, likely to happen but without foreseeable dates. All of these possible accessions have critical territorial implications—in the Balkans, Turkey, the former Soviet republics, and the Mediterranean.

The Western Balkans

In the Western Balkans, EU integration must cope with the political fragmentation of a space that, geographically speaking, is already fragmented. The new borders created since the breakup of Yugoslavia have to be managed; a new distribution of population must be accommodated; and a market economy has to be established. Croatia has just begun its accession negotiations, and Macedonia is now recognized as a "candidate country," but it still lacks the administrative capacity to implement Community policies.

Contrary to the global move toward integration in other parts of Central Europe, which is reducing the role of borders, the process of fragmentation in the Western Balkans has already created 2,339 kilometers of new borders, not taking into account the de facto borders that exist within Bosnia-Herzegovina and Serbia. Therefore, these "potential candidates" for EU accession are likely to present a huge number of territorial problems on a scale not seen since the end of World War II:

• Organizing a new territorial framework, facilitating relations with neighboring countries (now all members of the EU or due to accede in 2007), and becoming integrated within the EU framework

• Transforming the new border zones into cooperation areas and to some extent restoring the networks that had been functioning up to the end of the former Yugoslavia

• Taking into account the consequences of forced movements of population in a realistic way (some displaced persons are not likely to go back to their homes)

Turkey

With Turkey, the EU would have to prepare to expand into a troubled area beyond the classical limits of Europe. To some extent, the territorial implications of Turkish accession have already been considered within the framework of the spatial activities of the Council of Europe. But many issues have yet to be tackled within Turkey as well as in cooperation with its neighbors.

As a long-standing participant in the spatial planning activities of the Council of Europe, Turkey has had various opportunities to develop spatial planning policy at the national level. However, its accession raises very important territorial problems, which so far have received little consideration.

First, in addition to its large regional imbalances, Turkey is suffering from rather weak *territorial* management. Urban development, tourism, and development of transport infrastructure have all been pursued without consideration for the country's fragile and downgraded environment. Moreover, the urban population has grown for more than three decades at an annual rate of 5 percent. Meanwhile, lack of planning has resulted in problems that, unfortunately, were brought into focus by the 1999 earthquake. Insufficient legislation, poor enforcement capacity, and the little thought given to natural hazards have had, among them, tremendous consequences. Although some progress has been made since 1999, the general delivery mechanisms remain unable to meet the challenges of the near future.

Second, some of Turkey's border regions are facing a deplorable situation because of decades of neglect of the country's remote regions and the poor quality of relations with neighboring countries. Some borders were hermetically closed by the iron curtain and remain closed—for example, the border between Turkey and Armenia.

Third, Kurdistan's borders with Syria, Iraq, and Iran are more open to smuggling than to cooperation. Indeed, extending the future EU external borders in this area will present problems. The unknown future of Iraq, as well as the continuing instability of the Middle East region, will have an impact on neighboring countries, including Cyprus, which is already a member state. In Turkey itself, the underdevelopment of these border zones (especially in the lagging behind eastern half of Turkey) is a huge obstacle to the stability of the region as a whole, with a potentially negative impact on the implementation of some EU policies such as in the areas of justice and home affairs.

Fourth, unlike other eastern and southern Mediterranean countries, Turkey is not threatened by a scarcity of water. But its behavior in the upstream drainage basin of the Tigris and the Euphrates Rivers has resulted in a water dispute. Taking advantage of the absence of an international water-sharing agreement, Ankara has acted unilaterally, building dams and filling the reservoirs at the expense of its neighbors, depriving them of their water. For this reason, the huge GAP project[6] has not been financed by international institutions. Because European integration requires final settlement of such disputes, transnational cooperation must be enhanced so that a common development plan can be drawn up for Mesopotamia as a whole. This plan should provide for joint utilization of water and other resources, ensuring a complementary approach between the works to be completed upstream (stocking water in Turkey and Iran) and downstream (flood protection and irrigation of the lowlands in Turkey, Syria, and Iraq).

Fifth, although it has limited experience in cross-border cooperation (it launched a limited cross-border program with Greece in Thrace in 2003), Turkey has already entered into transnational cooperation agreements. In 1992 Ankara took the initiative in promoting the creation of the Black Sea Economic Community (BSEC). The BSEC comprises all the Black Sea countries, plus Greece, Albania, Serbia, and Azerbaijan. To date, the BSEC has achieved limited results, but it remains the relevant forum for developing large-scale cooperation to tackle territorial problems, such as the fragile environment of the Black Sea, which is already heavily polluted by Russian rivers and the Danube and is subject as well to the growing risk of oil spills from tankers navigating the Black Sea, the Dardanelles and Bosporus Straits, and the Aegean Sea.

Former Soviet Republics

Since the "Revolution of the Roses" in Georgia, followed by political change in Ukraine, the EU is confronted with the "territorial extension of democracy" in the former Soviet republics at an unprecedented speed. This process raises once again the question of the territorial limits of European integration, including the nature of the partnership with Russia. Because of the size of the Ukrainian territory and its Soviet heritage, in the long run its territorial integration would raise an important challenge to European financial instruments, already overburdened by the priorities brought by the new member states and the prospect of Turkish accession.

An unknown number of the former Soviet republics are likely to apply for accession to the EU as soon as their political and economic structures will allow them to do so. Whatever their final status, they share various territorial problems with the EU, as sadly demonstrated by the 1986 Chernobyl nuclear disaster. A joint analysis of these problems is therefore needed—for example, in the framework of the new Community neighborhood policy, launched in 2003 to accommodate various neighborhood problems, including discouraging accession hopes. To date, it looks like an "à la

---

[6] GAP (Güneydou Anadolu Projesi, in Turkish) is a great hydropower and irrigation scheme for the development of the upstream Euphrates and Tigris basins.

carte" policy in which 16 Mediterranean and ex-Soviet Republics select their cooperation priorities with the EU through commonly agreed upon action plans. As far as territorial cooperation is concerned, possible subjects to tackle are the construction of new transport and energy networks, agreed goals for reducing pollution in common catchments areas of rivers flowing to the Baltic and Black Seas, and the transnational aspects of nuclear safety. Because this region is of growing importance for its gas and oil resources, this analysis, as well as its territorial and policy implications, is of great urgency.

Mediterranean Countries

In the Mediterranean region, the importance of the territorial dimension of the EU's new neighborhood policy is obvious, in particular for the southern member states, from Portugal to Greece, which have complained about the "Eastern priority" and have asked Brussels to pay more attention to trans-Mediterranean issues. Up to now, neither cross-border nor transnational cooperation has really begun in the region. However, what concrete steps can be taken to address the huge territorial problems of this area through, for example, trans-Mediterranean cooperation? Is it worthwhile to offer partnerships as real alternatives to accession? Is partnership likely to attract Mediterranean countries as well as the former Soviet republics if and when democracy has been established?

The Mediterranean, as well as the beautiful landscapes surrounding it, has been suffering from four decades of unprecedented urban growth. This unfortunate heritage requires urgent measures at the trans-Mediterranean level, as already demonstrated in the Blue Plan. An intergovernmental meeting held in Split in 1977 established the Blue Plan mandate, specifically assigning it the task of "putting at the disposal of political leaders and decision-makers all information that will enable them to develop plans likely to ensure sustained optimal socio-economic development without degrading the environment" and "helping governments of coastal states in the Mediterranean region to increase their knowledge of the joint problems they have to face, both in the Mediterranean Sea and in their coastal areas."[7] Through its think-tank approach, the Blue Plan provides a package of data as well as systemic and prospective studies, combined in certain cases with proposals for action, intended to provide the Mediterranean countries with useful information for implementing sustainable socioeconomic development that does not result in degradation of the environment. However, the Blue Plan lacks systematic implementation because of the absence of delivery mechanisms and the scarcity of funding.

---

[7] See Guillaume Benoit and Aline Comeau, *A Sustainable Future for the Mediterranean, the Blue Plan's Environment and Development Outlook*, 2005.

The Future?

In many cases, then, extensions of the EU cannot be considered without a steady improvement in the decision-making procedures in Brussels. Because the EU missed the point when negotiating the Amsterdam Treaty and did even worse at Nice, it was thought that the constitutional treaty would contain the provisions needed to meet the challenge, or a least to present the EU with the capacity to better manage itself after its enlargement to 25 member states.

Now, however, after rejection, with clear majorities, of the constitution by two founding member states (France and the Netherlands), this challenge is unlikely to be met before some years have passed. The EU has already begun to move in the opposite direction, limiting its ambitions by adopting conservative financial perspectives in December 2005 and, de facto, taking a restrictive view of the enlargement issue, the expectations raised in Eastern Europe notwithstanding. Nevertheless, the dominant trends toward democracy, initiated at the end of the 1980s, remain, and major territorial changes remain likely.

As already demonstrated, the EU cannot avoid considering the territorial dimension of integration. Compared with the United States, Europe has less labor mobility and flexibility in the reallocation of space, and those factors are not likely to improve in the future (see Carbonell and Yaro 2005). Consequently, the EU needs to enhance its regional policy and spatial development, to meet the challenge of unavoidable and major changes of its territory and its surroundings.

Some experts are promoting the Euromed concept to favor a joint European development scheme that would include all of the Mediterranean. For instance, Euromed ministries responsible for transports have approved in 2005 an outline plan for their networks. But within that framework, some policy orientations still must be developed. First, whatever happens in the enlargement process, trends toward integration are already working, at least in the economic sphere. But the question of being or not being a European state leads to discrimination between the eastern and southern peripheries. As mentioned earlier, countries on the eastern periphery seem to be eligible for integration (but how far?) and those on the southern periphery appear to be excluded (but for how long?). Because territorial integration is already under way, why not establish common objectives—for example, for transport and environment policies? This question will be a key one in the "new neighborhood financial instrument" that the Commission intends to develop from 2007 onward in cooperation with a large circle of neighboring countries, from Russia to Morocco.

Second, as proposed in the Commission draft regulations for the Structural Funds (2007–2013), cross-border cooperation needs to be developed as a full-scale cooperation instrument (see box 8.3). A decade of development has already achieved much success, but, at least in comparison to mainstream operations, too many programs are facing too many implementation problems. Unnecessary procedural obstacles have to be removed and the instrument replacing Interreg streamlined to provide results at the level of its political expectations.

To enhance territorial cohesion, transnational cooperation has the greatest potential. Political umbrellas are quite often already available, even when practical achievements are fairly limited (see Danube and Black Sea cooperation[8]), taking the form of regular meetings of ministerial councils representing the states concerned.

The intermediate level between the EU level (being too large) and the national or cross-border levels (being too small) is appropriate. The question is how to organize adequate groupings relevant to such cooperation. From the Baltic experience, it is quite obvious that groupings based on geographic realities have a better chance of achieving practical results. Therefore, the Commission must convince member states and regions not to try to participate in as many cooperation areas as possible in order to maximize their chances of receiving EU funding, and thus to refrain from forming irrelevant and inefficient cooperation areas without common objectives.

Practical objectives can be selected in groupings based on geographic realities, in particular for environment and transport measures, which can play a fundamental role in such cooperation. The need to clean up the Danube drainage basin or the Black Sea is an excellent springboard for going beyond sector-based cooperation.

Finally, in the framework of an ERDF program, support from Community funding can be obtained through a joint program ensuring the implementation of commonly agreed upon objectives and the establishment of a delivery mechanism.

Based on the achievements of such a form of cooperation, a bottom-up process can revitalize spatial planning at the Community level and facilitate the identification of feasible priorities for the establishment of a global Euromed reference framework. However, the tasks remain politically and technically difficult. Such tasks were not achieved with 15 member states, and so can they be carried out with 30–35 member states, plus neighboring countries? To a significant extent, the reply to this question depends on successful achievements in the area of transnational cooperation.

---

[8] For this effort, the Directorate General for Regional Policy (DG Regio) commissioned two studies identifying major trends for transnational cooperation (see ÖIR 2000 and TAD 2001).

References

Biedenkopf, K., B. Geremek, and K. Michalski. 2004. *The spiritual and cultural dimension of Europe: Concluding remarks (Reflection group initiated by the president of the European Commission)*. Vienna/Brussels: Institute for Human Sciences. http://europa.eu.int/comm/research/social-sciences/pdf/michalski_281004_final_report_en.pdf.

Carbonell, A., and R. D. Yaro. 2005. American spatial development and the new megalopolis. *Land Lines* 17(2):1–4.

CEC—Commission of the European Communities. 1991. *Europe 2000: Outlook for the development of the Community's territory*. Luxembourg: Office for Official Publications of the European Communities.

———. 1994. *Europe 2000+: Cooperation for European territorial development*. Luxembourg: Office for Official Publications of the European Communities.

———. 1999. *European Spatial Development Perspective: Towards balanced and sustainable development of the territory of the EU*. Luxembourg: Office for Official Publications of the European Communities.

Drevet, J.-F. 2002. The European Union and its frontiers: Toward new cooperation areas for spatial planning. In *European spatial planning*, A. Faludi, ed. Cambridge, MA: Lincoln Institute of Land Policy, 159–178.

———. 2004. *L'élargissement de l'UE jusqu'ou?* Paris: Harmattan.

European Conference of Ministers Responsible for Regional Planning. 2002. *Guiding principles for sustainable spatial development of the European continent*. Strasbourg. http://www.coe.int.

Faludi, A., ed. 2002. *European spatial planning*. Cambridge, MA: Lincoln Institute of Land Policy.

———. 2005. Territorial cohesion: An unidentified political objective. In Territorial cohesion, A. Faludi, ed., special issue. *Town Planning Review* 76(1):1–13.

Meining, D. W. 1998. The shaping of America: A geographical perspective on 500 years of history. In *Transcontinental America*, 1850–1915, vol. 3. New Haven, CT: Yale University Press.

ÖIR—Austrian Institute for Regional Studies and Spatial Planning. 2000. *Regional and territorial aspects of development in the Danube countries with respect to impacts on the European Union*. Vienna: ÖIR.

Osborne, D. 1988. *Laboratories of democracy: A new breed of governor creates models for national growth*. Boston: Harvard Business School Press.

Rifkin, J. 2004. *The European dream: How Europe's vision of the future is quietly eclipsing the American dream*. Cambridge: Polity Press.

TAD—Territoires, Aménagement, Développement. 2001. *Territorial impact on the European Union of the evolution of the Black Sea countries*. Paris: TAD, November.

Turner, F. J. 1996. *The frontier in American history*. New York: Dover Publications.

Chapter 9

The Vienna-Bratislava-Győr Triangle

The European Model of Society in Action

GABRIELE TATZBERGER

The Vienna-Bratislava-Győr border region that straddles Austria, Hungary, and Slovakia has experienced huge changes over the last 15 years, especially since the fall of the iron curtain in 1989 and the European integration that followed. In view of these changes, the Vienna-Bratislava-Győr Triangle can be regarded as an important springboard for revitalizing East-West relations (ÖIR 2003b, 7). Indeed, for the first time in decades a common transnational view and intensive cooperation are possible, and yet vast differences remain. For that reason, disparities among regions became a new focus of the European Union (EU) with its enlargement to 25 member states in 2004. This enlargement was a momentous achievement that signaled Europe's unification after 50 years of division, while simultaneously creating a new political order that for the first time in contemporary history is based on common values and a shared desire to construct a space of security and peace.

With the addition of the 10 new member states, the population of the EU rose to over 455 million, its territory to 3.9 million square kilometers, and its official languages to 20. By comparison, the United States has 293 million inhabitants, 9.4 million square kilometers, and one official language, English.

The EU enlargement of 2004 had several specific features. First, it was the biggest enlargement the EU has ever undergone. Second, in 2001 most of the regions within the new member states had a gross domestic product (GDP) per capita adjusted for purchasing power parity of less than 75 percent of the EU15[1] average (CEC 2004b). And, third, the new member

---

[1] EU15 refers to the 15 member states that made up the EU prior to the 2004 enlargement to 25 member states (EU25).

states in Eastern Europe are former socialist countries and therefore have undergone huge changes in becoming democracies and market economies. Even though entry to the EU might seem to imply the end of transition by these countries, which are now well-established market economies, it would be a mistake to imagine that history can be wiped out in such a short period and that no structural traces of the former communist system remain (Mercier 2005).

The EU is now the largest internal single market and trader of goods and services in the world (Rifkin 2004) and one of the strongest regions economically. Yet it still suffers from major regional disparities that were intensified with the enlargement of 2004. Europe's "pentagon" (defined by the metropolises of London, Paris, Milan, Munich, and Hamburg) comprises 15 member states that cover 20 percent of the territory of the EU, contain 40 percent of its population, and produce 50 percent of its GDP. Once the EU expands to 27 member states (Romania and Bulgaria are scheduled to join in 2007), the very high concentration of activities in the central part of the EU will resist, with the "pentagon" comprising 14 percent of the EU territory, 32 percent of the population, and 46.5 percent of the GDP. These increasing disparities and the high concentration in the EU were the main drivers of the emergence of the concepts of territorial cohesion and polycentric development. The next section describes how these concepts emerged at the European level and their importance.

Polycentric Development, Territorial Cohesion, and the European Model of Society

Polycentric development means enhancing competitiveness through cooperation, but also fostering regional balance while keeping in mind urban-rural relationships. The traditional response to the problems of disadvantaged or peripheral regions was to connect them to the core, but polycentric development also means fostering internal connections in order to create a network of internationally accessible urban areas and their linked hinterland (Hague and Kirk 2003). Polycentric development is not, morphologically speaking, intended to make monocentric structures more polycentric, but rather to use territorial capital through the creation of a win-win situation so that an urban area can play a role in the next higher league through cooperation.

The concept of polycentric development was introduced at the European level in 1999 through the European Spatial Development Perspective (ESDP) as a response to the wide gaps in competitiveness persisting between the central parts of the European Union and its peripheries (CEC 1999). The aim is to develop alternatives (global economic integration zones) to the "pentagon" at the European level by promoting more polycentric development at both the European and transnational levels. Polycentric development is assumed to be more efficient, sustainable, and equitable than either monocentric or dispersed urban development. The concept has spawned, in turn, the concept of balanced competitiveness or equity. These topics are very much related to the concept of territorial cohesion that was included in the Treaty of Amsterdam in 1997 in connection with services of general economic interest (European Communities 1997). Different interests, however, underlay the inclusion of the concept of territorial cohesion in the Treaty of Amsterdam.

Territorial cohesion combines different political purposes such as mitigating liberalization arising from the EU in order to ensure equal access to services of general economic interest and to resist complete market liberalization—market failures served as arguments for reining in the forces of competition (Faludi 2004). Some analysts would like to give more consideration to the territorial dimension and effects of sector policies at the European, national, and regional levels and to improve the horizontal and vertical coordination between levels and policies (Robert et al. 2001). The debate around the concept of territorial cohesion also aims to frame European regional policy after 2006—the Structural Funds are the EU's second largest budget item.

Territorial cohesion is regarded as an argument for continued support for those regions that are lagging behind or are on the periphery, but, in combination with polycentric development, arguments have also been made about supporting towns and cities as the motors for regional development. The traditional strategy of regional policy in the EU focused on structurally weak and disadvantaged regions, whereas the new emphasis is more on the developmental potentials of a region (Tatzberger 2003). Another very much related factor is the goal of distributing economic activities more evenly over the territory of the EU, whereby services of general economic interest are regarded as a basic precondition to use territorial capital. (In chapter 3, Waterhout sums up these issues in the different discourses underlying territorial cohesion.) Finally, the concept of territorial cohesion has gained prominence since it recently became an objective in its own right and gained an equal footing with economic and social cohesion in the Treaty establishing a Constitution for Europe (European Union 2004). The treaty will come into force if and when the member states ratify it, but that prospect is receding now that voters in France and the Netherlands have refused to ratify the treaty.

Both concepts, territorial cohesion and polycentric development, reflect the idea of a European model of society, which, so far, has not been clearly defined and contested (see chapter 1), but is understood to foster competitiveness while heeding concerns about social welfare, good governance, and sustainability. Rifkin (2004) has analyzed the differences between the European and American dreams, which are also related to the European model of society. Europeans are described as placing more emphasis on collective responsibility and global awareness. Thus, the European model is more oriented to the socialist idea of collective responsibility for the welfare of the community. European society is also much more willing to entertain government intervention to redress inequalities, and the European model is based on the belief that market forces are often unfair and therefore must be tamed. By contrast, the American dream is described as based on an unswerving belief in the preeminence of the individual and personal responsibility and accountability; freedom is associated with autonomy. Americans are said to prefer to keep taxes low and limit government involvement in the community in order to optimize individual accumulation of wealth and ensure greater personal control.

The EU has always defended the traditional European model of society by seeking to balance regulation and liberalization efforts. Its goal is to close the gap with the U.S. economy, but without following the U.S. model (Martens 2002). Solidarity and equal treatment within an open and dynamic market economy are therefore fundamental EU objectives. General interest services are regarded by many people as social rights that make an important contribution to economic and social cohesion and thus are at the heart of the European model of society (Labour Associates 2003). Basic elements of that model are, for example, employment and quality of jobs, access to services of general interest, social justice, equity, and balanced, dynamic, sustainable economic development. One action taken in line with the ideas underlying the European model of society was the introduction of regional policy and the Structural Funds in 1986 in the Single European Act. Ratification of the act was a reaction to the existing regional disparities within the Community. Today, the neoliberal logic is gaining strength at the European level. Of the 25 commissioners of the European Commission (the executive body of the EU), only six are Social Democrats; the rest are neoliberals, who form the center-right. The top jobs in the Commission—such as competition and internal market—are in the hands of committed neoliberals (Mahony 2004).

Polycentric development and territorial cohesion are thus concepts that have great political relevance and are intensively discussed in Europe. But does this discourse influence planning in a transnational area like the Vienna-Bratislava-Győr Triangle? How would these concepts fare in this area? Both concepts have underlying ideas that could be highly relevant to the functional integration of the area. Territorial cohesion includes the notion of reducing socioeconomic disparities, while enhancing differences in spatial characteristics (Vogelij and Nauta 2004). As Zonneveld and Waterhout (2005) emphasize, for both concepts it is necessary to attend to the spatial structure and qualities of areas in order to set priorities. For the Vienna-Bratislava-Győr Triangle, the disappearance of national barriers and the possible emergence of new transnational polycentric functional areas are regarded as a great asset.

The Vienna-Bratislava-Györ Triangle

No common definition exists of the Vienna-Bratislava-Györ Triangle, nor is any administrative institution responsible for it. On the contrary, the three cities are part of three different countries that once were part of the same empire, but then were separated and have just been reunited in the wake of the political changes in 1989 and EU enlargement in 2004. Although these political events caused huge changes within the area, vast differences remain. The three countries have turned inward, orienting themselves toward their national territories. Their capitals are the primate cities dominating the respective urban hierarchies. In other words, with the exception of Slovakia, which has a more balanced urban system, the situation in each of the countries is far from polycentric. As for territorial cohesion, each of the three countries is found wanting. A particular characteristic of the area is that Vienna and Bratislava are one of the closest pair of capitals in the world (60 kilometers apart from center to center), resulting in potentially easy commuting and functional integration.

The area of the Vienna-Bratislava-Györ Triangle is delineated differently, depending on the topic of cooperation or the themes of study. In figure 9.1, the study area is defined by following NUTS 3 regions:[2] Mittelburgenland, Nordburgenland, Niederösterreich-Süd, St. Pölten, Weinviertel, Wiener Umland/Nord, Wiener Umland/Süd, Wien (Vienna), Györ-Moson-Sopron, Bratislava, and Trnava.

This area is characterized by huge historical changes, especially in the last 15 years; three countries with three different administrative structures and languages; different socioeconomic development levels in close proximity to each other, but high dynamics; medium-size agglomerations alongside the economic core areas, two of them capital cities that are facing further suburbanization; and a distinct urban-rural disparity.

Vienna and Bratislava are the national capital cities and thus the administrative, economic, and political centers of their respective countries, Austria and the Slovak Republic. Györ, which lies halfway between Budapest and Vienna, is the regional administrative and economic center of western Hungary. In terms of population, Vienna with 1.5 million inhabitants, Bratislava with 428,000, and Györ with 129,000 are the three largest cities in the Triangle, followed by Trnava (70,000), Sopron (56,000), and St. Pölten (50,000).

Relations between the three countries are influenced by their different characteristics, but also by political events of the past. Slovakia is a very young state that came into existence in 1993 through the peaceful dissolution of the federation with the Czechs. Originally, Slovakia was not a candidate for the 2004 enlargement, because from 1992 to 1998 (with a break of

---

[2] NUTS (Nomenclature of Territorial Units of Statistics) is a geocode standard developed by the EU for classifying territorial units for statistical purposes.

Figure 9.1

The Vienna-Bratislava-Györ Triangle

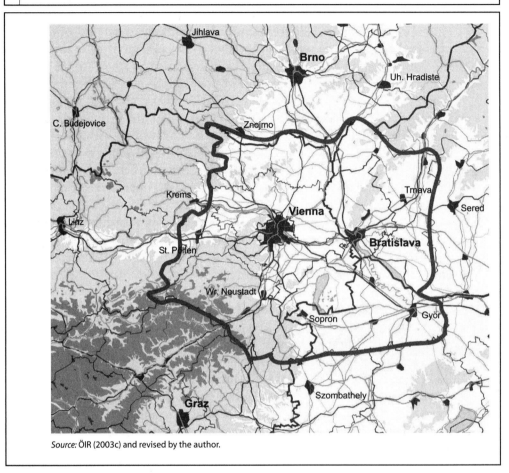

Source: ÖIR (2003c) and revised by the author.

a few months) Vladimír Mečiar's semiauthoritarian party ruled Slovakia, seriously breaching democratic norms and the rule of law. This difficult start during the Mečiar era, as well as Mečiar's negative attitude toward accession to the EU and the North Atlantic Treaty Organization (NATO) led to Slovakia's political isolation. However, after 1999 Slovakia made huge political and economic progress, and today is one of the most promising new member states.

As for the administrative structure of the three countries, Slovakia has a more regionalized administrative structure than Hungary, whose capital, Budapest, which is larger than Vienna, and whose regional center Györ are very much dependent on the national government. Austria has a federal structure in which the *Länder* (provinces) have many powers. Vienna, which is both a province and municipality, thus has far more room to maneuver in terms of its powers and budget than Bratislava and Györ.

Historical Development

When Vienna, Bratislava, and Györ were still part of the Austro-Hungarian Empire, which stretched over some 680,000 square kilometers and was home to 52 million inhabitants (the two parts of the empire were linked only through the common monarch, foreign policy, military, and common finances[3]), the two agglomerations of Vienna and Bratislava[4] interacted particularly intensively because of the absence of significant trade barriers. The transport infrastructure, which was adequate, mostly consisted of railroads and waterways. In 1914 a direct tram connection was launched with great success between the Vienna and Bratislava city centers (Kleindel 1995, 304). But this close relationship changed radically after World War II, when the 40 years of separation began, and the cities coexisted—despite their close historical relations before 1945—without any form of institutionalized cooperation. The iron curtain, which ran precisely along the border between Austria and Slovakia and Hungary, precipitated a fundamental change in the geographic position of the Triangle. Once at the core of Europe, the three cities found themselves at the periphery, each oriented toward its respective country and cut off from its regional hinterlands.

After the fall of the iron curtain in 1989 and the subsequent political and economic changes in the Central and Eastern European countries (CEECs), Vienna, Bratislava, and Györ began to become reacquainted. The transformation process in the CEECs began, however, with a radical economic downturn. This restructuring process was characterized by high levels of uncertainty, a decline in production, unemployment, and much social degradation. Most countries turned toward the West because they were seeking to replace the trade from the Council for Mutual Economic Assistance (CMEA),[5] which collapsed. Today, five CEECs including Hungary and Slovakia have moved beyond the economic performance they had in 1989. Meanwhile, for Vienna, Bratislava, and Györ the dismantling of the iron curtain once again changed their geographic position—they reassumed a core position that has influenced the area's economic and spatial development.

Economic Performance

Vienna's economic situation in relation to that of Austria's other regions is revealed by the fact that about 30 percent of Austria's GDP is produced in Vienna and about 26 percent of its labor force works there. In 2001 Vienna

[3] A common monetary and customs union was established to guarantee economic stability. The crown (German krone) was introduced by the Austro-Hungarian monarchy on 11 August 1892, as the first modern gold-based currency in the area (Kleindel 1995).
[4] Bratislava was part of Hungary at that time.
[5] COMECON/CMEA, which existed from 1949 to 1991, was an economic organization of communist states and a kind of Eastern European equivalent of the European Economic Community.

had an unemployment rate of 4.9 percent, above the Austrian average of 3.4 percent but far below the EU15 rate of 7.6 percent. Vienna and its immediate hinterland to the south enjoy the country's highest economic status. Their respective GDPs per capita are 60 percent and 35 percent above the comparative EU value. Conversely, the regions north and east of Vienna are below average; in those regions agriculture plays a major role in the economy. Another feature of the economic structure of Vienna is its large share of small and medium enterprises, and it is home to the headquarters of many international organizations such as the International Atomic Energy Agency (IAEA) and the Organization for Security and Co-operation in Europe (OSCE).

Likewise, in the Slovak part of the study area economic activities are concentrated in the urban region of Bratislava. At the turn of the millennium, Bratislava already had a GDP per capita that was about on the same level as the EU average (measured by purchasing power parity). But the disparities within Slovakia are huge: Bratislava has a value of 200 percent compared with the average national index (measured in GDP at purchasing power parity/inhabitant whereby the national index = 100).

The economic disparities in Hungary are also significant. Budapest is the wealthiest area, followed directly by the region of Győr with 120 percent of the Hungarian GDP per capita (ÖIR 2003c). Indeed, the western part of Hungary has a strong economy and is one of the most dynamic regions of the country (ÖIR 1998; OECD 2003; see figure 9.2). But the disparities between countries are large, presenting huge threats to territorial cohesion. Austria belongs to the wealthiest countries in the EU with a GDP per capita of 113 (Index EU15 = 100) in 2001 (figure 9.2). The comparable figure for Hungary is 51 and for Slovakia 45. But over the past several years the GDP growth rates of Slovakia and Hungary have been rising (+5.7 and +4.3 percent, respectively) at rates far above the EU average (2.5 percent).

The economic structure of the study area is dominated by the secondary sector, which is more important in Slovakia and Hungary than in Austria. This high level of industrialization in Hungary and Slovakia is a legacy of the past, because before 1989 economic policy was directed at expanding industrial production (ÖIR 2003a). The existing human capital in this sector, combined with low wages and taxes, is a motor for a highly dynamic development. During the last few years, especially Győr and the area around Bratislava have become important centers for the automotive sector, benefiting from huge foreign direct investment (FDI). Audi invested €1.5 billion in Győr, and Volkswagen established a factory near Bratislava that is now the second largest employer in Slovakia. Peugeot-Citroën and Hyundai also decided to invest in the area near Bratislava and are planning to construct factories (*Die Presse* 2003, 2004; *Die Zeit* 2004).

FDI plays an important role in restructuring and improving the competitiveness of industry and manufacturing by helping to raise productivity and to expand exports. It has been one of the driving forces behind

Figure 9.2

The Vienna-Bratislava-Györ Triangle:
Differences in GDP per Capita, 2001 (Index EU15 = 100)

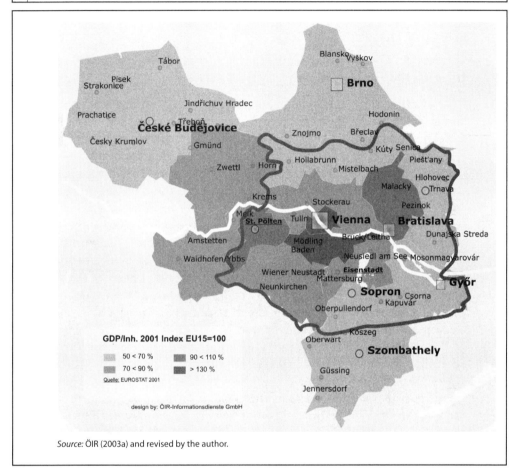

Source: ÖIR (2003a) and revised by the author.

industrial restructuring in Hungary and Slovakia. The majority of Austria's direct investment during the first years of transformation went to Hungary, which received approximately 70 percent of the total during 1989–1992. This factor explains the head start that Austrian enterprises received in the Hungarian market. Apart from geographic proximity, Austria's interest in Hungary can be attributed in particular to its good economic and political contacts there, dating back long before 1989 (Altzinger et al. 2000).

The trend in recent years toward economic integration within the Vienna-Bratislava-Györ Triangle has been supported by more favorable endogenous market conditions on the Slovak and Hungarian sides:

• A diversified economic base undergoing progressive structural change toward the tertiary sector, particularly production-oriented services, but also huge knowledge resources in the industrial sector

- A large share of qualified, motivated human capital supplied by a network of educational facilities but working at low wage levels

- The development of a broader educational and scientific research basis

- A potentially advantageous location, with the urban region serving as an intersection of the transport corridors

- Investment-friendly fiscal regulations (a flat tax in Slovakia and Hungary that is especially low in Slovakia)

The original assumption underlying Austria's goal of locating more labor-intensive functions in the neighboring states and concentrating more highly qualified functions in Austria is no longer valid. Over the last few years, the experiences of the Western European automobile industry in Hungary and Slovakia have revealed that production at the highest technological level can succeed there, and the commensurate research and development capacities will follow immediately. Thus, over the next few years a pattern of integration will develop that will depend much more on existing know-how and functions within international research and production networks than on factors such as wage levels, rents, and the price of land. An integrated regional economic structure will therefore emerge, covering both sides of the border, and the domination of one part will be a thing of the past.

The low level of wages in the postsocialist countries was one of the factors attracting investment from labor-intensive industries. In times of rising unemployment rates, the integration of the CEECs adds to friction in the labor market and the social system, which intensifies when workers from the CEECs look for better-paying jobs in Western countries. This friction and the corresponding fears of the population have led some countries to adopt restrictive migration and labor market access policies. The Organisation for Economic Co-operation and Development (OECD) finds such policies short-sighted, however, because they do not take into account the relationship among employment, trade, and foreign direct investment (Altzinger, Maier, and Fidrmuc 1998).

So far, labor migration in the Vienna-Bratislava-Győr Triangle—regarded as an important force in enhancing economic integration of a region—remains underdeveloped and fragmented mostly because of Austrian restrictions. Under the terms of EU accession of the Slovak Republic and Hungary, these restrictions will gradually be phased out (OECD 2003); however, serious fears persist. The implementation of freedom of movement for services and people could lead to economic and social problems on both sides of the borders by causing displacement of the labor market, especially for low-qualified persons. The tendency for segmentation could also increase with an increase in flexible, short-term work. Other threats are a brain drain from Hungary and the Slovak Republic to the West and from public to private enterprises and a traffic overload in the agglomeration areas because of an increase in commuting traffic. Yet new opportunities will emerge that should be perceived and used, for example, to benefit from the qualifications and the networks of immigrants and to develop cooperation networks.

Transport Infrastructure

The development of the Vienna-Bratislava-Györ area has always been influenced significantly by its spatial position in the wider European context. It features several important geomorphological formations such as the Alps, the Carpathians, the Pannonian Basin, and the Danube River, which have defined the most important European transport networks going both north-south and east-west.

Transport infrastructure is regarded as a central element of efforts to foster integration. The Vienna-Bratislava-Györ area lies at the crossroads of four Trans-European Network for Transport (TEN-T) corridors. The Danube is defined as Corridor VII connecting Eastern and Western Europe. Corridor VI extends from Gdansk-Warsaw-Zilina to Vienna. One branch of Corridor V connects Lvov with Bratislava, and Corridor IV runs from the North Sea and Berlin to Istanbul. The trans-European transport network seeks to ensure mobility of persons and goods and high-quality infrastructure, and to that end in 2003 the European Commission drew up a new list of 30 priority projects to be launched before 2010. Speeding up the completion of the border crossing sections has been designated as being in the Community's interest. In addition to Corridors IV, V, VI, and VII (see figure 9.3), the rail axes Paris-Stuttgart-Vienna-Bratislava and Gdansk-Warsaw-Brno-Bratislava-Vienna and the motorway axis Gdansk-Brno-Bratislava-Vienna are directly relevant to the Vienna-Bratislava-Györ Triangle (CEC 2004a).

The Commission's concerns reveal that—as a legacy of the political divide of Europe—the cross-border transport infrastructure is still disjointed and poorly connected to international networks. Furthermore, crossing a border requires a considerable amount of time and imposes costs on regional trade. So far, commuting problems caused by traffic jams occur only within centers and their surrounding areas but not between centers, because there is little commuting between them. As integration progresses, however, more congestion is likely, with all the attendant problems.

Although the traffic forecasts point to an increase in international and cross-border transport, the policies for all types of transport are unfortunately still weakly coordinated (OECD 2003). It is only during the past few years that the issue of cross-border transport routes has been addressed. The trilateral border area of Austria-Hungary-Slovakia is linked internally by both road and railway, though with some qualitative shortcomings in infrastructure and transport organization. These links are inadequately developed in some parts south of the Danube. The inadequacies in large parts north of the Danube stem mainly from the peripheral location of this

Figure 9.3

TEN-T Corridors IV, V, VI, and VII in the Case Study Area

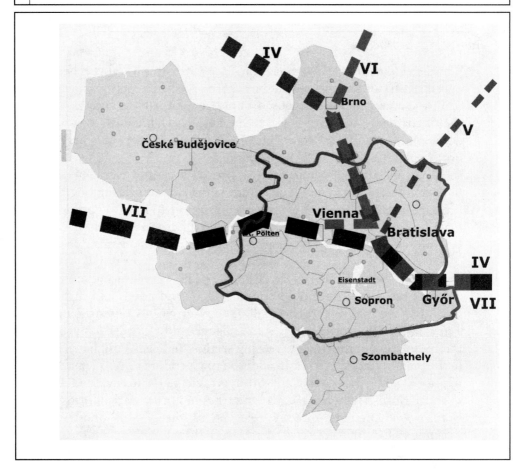

area and the barrier formed by the Morava River, but also from persistent delays on the Austrian side (ÖIR 2003c). As a consequence, no road connects Vienna and Bratislava north of the Danube, and the road connection south of the Danube is a trunk road with a bottleneck in the city of Hainburg. In 2004, and thus years after the motorway on the Slovak side had been completed, the construction of the counterpart on the Austrian side began.

A direct, fast rail link between Vienna and Bratislava was opened in 1999, but it is poorly linked to both city centers. A further improvement of the rail link between Austria and Slovakia is under discussion, focusing at the moment on the electrification of the line north of the Danube (Devínska Nová Ves-Marchegg-Gaenserndorf) and a double-track connection south of the Danube on the line Kittsee-Petrzalka.

The international airports Vienna-Schwechat and Bratislava-Ivanka are

40 kilometers apart. The idea of cooperation between the two airports began with a General Agreement on Air Traffic signed between Austria and Slovakia in 1993, but so far these efforts have had relatively little impact on actual operations of the airports and on air traffic. Improving the Danube waterway for tourist traffic and for goods transport is under discussion as well. Over the next 20 years, it is foreseen that some €280 million will be devoted to improving the Danube route east of Vienna (ÖIR 2003c).

In general, it can be concluded that in the Vienna-Bratislava-Györ Triangle accessibility is high and transport infrastructure is well developed, but insufficiently oriented toward the future challenges of the border area.

A High-Quality Landscape

Bearing these infrastructure improvements in mind, a look at an aerial photograph of the Vienna-Bratislava-Györ area will demonstrate the presence of more spatial tensions. Between the metropolitan areas, there is high-quality landscape such as national parks and numerous nature conservation zones of national and international importance that could come under pressure to make way for additional business locations and provide land for housing and shopping malls and new transport infrastructure. The national parks in the Triangle are recognized as the green axis or "Green Core" of the area, and proposals have been made for their management as a complementary soft factor for the location profile (ÖIR 2003c; Zech, Schaffer, and Schremmer 2004).

Polycentric Development and Territorial Cohesion in Transnational Planning

Because no established policies or institutions for transnational planning are in place in central and southeastern Europe, any new visions or policies have to be related to national or European policies. Nevertheless, transnational or cross-border cooperation presents an added value that is necessary to actively create new development potential.

The EU Community initiative Interreg is currently one of the most important support programs fostering transnational cooperation. For example, the first priority of the Interreg IIIB CADSES (Central Adriatic Danubian South-Eastern European Space) program is to promote spatial development approaches and actions for social and economic cohesion. It also includes a measure aimed at shaping urban development and promoting urban networks and cooperation. Interreg offers good opportunities for establishing networks, exchanging information, developing common strategies, and increasing mutual know-how about the partners.

Interreg projects, especially transnational ones, often require huge administrative efforts at the project level. Furthermore, because program structures are not continuous (the programming period is only six years), management structures and rules for project applicants can change radically. In addition, especially within central and southeastern Europe a balanced partnership was and still is difficult to achieve because of different regulations, programs, and budgets. Thus, despite commitments for cooperation in principle, the current regulations do not seem to solve the constraints (see chapter 6 in this volume), but this situation will change, especially with EU enlargement and the next programming period. In this context, the first discussions are already under way in Austria, because the weak peripheral areas at the border will be confronted with neighboring regions that are benefiting from large Structural Funds allocations.

Transnational cooperation between cities and metropolitan regions confronts not only economic challenges but also political ones. These political challenges consist of coordinating a variety of political and economic actors embedded in mostly nonhierarchical relations. Networking and cooperation between cities is always marked by the coexistence of cooperation and competition. Nevertheless, networks enjoy several advantages over hierarchical structures. For one thing, the integration of different actors improves the quantity and quality of information used as the basis for decision making. For another, the decision-making process supports the recognition, consideration, and—where appropriate—acceptance of different and even conflicting interests, resulting in a greater probability that decisions will be accepted or that decisions are at least better legitimized. Typical impediments to cooperation are the fears of representatives or politicians that they will lose their influence, but also the higher transaction costs arising from the longer time spans needed for decision making in the negotiation processes (Heeg, Klagge, and Ossenbrügge 2003).

Polycentric development has two integral dimensions: the morphological and the relational (Cattan 2003). The relational dimension comprises different forms of cooperation and networking activities (such as bilateral or multilateral, institutionalized, and informal), but also flows of goods, people, money, and information such as foreign direct investment, air transport, exports and imports of goods, and migration. In what follows, the emphasis is on cooperation and networking activities. The general information presented in this section on the morphological dimension and comments on cooperation activities and their relationship with competition, coordination, and governance issues will lead to a description of the experiences in the Vienna-Bratislava-Győr Triangle.

The morphological distribution patterns of urban areas in Austria, Slovakia, and Hungary are still very much influenced by national points of view, and usually these national perspectives and maps are used for decision making at national and regional level (see figure 9.4). It would be much more useful for any map of the urban and settlement structure to also cover areas of the neighboring countries. In fact, a new interpretation is needed of this structure and its developmental tendencies in the European context, referring to the transnational/European level (with a focus on the global

Figure 9.4
Settlement Structures in the Vienna-Bratislava-Györ Triangle

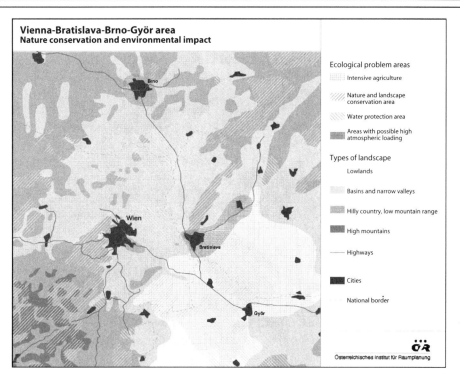

Vienna-Bratislava-Brno-Györ area
Nature conservation and environmental impact

Ecological problem areas

Intensive agriculture

Nature and landscape conservation area

Water protection area

Areas with possible high atmospheric loading

Types of landscape

Lowlands

Basins and narrow valleys

Hilly country, low mountain range

High mountains

Highways

Cities

National border

Österreichisches Institut für Raumplanung

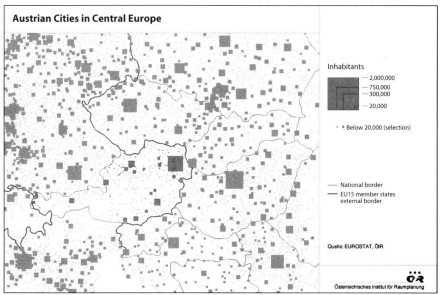

Austrian Cities in Central Europe

Inhabitants

—2,000,000
—750,000
—300,000
—20,000

Below 20,000 (selection)

National border
EU15 member states external border

Quelle: EUROSTAT, ÖIR

Österreichisches Institut für Raumplanung

Source: Schindegger and Tatzberger (2002).

(continued)

Figure 9.4 (continued)

Settlement Structures in the Vienna-Bratislava-Györ Triangle

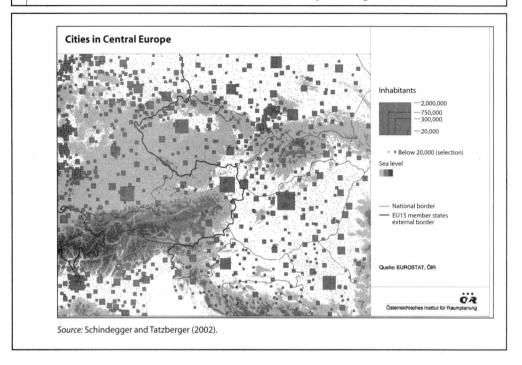

Source: Schindegger and Tatzberger (2002).

economic integration zones) and intraregional level (decentralized urban structures in order to guarantee balanced intraregional development).

The crucial question about transnational cooperation is how the relatively stable structure of the last 50 years would develop under the influence of European integration within the Vienna-Bratislava-Györ area. For example, would there be a repositioning of the city regions of Vienna, Bratislava, and Györ, but also other cities such as St. Pölten, Wiener Neustadt, Trnava, or Sopron, in the European space? Would the area gain synergistic advantages through developing cooperation, the common use of location potentials, and a division of labor between cities and urban areas within daily commuting distance? Would the centers in the Vienna-Bratislava-Györ area see further nearby suburbanization because of inadequate governance structures? The next section discusses a selection of relevant studies and cooperation initiatives to highlight activities going on in a transnational context.

Studies and Cooperation Initiatives in the Case Study Area

One study that deals with the concept of polycentric development and its morphological dimension in the Vienna-Bratislava-Györ Triangle in order to foster a decentralized settlement structure assumes positive developmental effects, especially for the suburbs, which will have to face high pressure from commercial development (ÖIR 2003b). Because of infrastructure improvements, the outskirts of Vienna and Bratislava will gain locational advantages. Planners within the area are also aware that, unless development in the hinterland or the suburbs of larger towns is better managed, there will be negative consequences overall: greater demand for transport, negative impacts on the environment, and deterioration of the landscape and the quality of the environment. Thus, planners must pay attention to promote fast regional public transport and to integrating services.

The goal of a balanced spatial distribution of opportunities can be pursued by means of high-quality transport and economic infrastructure in small and medium-size towns, such as freight terminals in the cities of Sopron or Tulln, technology parks in the town of Eisenstadt, as well as several business and industrial parks in the Sopron-Eisenstadt-Wiener Neustadt region. The areas south of the Danube in Vienna and north of the Danube in Bratislava have a head start in the development of where workplaces are mainly located, and this head start will continue for years to come. Over the long term, however, the counterparts will be strengthened. Along with the new transport infrastructure, large land reserves for building will appear, and thus the focus should be on developing specific locations in combination with public transport in order to reach magnitudes capable of supporting a self-contained dynamics and to avoid urban sprawl.

Several European studies confirm that the Vienna-Bratislava-Györ Triangle could be regarded as the core area of a possible new global economic integration zone (French Presidency 2000; IRS, 2003; Nordregio et al. 2004). Indeed, these studies demonstrate the great morphological and economic potential for the development of European and transnational polycentric structures. But how do the decision makers and key actors of the Vienna-Bratislava-Györ area react to these findings? The twin goal of achieving polycentric development and territorial cohesion as such is not mentioned as a driving force behind cooperation initiatives, but the central actors in the area are aware, nevertheless, of the challenges and opportunities of European integration. In recent years, several interesting transnational cooperation initiatives have come up that are very much in line with the ideas underlying polycentric development and territorial cohesion.

First, the Danube River as such has metaphoric power for Central and Eastern Europe, especially for Vienna, Bratislava, and Györ. The Danube Space thus defined is an important issue in spatial development policy, and many cooperation initiatives are under way, especially related to environmental issues, political reintegration of the Western Balkans, and the use of the Danube as an inland waterway and for tourism (ÖIR 2002). The scenario "ProDanube 2010" defines the Danube belt of transnational cooperation as involving eight European cities: Munich, Prague, Vienna, Bratislava, Budapest, Belgrade, Sofia, and Bucharest. In terms of economic and business development, this Danube Belt represents the strongest cohesive power (CEC 2000).

The Interreg IIIB CADSES project PlaNet CenSE (Planners Network of Central and South East Europe) deals with information and knowledge exchanges on European spatial planning matters from a central and south-eastern European point of view. Two pilot projects are directed at developing metropolitan networks and their potential for becoming a global economic integration zone supported by a "backbone" of improved transnational north-south rail corridors from the Baltic to the Adriatic. The main goal of the pilot study Metropolitan Networks is to further develop and use its network of experts to obtain data and information on existing spontaneous or institutionalized types of cooperation between cities and metropolitan areas as a launch pad for using these networks to promote the idea of polycentric development.[6]

The "CENTROPE—Building a European Region" initiative is seeking to establish a Central European Region that supports dynamic development in important fields such as science, politics, administration, culture, and regional development. The CENTROPE area covers parts of Austria, the Czech Republic, Slovakia, and Hungary. In September 2003, all regional governors in the area and the mayors of Brno, Bratislava, Trnava, Győr, Eisenstadt, St. Pölten, and Vienna signed a political declaration of intent to form a "European region" that would seek opportunities for more prosperity and sustainable growth. CENTROPE activities are directed at joint location marketing, in order to reach a critical mass of 4.4 million inhabitants and therefore to become visible on a global scale, and at the establishment of adequate cross-border organizational structures.[7]

The JORDES+ (Joint Regional Development Strategies for the Vienna-Bratislava-Győr Region) project, which began in April 2002 and was completed in 2005, was cofinanced by Interreg IIIA. JORDES+, an instrument for the territorial administration of the cross-border region, helped planners to prepare and implement projects of common interest. JORDES succeeded in defining strategic development goals, establishing a basis for common planning and understanding, initiating the cooperative development of projects, and providing organizational structures for implementation. The common regional development strategy is a joint program of activities and provides recommendations for political decisions and private investments.

All of the projects described here are trying to bring experts and stakeholders together to exchange information and improve their knowledge about regional development and the potential for cooperation and to develop a new common identity. The cooperation area is delineated variously, from the whole of the CADSES area to just the Vienna-Bratislava-Győr area. All these projects have Austrian lead partners not only because of the different program structures, but also because the other partners are suffering from

[6] For more information on this study, see http://www.planet-cense.net.
[7] For more information on this initiative, see http://www.centrope.com.

budgetary constraints. Here, too, the importance of benefiting from the Structural Funds (in order to plow EU money back into a country) is a highly political issue in Austria and will soon become one in Slovakia and Hungary as well. So far, political support for cross-border and transnational cooperation has not been that high in the new member states, resulting in great differences in participation in individual projects.

Many other initiatives are under way, but all of these efforts are still sporadic attempts that have emerged where the opportunity arises or where money is available. Another challenge for future development is that often transnational or cross-border cooperation is more intensive than cooperation between cities in the same country or cities and their surrounding region, such as Vienna and Niederösterreich (Lower Austria) and Bratislava and its surrounding cities. Interviews with key actors in the Vienna-Bratislava-Györ Triangle revealed that transnational and cross-border cooperation is regarded as crucial and that Vienna is the recognized *primus inter pares* in the region. However, Vienna is keen to dispel any idea of presenting itself as the capital of the former Austro-Hungarian monarchy. Rather, it presents itself as the capital of Austria, a country smaller than either Hungary or the Czech Republic. Nevertheless, partnership within the different cooperation initiatives was not always seen as equal. The reasons given during the interviews were different program structures and the dominance of Vienna.

Future Opportunities

As for future cooperation among Vienna, Bratislava, and Györ, the emphasis will clearly be on Bratislava and Györ's cooperation with Vienna; there are almost no official cooperation initiatives between Györ and Bratislava. This lack of cooperation can be attributed to different reasons, but mainly historical tensions. The fact that Slovakia was once dominated by stronger political entities and Slovaks suffered from ethnic domination, "Magyarization," during the Austro-Hungarian Empire is one example of the historical root of a modern tension. This history bred a psychology of ethnic superiority among Hungarians and still influences relationships between the two countries.

Another reason for lack of cooperation between the two countries is the Gabcikovo Dam dispute. In 1977 Hungary and Czechoslovakia initiated the project with the goal of tapping the resources of the Danube between Bratislava and Budapest to produce hydroelectric power and to reduce air pollution in the area. In addition, the Soviet Union was hoping to improve the navigability of the river. In 1992 Hungary terminated the project, using environmentalism as political cover. In the same year, Slovakia began to divert the river, thereby extracting 90 percent of the water from the old riverbed, which caused the water level to drop by 2 meters. The ensuing conflict took on an international dimension and was submitted to the

International Court of Justice in The Hague, which led to the exploitation of the Danube project as an arena for a struggle over power and minority issues. Hungary protested that the Hungarian minority in Slovakia had been squeezed into a thin strip of land between a canal and the Danube, and it claimed that the Hungarian population structure was undermined, because Slovakian construction workers were settling in the region. Since 2002, the Hungarian government has objected to even the construction of a lower dam. Meanwhile, Slovakia has signaled its willingness to compromise on the condition that Hungary pays compensation. Thus, the fundamentally different interpretations of the problems by two conflicting parties remain and could probably continue to affect prospects for future cooperation (Fürst 2003).

In general, the cooperation between Austria and Hungary began earlier and is more intensive than that with Slovakia. This difference stems from the political isolation during the Mečiar era in Czechoslovakia, Austria's long opposition to the construction of bridges over the Morava River between Austria and Slovakia (before World War II there were 12 crossings, but today there are two), Austria's resistance to the atomic power plants near the Slovakia-Austria border, and the conflict over the hydroelectric power plant in Gabcikovo (Austrian environmentalists were in the forefront of the fight against the plant).

Although considerable efforts are being made to promote cooperation in the Vienna-Bratislava-Györ Triangle, there is, especially on the Austrian side, lingering awareness of the formerly impermeable border. The border along the former iron curtain has changed in meaning and function in that a largely impermeable border separating two different political and economic systems has become semipermeable. Actors on both sides of the border have developed feelings of either superiority or inferiority and a social hierarchy that reproduces the differentiating effects of the national border. Differences in language, fundamentally different legal and administrative systems, as well as the populist statements and activities of individual Austrian and Slovak politicians urging recourse to scare tactics support and strengthen differentiation.

The rejoicing and raised hopes aside, the border opening itself was also a disillusionment. The Austrian view of the border opening was associated with the loss of familiar feelings of security and peace, which were replaced by feelings of insecurity because of phenomena such as illegal border crossings and the loss of the economic impulses. For Slovaks, the border opening brought two kinds of disappointments: exclusion from the Western consumer world and the refusal of Austrians to pursue contacts with Slovaks. In general, Austrian behavior after the border opening can be characterized as defensive-preserving, and the attitude on the Slovak side can be characterized as offensive-dynamic (Fridrich 2003). These findings demonstrate that cooperation between the two countries is still at a very early stage and that further investments in cross-border and transnational initiatives are badly needed to improve the relationship.

All actors are aware that cooperation and competition always exist in parallel, which is also regarded as positive. For example, under the CENTROPE initiative the area can undertake location marketing on a global scale and thus become visible. But as soon as concrete location inquiries materialize, the regions within the area will be competing with each other. Indeed, Vienna will find itself no longer alone in marketing in specific fields such as tourism, conference locations, or regional headquarters of multinational firms and recognizes that cooperation is important in those fields.

But nevertheless, in parallel to good cooperation initiatives, there always will exist political issues that will be pursued even against the interests of the neighboring partners.

Conclusions

Important preconditions for polycentric development within the Vienna-Bratislava-Győr Triangle, including small and medium-size cities and the more rural and peripheral areas, are in place: unique location factors such as the high quality of the landscape; the strong economic dynamics together with the existence of great differences in the level of development; the expected radical conversion of the economic structure when Slovakia and Hungary catch up with their European neighbors; and the incentives and transfers from the EU budget under the Structural and Cohesion Funds to Slovakia and Hungary.

Currently, however, the cooperation structures are insufficient to face the future challenges of governance, networking, and cooperation. Furthermore, because of increasing liberalization and privatization, the opportunities for public initiatives are decreasing. One of the remaining key questions for the area is how a historically unique economic situation of competition in a very small area can be used in a sustainable way to benefit both sides of the borders. The use of synergy effects requires optimal coordination of subareas based on the hypothesis that coordinated development results in a more positive outcome for all. The Vienna-Bratislava-Győr area is a prototype for a situation in which, given strong competition, cooperation in different fields is of advantage to both sides of the borders.

From an economic point of view, the development perspective of the region is characterized by different developmental levels and dynamics and tensions, which result from catching-up processes in the new member states. It is assumed that both new member states will have higher economic growth rates than Austria, which would lead to slowly decreasing differences in income and the price of land, housing, and convenience goods in Slovakia and Hungary, but not necessarily equally distributed within these countries. If and how well the existing potentials will be used also depends on how the area copes with the tension related to developments such as commuting, displacements in the labor market, wage pressure on the Austrian side, and whether the cross-border spatial functional integration of the urban areas can be promoted.

Currently, the ideas underlying the European model of society do not seem to be central political issues in the three countries. Their priority is to increase competitiveness in a sustainable way. According to some interpretations, the combination of competitiveness, sustainability, and social concerns is what the European model is about. In this realm, Slovakia especially, with its flat tax on income, has provoked discussions beyond the Vienna-Bratislava-Györ Triangle. For example, when U.S. president George W. Bush visited Bratislava in February 2005 he praised Slovakia's tax reform with its uniform 19 percent flat tax, which puts pressure on Western Europe. Compared with companies in Austria, France, and Germany, Slovakian companies pay almost half the taxes at the moment. Especially France and Germany voiced disapproval and argued that if new member states could "afford" a flat tax (which is assumed to lead to a decline in tax revenues) they would not need all that much financial help from the EU. After all, these transfers could be construed to finance tax competition (Tzortzis 2005).

The European model can also be linked with the ongoing discussions about the liberalization of the market for services. Some EU member states, especially the U.K., Ireland, and Eastern European countries, support this idea, because they believe it will create thousands of jobs. The opponents, mainly France and Germany, argue that such liberalization would lead to lower wages and poorer working conditions and therefore lead to social dumping. Be that as it may, from the Austrian point of view one important question remains about the Vienna-Bratislava-Györ Triangle: can integration-connected advantages moderate or even outweigh the expected disadvantages during the transition phase, especially the pressure on wages and output; the displacement in the labor market, and the increase in traffic to an extent so far unknown?

How the area will cope with these challenges remains unknown. But it is true that, especially in competitive situations, the public institutions become very much focused on the economy. Actors in the Vienna-Bratislava-Györ Triangle point out that it is essential that they not wear themselves out in internal competition with the result that the area is no longer visible at the European or global level. It is thus up to a point better to permit redundancies that have their positive sides in order to allow quality competition, but also to look for opportunities for cooperation. As the EU continues to enlarge, the number of attractive locations for investment equipped with specific advantages and disadvantages will increase. It will then be crucial that the Vienna-Bratislava-Györ Triangle develop excellent management structures and produce attractive environments as location factors. Transnational planning can assist importantly in this effort by gathering knowledge about different areas and their cultures. Actors dealing with transnational planning are highly aware of existing opportunities and tensions, and they try to find ways to guide development in order to guarantee access to services and to foster balanced and sustainable economic development combined with equity. This goal is exactly what the European model of society stands for by keeping in mind the territorial and political circumstances.

References

Altzinger, W., P. Egger, P. Huber, K. Kratena, M. Pfaffermayr, and M. Wüger. 2000. *Transnationale direktinvestitionen und kooperationen*. Subproject 5, Interreg IIC, Preparity. Vienna, December.

Altzinger, W., G. Maier, and J. Fidrmuc. 1998. Cross-border development in the Vienna/Bratislava region: A review. In *Sustainable development for Central and Eastern Europe: Spatial development in the European context*, U. Graute, ed. Berlin: Springer.

Cattan, N. coord. 2003. Critical dictionary of polycentrism. In *The role, specific situation and potentials for urban areas as nodes of polycentric development*, 26–43. ESPON 1.1.1. Second interim report. Stockholm: Nordregio.

CEC—Commission of the European Communities. 1999. *European Spatial Development Perspective: Towards balanced and sustainable development of the territory of the EU*. Luxembourg: Office for Official Publications of the European Communities.

———. 2000. *Danube space study: Regional and territorial aspects of development in the Danube countries with respect to impacts on the European Union*. July.

———. 2004a. Decision No. 884/2004/EC of the European Parliament and of the Council of 29th April amending Decision No. 1692/96/EC on Community guidelines for the development of the trans-European transport network. *Official Journal of the European Union* L167.

———. 2004b. *A new partnership for cohesion: Convergence, competitiveness, cooperation. Third report on economic and social cohesion*. Luxembourg: Office for Official Publications of the European Communities.

Die Presse (Austria). 2003. Györ: Zentrum der Wirtschaft in Ungarn. 3 December.

———. 2004. Europas Mitte: Interessanter Standort. 20 January.

Die Zeit (Germany). 2004. Turbodiesel statt Tokaier. 7 April.

European Communities. 1997. Treaty of Amsterdam amending the Treaty on European Union, the treaties establishing the European Communities and related acts. http://europarl.europa.eu/topics/treaty/pdf/amst-en.pdf.

European Union. 2004. Treaty establishing a constitution for Europe. *Official Journal of the European Union* C310/1, vol. 47, 16 December. http://europa.eu.int/eur-lex/lex/JOHtml.do?uri=OJ:C:2004:310:SOM:EN:HTML.

Faludi, A. 2004. Territorial cohesion: Old (French) wine in new bottles? *Urban Studies* 41(7):1349–1365.

———. 2005. Polycentric territorial cohesion policy. In Territorial cohesion, A. Faludi, ed., special issue, *Town Planning Review* 76(1):107–118.

French Presidency. 2000. *Contribution to the debate on the long-term ESDP polycentric vision of the European space*. Final report, vol. 2. Paris: DATAR.

Fridrich, C. 2003. Kooperation versus Abgrenzung auf lokaler Ebene: Fallstudie österreichisch-slowakisches Grenzgebiet. In *Mitteilungen der österreichischen geographischen Gesellschaft*, 145: 95–118.

Fürst, H. 2003. *The Hungarian-Slovakian conflict over the Gaãikovo-Nagymaros dams: An analysis*. Vol. 6, no. 2. New York: East Central European Centre, Columbia University.

Hague, C., and K. Kirk. 2003. *Polycentricity scoping study*. Report commissioned and published by the Office of the Deputy Prime Minister (ODPM). Edinburgh: School of the Built Environment, Heriot-Watt University.

Heeg, S., B. Klagge, and J. Ossenbrügge. 2003. Metropolitan cooperation in Europe: Theoretical issues and perspectives for urban networking. *European Planning Studies* 11(2):139–153.

IRS—Institute for Regional Development and Structural Planning, European Policies Research Centre, and Centre for Regional and Tourism Research. 2003. *Pre-accession aid impact analysis.* ESPON 2.2.2. Second interim report. http://www.irs-net.de/anzeigen .php?choice1=projects&choice2-espon.

Kleindel, W. 1995. *Österreich: Daten zur Geschichte und Kultur.* Vienna: Ueberreuter.

Labour Associates. 2003. *Analysis of the impact of Community policies on regional cohesion.* Study commissioned by the European Commission, Directorate General of Regional Policy. October.

Mahony, H. 2004. Socialists wary of neo-liberal Commission. *Euobserver,* 10 December.

Martens, H. 2002. The liberalism and regulation: A European model? *EurActive,* 3 June. http://www.euractiv.com.

Mercier, G. 2005. Which territorial cohesion policy for the new EU members? The example of Slovakia. *Town Planning Review* 76(1):57–68.

Neubauer, J. 2004. Spatial diagnosis of enlargement. In Part 2, ESPON 1.1.3. *Particular effects of enlargement of the EU and beyond on the polycentric spatial issue with special attention on discontinuities and barriers.* Third interim report. Stockholm: ESPON.

Nordregio et al. 2004. *Potentials for polycentric development in Europe.* ESPON 1.1.1. Final report. Stockholm: Nordregio.

OECD—Organisation for Economic Co-operation and Development. 2003. *Territorial reviews, Vienna-Bratislava, Austria/Slovak Republic.* http://www.oecd.org/document /18/0,2340,en_2649_37429_6282834_1_1_1_37429,00.html.

ÖIR—Austrian Institute for Regional Studies and Spatial Planning. 1998. *Planning the gateway: Wege zur Planungskooperation im Städtenetz Wien-Bratislava-Brünn-Györ.*

———. 2002. *Danubian cooperation, issues and perspectives.* Study commissioned by the Austrian Ministry for Foreign Affairs, City of Vienna and Bank Austria. Vienna, May.

———. 2003a. *Centrope region: Regional analysis.* Final report. Study supported by European Commission and the Centrope Partners. Vienna, September.

———. 2003b. *Regionales Organisationsmodell Siedlungs- und Verkehrsentwicklung und Wirkungsbeziehungen. In the framework of the Interreg IIIA project JORDES+ Joint Regional Development Strategy for the Vienna-Bratislava-Györ region.* Vienna, December. http:// www.pgo.wien.at/jordes_hp.

———. 2003c. *Vienna-Bratislava region.* Austrian background report for OECD territorial review and "assessment and recommendations" of the OECD. Summary of main results. Study commissioned by the City of Vienna, Werkstattberichte NR. 59A of City of Vienna.

Rifkin, J. 2004. *The European dream: How Europe's vision of the future is quietly eclipsing the American dream.* New York: Penguin.

Robert, J., T. Stumm, J. M. de Vet, C. J. Reincke, M. Hollanders, and M. A. Figueiredo. 2001. *Spatial impacts of Community policies and cost of non-co-ordination.* Study carried out at the request of the Directorate General Regional Policy, Commission of the European Communities.

Schindegger, F., and G. Tatzberger. 2002. *Polyzentrismus ein europäisches Leitbild für die räumliche Entwicklung.* Vienna: ÖIR Forschungsberichte.

Tatzberger, G. 2003. The concept of territorial cohesion in Europe: Its genesis and interpretations and link to polycentric development. Paper presented at the 2003 Third Joint Congress of the AESOP/ACSP, Leuven, Belgium, 9–12 July.

———. 2004. Polycentric development: Really an appealing concept with political relevance? Paper presented at the AESOP Conference, Grenoble, France, 30 June–3 July.

Tzortzis, A. 2005. Flat tax revolution puts Europe on edge. *Deutsche Welle,* 28 February. http://www.dw-world.de.

Vogelij, J., and C. Nauta. 2004. *Territory and innovation: The Lisbon strategy.* Royal Haskoning Nederland BV Spatial Development, commissioned by VROM–DG Ruimt. February.

Zech, S., H. Schaffer, and C. Schremmer. 2004. *Biosphärenregion und Leitbild Grüne Mitte: In the framework of the Interreg IIIA project JORDES+ Joint Regional Development Strategy for the Vienna-Bratislava-Györ region.* Final report. Vienna, March.

Zonneveld, W., and B. Waterhout. 2005. Visions on territorial cohesion. *Town Planning Review* 76(1):15–27.

Chapter 10

Unraveling Europe's Spatial Structure Through Spatial Visioning

WIL ZONNEVELD

The making of the European Spatial Development Perspective (ESDP) has revealed deep conflicts over the organization of European Union (EU) space. It can be interpreted as an ongoing dialectic between two principles that, according to former European Commission president Jacques Delors, the European model of society should combine: competitiveness and cohesion. These principles relate to whether Europe's territorial organization was and will be shaped by competition between countries and (urban) regions or whether there are—and also should be—forces of cohesion at work. The ESDP puts forward the image of the "pentagon" (London-Paris-Milan-Munich-Hamburg) to describe Europe's current spatial structure. It also enters a plea for an alternative spatial image, a kind of archipelago made up of numerous little pentagons. The synthetic image or spatial concept is that of polycentricity.

As a result of the political deliberations during its making, the ESDP also discusses many issues other than the European urban system and its effects on economic and social development. At the recent Informal Ministerial Meeting on Territorial Cohesion held in Rotterdam in November 2004, the ministers decided to focus future European territorial cooperation on, among other things, the structuring elements of the EU territory. This approach was endorsed at their meeting in Luxembourg in May 2005.

The novel concept of structuring elements could be interpreted as an effort to pursue a more selective approach to territorial cooperation. Interestingly, since the Rotterdam meeting the issue of European territorial governance has been explicitly linked with the principle of territorial cohesion and the Lisbon/Gothenburg Strategy aiming for economic growth and the creation of jobs. The idea is to link the discussion on European territorial governance to the wider debate on the goals of the European Union. This linkage can be viewed as an effort to demonstrate that territorial governance is highly relevant to these goals and that the European Union cannot do without it.

In a nutshell, then, the reasoning behind this territorial approach is that improved territorial governance in the European Union should contribute to achieving territorial cohesion and to the realization of the ambitions, newly confirmed in revised form in 2005, of the Lisbon/Gothenburg process. Toward this end, territorial governance should focus on structuring elements. In the documents put before the Luxembourg ministerial meeting, there was a clear tendency to equate structuring elements with territorial structure. So it makes sense to ask how to interpret space and territory in terms of territorial structure. However, there is another reason to ask this question as well. The idea of services of general economic interest is the notion underlying territorial cohesion—Article 16 of the present Treaty on European Union is evidence. But the provision of such services is no longer self-evident. In determining where the provision of services of general economic interest is under threat and where action is needed, it is important to discuss territorial structure.

Analysis of the territorial structure of the European Union began during the first half of the 1990s with the issuance of analytical documents such as *Europe 2000* and *Europe 2000+* (CEC 1991, 1994)—for the underlying reasoning, see chapter 8 by Drevet in this volume. Efforts to unravel Europe's territorial structure entered a political phase with the onset of the drafting of the European Spatial Development Perspective during the 1990s, a process that came to an end with the adoption of the ESDP by the European Commission and the member states of the EU15 in 1999.[1]

The goal of this chapter is to analyze the making of the ESDP and the member state initiative in its wake as exercises in visioning—that is, interpreting Europe's spatial structure from the perspective of territorial cohesion and the underlying notion of services of general economic interest as they relate to the European model of society. This chapter therefore focuses on two issues: the drafting of the ESDP and its follow-up. The discussion of these two issues is, however, prefaced with an exploration of the theoretical notions invoked in this chapter: spatial concepts, spatial structure, and spatial visions. These notions are a kind of toolbox for discussing issues of territorial cohesion. The concluding section returns to the main question: what is the relationship between spatial visioning and the principle of territorial cohesion and the underlying notion of services of general economic interest as they relate to the European model of society?

---

[1] EU15 refers to the 15 member states that made up the EU prior to the 2004 enlargement to 25 member states (EU25).

Theoretical Concepts and Issues

The European Spatial Development Perspective of 1999 and the transnational spatial visions developed since can be interpreted as efforts to interpret territorial structure and territorial developments beyond the national scale (CEC 1999). Thus, the question is one of how space and territory are being perceived. The point is that people construct problems "through frames in which facts, values, theories and interests are integrated." Framing, then, is "a way of selecting, organizing, interpreting and making sense of a complex reality so as to provide guideposts for knowing, analyzing, persuading and acting. A frame is a perspective from which an amorphous, ill-defined problematic situation can be made sense of and acted upon" (Rein and Schön 1986, 4).

Planning Concepts

In the context of spatial planning, planning concepts play a key role in framing. Such concepts bring forward "ideas about spatial organization" (Healey 2006, 78). They also express in a condensed and synthesized form, through words and images, how people look at the intended spatial organization of an area (Zonneveld 1991). In terms of framing, spatial planning concepts have—in different proportions—five different dimensions: cognitive, intentional, institutional, communicative, and action.

The *cognitive dimension* stems from the fact that spatial planning concepts are based on interpretations of the actual spatial organization of an area. Such interpretations can be based on different sorts of knowledge, from tacit to scientific.

The *intentional dimension* arises from the fact that spatial planning concepts are based on *norms* about spatial organization and spatial development—that is, an assessment of what is to be desired or to be avoided. The principle of territorial cohesion provides such a normative perspective.

The *institutional dimension* relates to the competences and roles of stakeholders. On the European scale, this is a rather complex issue. Unlike the situation in most countries, the EU has no formal spatial planning competence, and thus who assumes which role is not obvious. This means, for example, that it is very difficult to determine the "authorship" of policy documents. Delicate decisions must then be made about who is actually responsible and in what way and who is validating a document and what such a validation means in practice.

The *communicative dimension* is extremely important. The role of persuasion and language, long recognized in planning theory, has led to what is often referred to as the communicative turn in planning (see, for example, Healey 1996). Even after nearly 15 years of European discussions on what territorial governance is about, there is as yet no established tradition. An indication is the constantly changing language. When the ESDP was being formulated, it was common practice to speak about spatial planning and spatial development, but these designations have become obsolete. At present, it is customary to define the policy domain in terms of territorial governance. Furthermore, spatial planning concepts are expressed in two language domains: the verbal language, or the language of text, and the visual language of spatial images and maps.

In the action dimension, planning concepts are positioned between goal setting and concrete policy instruments. They indicate what kind of subsequent decisions is needed. But not all concepts have a clear-cut action dimension. Some concepts are more about perceptions of territorial organization. Others define exactly the places and areas where certain policy instruments are to be deployed. In a policy domain that is still evolving, it is likely that instrumental spatial planning concepts will find only limited use. The need, then, is for a limited number of strategic spatial concepts that emphasize the first three dimensions discussed here. The fact that this is the case in European territorial governance accounts for the recent emphasis on identifying structuring elements of the European territory. This step could be one toward the application of concrete policy instruments in concrete areas, possibly through the adaptation of existing policies defining kinds of necessary action. As described later in this chapter, the notion of structuring elements has been introduced into the search for selectivity, starting with the desire to focus policy instruments on areas and territorial structures that really matter.

For all these reasons, planning concepts are the bread and butter of spatial planning. They not only serve as guideposts in concrete decision making, but also frame the attitudes toward spatial development and the structure of territories. Their presence and content are not undisputed, however. Almost by definition, planning concepts are biased. They do not just simplify reality; they "capture and frame certain ideas, relations, realities and potentials, whilst excluding others" (Jensen and Richardson 2003, 11). Mechanisms of power are at work here. Although not a central issue in this chapter, this aspect of planning concepts must be kept in mind. Planning concepts do not just name and frame; they also claim reality. They do not just represent space and spatial relations; they posit priorities and interests (Duinen 2004, 23).

The Content of Planning Concepts: Territorial Structure

Territorial cohesion is still in a framing stage. In the current follow-up to the ESDP process, dubbed the Agenda 2007 Process, territorial cohesion is being linked to the concept of *territorial capital*, a term coined by the Organisation for Economic Co-operation and Development (OECD). This linkage implies a wider interpretation of the concept, which originally was about services of general (economic) interest. In order to form images of territorial cohesion, in particular about services of general interest, it makes sense to identify certain categories of spatial planning concepts according to their content.

Planning concepts on a lower scale are often about spatial arrangements and spatial layout—that is, the exact location and nature of activities (such as size, location, design, type of function, and intensity of use). On a higher scale, territorial structure comes to the fore, a term that, although basic, is rather aggregate and complex. It can be made more comprehensible by differentiating between three elements: a zonal structure, made up of spaces and areas; a nodal structure formed by functions and activities concentrated at certain locations (nodes); and a communicative structure mostly formed by linear elements that together form networks. Presented in graphic form, these three structures translate into a visual language using the three archetypal symbols of planes, dots, and lines.

All three structural elements are relevant in discussing territorial cohesion and the specific issue of services of general interest. Zonal elements are invoked when certain indicators related to territorial cohesion are associated with areas. Here the basic policy issue to be answered by invoking these indicators is whether some areas are lagging behind and, if so, which ones they are. The EU Structural Funds operate largely in this way, using the NUTS system[2] as the basis to define areas (see Williams 1996, 118–119). Although the zones do form a pattern, the outcome of applying this zonal approach hardly deserves to be called a structure, because the areas and regions thus described have no territorial relations. The Netherlands advocated such an approach in the Rotterdam document (Dutch Presidency 2004), which leads to the suggestion that the EU focus the discussion of territorial governance on structuring elements—that is, the structures that really matter in terms of the development of the European territory.

Nodal elements become relevant when discussing whether urban settlements in general or the (nodal) systems used for the distribution of services in particular are showing certain *gaps*. Here the policy issue is whether certain categories in these systems are missing or will be missed because of the combined effect of ever higher demographic thresholds and of rationalization measures by the suppliers of services of general interest. Actually, the same issues play a role in communicative systems—that is, the networks of traffic and transport. These systems, too, can display gaps in terms of space (no connections available at all or just connections of poor quality) or time (connections only available at certain times). This highly sensitive matter is reflected in the decision-making process surrounding the Trans-European Networks (TENs).

[2] NUTS refers to the Nomenclature of Territorial Units of Statistics (the acronym is based on the French version of this title).

Territorial Structure and Spatial Positioning

Territorial structure as such does not exist; it has to be discerned through the conceptualization of space and territory. Politically, this is a highly sensitive matter; intellectually, it is challenging as well. Dealing with territorial structure could be described as *spatial positioning*. Williams (1996) has made some important observations, distinguishing between positioning in a national context and at the European level: "Most local planners have a clear sense of the location within national space of the place for which they are responsible, often without thinking very consciously about it. The capacity to conceptualise or think about one's location or situation within the spatial structure of Europe as a whole is a skill which often needs to be developed. Spatial positioning is the term proposed for this skill. . . . In many ways, it requires imagination and lateral thinking rather than any particular skill" (Williams 1996, 97).

Because spatial positioning is all about the conceptualization of space, there is a direct link with the theoretical notions of planning concepts and spatial structure. Images of spatial positioning are normatively charged perceptions of space and spatial relationships. Thus, spatial positioning involves the art of "structural thinking." The challenge is to identify territorial elements that structure the area in question (Vermeersch 1994, 137). These elements are not confined to the "plan area"; many territorial relations extend beyond them. Structural thinking is, above all, selective, aiming to identify essential forms of territorial integration, including the social agents behind particular functions that have an impact on the spatial structure of an area (de Vries 2002, 189).

An Unfinished Story of Unraveling Europe's Spatial Structure

One class of planning documents called spatial visions is an important vehicle for conceptualizing space and for spatial positioning. One such document is the European Spatial Development Perspective.

The Importance of Balance

Like many political documents, the ESDP has three layers: one layer formed by the three principal policy objectives, one formed by the three policy guidelines, and one presenting 60 policy aims and options.

Combining three very different principal policy objectives, the first layer in itself represents a territorial version of the European model of society. Briefly, the ambition is to achieve "balanced and sustainable spatial development" (CEC 1999, 10). This ambition is elaborated in what is often referred to as the ESDP's policy triangle of society, economy, and environment. European policy should contribute to (1) economic and social cohesion; (2) conservation of natural resources and cultural heritage; and (3) more balanced competitiveness of the European territory. Thus, the remit of spatial development policies is quite varied.

Leaving the field of abstract policy objectives behind and moving closer to the realm of planning concepts, the ESDP arrives at the notion of *balanced spatial structure*, once again one of those very general statements that is doing well in the political domain. This second layer, policy guidelines, again consists of a trinity of political statements, some more tangible in a territorial sense and thus potentially at least presentable in graphic form. This is where the only genuine spatial planning concept of the entire ESDP crops up. One of the three policy guidelines derived from the triangle of underlying objectives is the idea of developing a balanced (again!) and therefore polycentric urban system, mentioned in the same breath as the development of new urban-rural relationships. In full, the three policy guidelines are (1) developing a balanced and polycentric urban system and a new urban-rural relationship; (2) securing parity of access to infrastructure and knowledge; and (3) pursuing sustainable development, prudent management, and protection of nature and cultural heritage.

Much has already been written about polycentricity (see, for example, Davoudi 2003 and Faludi 2005). Like the majority of spatial planning concepts, it links spatial analysis with goal setting and the formulation of normative viewpoints, which, together with finding the right sort of communicative devices in the domains of verbal language and spatial imagery, is the essence of conceptualization in spatial planning. However, although spatial imagery is an inextricable part of conceptualization, in making the ESDP there was, with one exception, no attempt to use spatial imagery. This is all the more striking because the way in which the concept of polycentricity is presented calls for a spatial image. But all that is presented is a verbally articulated image, together with an abstract icon that cannot be related to specific areas and urban regions.

The makers of the ESDP more or less began with the image of a blue banana, the almost infamous symbolic picture of the economic core area of Europe. In the verbal imagery of the ESDP, this banana-shaped European core area is amended by including the Paris region. Thus, the core area according to the ESDP is pentagon-shaped, defined by the metropolises of London, Paris, Milan, Munich, and Hamburg (CEC 1999, para. 68). As soon as it was put on paper, the blue banana was attacked. An opposing view of the spatial structure of Europe was portrayed in metaphorical language as striking and provocative as the blue banana—a bunch of grapes (Kunzmann and Wegener 1991). This metaphor conveys a polycentric image of Europe's urban and economic structure.

In the ESDP, both conceptions are combined. Justifying this, the makers of the ESDP revert to the language of the pre-ESDP period in which antagonism between a small core and a large periphery dominates: "Previous policy measures affecting spatial development were primarily concerned with improving the links between the *periphery* and the core area through projects in the field of infrastructure. However, a policy is now required to offer a new perspective for the peripheral areas through a more polycentric arrangement of the EU territory" (CEC 1999, para. 70, emphasis added).

Although it is open to question whether the image of a pentagon-shaped core area is a caricature of reality developed for political reasons, it is important to underline that the ESDP sketches a cohesive picture of Europe. The concept of polycentricity combines cohesion and competitiveness. As such, one is dealing here with a territorial model of society. It is noticeable that there is no reference to services of general interest. The only exception is where the ESDP talks about *urban-rural relationships*. There, the text stipulates that the "urban and rural diversity of the EU" should be maintained (CEC 1999, para. 71). Rural "problem" regions are noted, however (CEC 1999, para. 93); they are often regions less densely populated with a peripheral location (CEC 1999, paras. 76, 79). In such regions, the towns are capable of "offering infrastructure and services for economic activities" (CEC 1999, para. 93). Often, though, because of their small size, individual cities and towns can no longer fulfill this role satisfactorily. Thus, the ESDP recommends networking and cooperation so that urban centers can complement each other. Within the ESDP, then, the issue of services of general interest is rather limited to the sphere of urban-rural relationships. But if the notion of services of general interest is expanded to include the provision of infrastructure or, in a more abstract sense, accessibility and connectivity, services are then regarded as of critical importance.

"Securing parity of access to infrastructure and knowledge" is the second of the three policy guidelines for spatial development of the EU (CEC 1999, para. 19). Prime attention is given to the cohesive aspects of infrastructure and knowledge networks: "Efficient transport and adequate access to telecommunications are a basic prerequisite for strengthening the competitive situation of peripheral and less favored regions and hence for the social and economic cohesion of the EU. Transport and telecommunication opportunities are important factors in promoting polycentric development" (CEC 1999, para. 26). And as it is for the concept of polycentricity, abstract icons apart, no spatial images are presented on what constitutes a network that gives parity of access.

Within the sphere of action of the European Union as such, the guideline to strive for parity of access to infrastructure and knowledge is linked to the Trans-European Networks, a program of investment explicitly intended to fill missing links in the communication networks of the EU. On the basis of a Transport Infrastructure Needs Assessment (TINA), the TEN program has been extended eastward, with the goal of integrating the infrastructure systems of the new member states in the overall European networks. A main criticism, though, is that the extension of the TEN is dictated by the existing east-west corridors within the EU15, which are merely extended eastward, without regard for missing links in a north-south direction at the national level regarded by the new member states as almost of the same importance. According to Fleischer (2004) this means to overestimate the supranational level of territorial cohesion: "Without good local networks the expected advantages can not penetrate into the local economy—to achieve cohesion" (Fleischer 2004, 9). Here Fleischer is pointing at the problem of scale in dealing with issues of territorial cohesion.

Similar discussions have taken place and are taking place in relation to the concept of polycentricity. For example, the 1990s was a period of rapid growth in the Irish economy, especially in the Dublin area. From a European perspective, this is exactly what the makers of the ESDP meant by polycentricity: Dublin and Ireland became integrated into the European and global economy (for very similar effects in Slovakia, see chapter 9 by Tatzberger in this volume). In Ireland, however, regional and social disparities within the country have increased (see Davoudi and Wishardt 2005). Such discrepancies probably were not foreseen when making the ESDP, but they are surely gaining political weight. It relates to an obvious but often overlooked aspect of spatial concepts: the same concept can be stretched over different scales, but with each step the concept changes, often resulting in contradictions within the concept.

The third and final policy guideline of the ESDP entails sustainable development and prudent management and protection of nature and cultural heritage. Because the other two guidelines mainly address spatial structures of the nodal or network type, this "conservation" guideline mainly addresses zonal structures. Bengs (2000) points out that this protection guideline is not just included for the intrinsic values of Europe's natural and cultural heritage: "The natural and cultural heritage are economic factors which are becoming increasingly important for regional development" (CEC 1999, para. 134). This guideline is an indication of the fact that the pages of the ESDP are awash in the issue of economic development, in particular its distribution across European space. Yet on this issue, the ESDP does not stand on its own. As will become evident, natural and cultural heritage has been brought under the umbrella of *territorial capital*. This in itself indicates a very broad notion of what constitutes a European territorial model of society.

The ESDP as a Vision

The drafters of the ESDP call the document a perspective, a "vision." Nevertheless, the reader would be hard put to find in it spatial planning concepts, the important exceptions being the European polycentric urban system and networks of infrastructure and knowledge. Although concepts do present images of a desired territorial structure, many questions remain, in part because, with the exception of the abstract graphics in the form of icons, the ESDP presents no spatial images as such. It discusses all types of territorial structures—zonal, nodal, and network—but in an abstract, almost generic way, unrelated to specific parts of the EU territory.

So does the ESDP present a vision? The answer depends on what constitutes a vision. It is clear that the ESDP as a spatial vision remains in the realm of what Shipley and Newkirk (1999) call goal setting and the identification of values and decision criteria—one of 10 different variants of a "vision" they have identified. The ESDP does not belong in the class of "future imaging," although Shipley and Newkirk unjustly equate future imaging with a master plan. This is a fundamental misconception of spatial visioning. Between visioning as "goal setting and the identification of values and decision criteria"—which constitutes visioning as a verbal exercise—and "conceiving a masterplan" there are several other possibilities, although they are very difficult to achieve. This is precisely why, though widespread, equating visual imaging with making a master plan is a misconception.

This misconception became evident in efforts to make transnational visions in the aftermath of the ESDP (see Zonneveld 2005a, 2005b). In the end, all policy maps were erased from the ESDP. Dühr (2005), in her research on the use of cartographic representation in European spatial planning, gives two explanations for this omission. The first is that whereas planning concepts in policy documents can be subject to a multitude of interpretations—the concept of polycentricity is one example—cartographic representations of spatial policy require a higher degree of consensus (see also Faludi 2002). Seen from this angle, it is understandable that the drafters of the ESDP chose to illustrate their policy messages with graphic icons rather than maps (for an example of a map that proved to be politically unacceptable, see figure 10.1). And yet in terms of the communicative dimension of spatial planning concepts, this decision results in very limited use of the possibilities and potentials of visual language.

The second reason Dühr gives for the omission of policy maps from the ESDP has much to do with what was described earlier as the institutional dimension of planning concepts. Although the ESDP clearly states that it is a legally nonbinding document (CEC 1999, para. 22), many participants in the process have associated "spatial planning" with land use regulation, which is a competence of national and subnational authorities. In land use planning, maps are being invoked in concrete decisions on issues for which only the authorities within member states are competent.

Dühr also makes clear, though, that cartographic representations in a policy document are often associated with analytical maps, such as those found in atlases or research reports. Only a few planning systems have had some experience with fuzzy, conceptual maps. Between the almost abstract icons of the ESDP and the clear, analytical, atlas-type maps lies an area of imaging hardly touched on in European planning. Following Kunzmann (1993), Dühr calls this type of mapping *geodesign*. It was a topic in the Study Programme on European Spatial Planning carried out during the finalization of the ESDP and cofunded by the Commission and the member states

Figure 10.1

Example of the Type of Policy Map That Proved Unacceptable in the ESDP Process

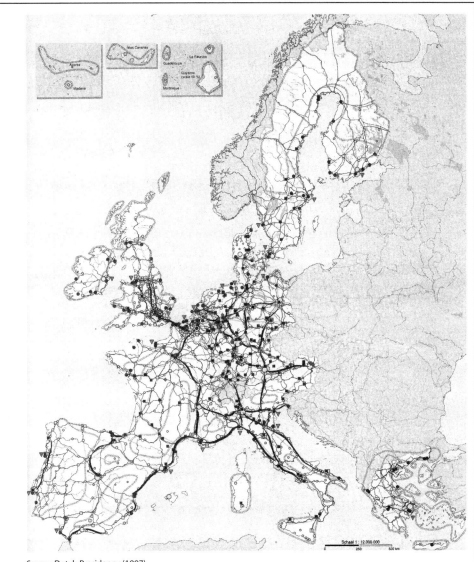

Source: Dutch Presidency (1997).
Note: A draft version of the ESDP contained this image of accessibility and transport systems in the EU15. Because the map emphasized too much the poor linkages in certain parts of Europe, it was not used in the final ESDP. Mapping the EU's territorial capital in terms of accessibility is currently left to the European Spatial Planning Observation Network (ESPON).

(see Jensen and Richardson 2004, 119–120). Surprisingly, though, the subject has not been picked up in the European Spatial Planning Observation Network (ESPON) 2006 program, which is something of a missed opportunity.

A broad evaluation of the use of planning concepts in the ESDP thus reveals a very limited use of such concepts. A consensus could only be reached on an elaborate set of policy goals, aims, and options that brought together the fundamentals of the different spatial planning policy systems in the EU member states. Spatial concepts related to the structure of the European territory and the spatial position of concrete areas proved to be politically contentious, and the relevant controversies could not be settled. Seen in this light, it is not surprising that there are no policy maps in the ESDP. Broad, generic policy goals cannot be mapped; they can only be illustrated through symbols, and that is exactly what happened.

The Rotterdam Process

After publication of the ESDP in 1999, the process came more or less to a standstill; only meetings between EU ministers and the Commission kept the ESDP machinery going. The last meeting was held in Tampere, Finland, in October 1999, six months after adoption of the ESDP in Potsdam. In Tampere, an action program was adopted, but, apart from a few low-key events, nothing further was done. It thus came as a surprise that the routine of informal ministerial meetings was resumed with a meeting in Rotterdam in November 2004. There, an agreement was reached on a working agenda for the next two to two and a half years: the Rotterdam Process.

Out of the Doldrums

According to the Dutch who took the initiative, the moment was ripe (see Faludi and Waterhout 2005 for an account of this meeting and also chapter 2 in this volume). For one thing, the principle of territorial cohesion was gaining in political importance thanks to its insertion in the constitutional treaty (although its ratification is now running into severe difficulties). It therefore seemed to be an opportune time to discuss the kind of territorial governance needed to achieve territorial cohesion. The second development in the wider political context was the efforts to breathe new life into the Lisbon/Gothenburg Strategy. In this strategy, the major issue is the competitiveness of the European economy, the proviso being that economic development should also be ecologically sound. So on the table were the issues of territorial cohesion and competitiveness, but this time not *within* a policy trajectory focusing on territorial development but deriving from the wider EU context.

An Exercise in Focusing?

When the ESDP was drafted, the prime question was the meaning of the spatial approach at European level. Answering this question implied holding fundamental discussions. Now, after two meetings (the Rotterdam meeting was followed by a meeting at Luxembourg in May 2005; see chapter 7 in this volume), the key issue is "the identification of a territorial approach for a better integration of the territorial dimension into EU (and national) policies" (Luxembourg Presidency 2005, 2). The phrase "EU policies" is not referring to the wide variety of policies that might be relevant from the viewpoint of territorial development. Rather, it is referring to territorial cohesion policies and the Lisbon/Gothenburg Strategy: "Towards a stronger European territorial cohesion in the light of the Lisbon and Gothenburg ambitions," which is the subtitle of a paper produced by the Luxembourg Presidency (2005).

This act of focusing (*scoping* is the official term) seems to require a change of language. Because, as Rein and Schön (1993) point out, naming is framing, the adjective *spatial*, as in spatial development and spatial development policies, is being replaced by *territorial*, as in territorial governance. It is not difficult to understand why. For those trying to influence the wider EU political agenda, there is no alternative to adopting the language of this agenda. An analysis of the Luxembourg paper seems to reveal that the Rotterdam Process implies pursuing two trajectories. Under the first trajectory, the goal is to influence the discussion on territorial cohesion and the Lisbon/Gothenburg ambitions. Here a new concept is invoked, that of *territorial capital*. The second trajectory is all about territorial cooperation. At present, a territorial cooperation takes place within the context of the Community initiative Interreg, but it will become one of the three main objectives of the Structural Funds. At the Rotterdam and Luxembourg meetings, an agreement was reached to focus this type of cooperation, including the funds, on *trans-European structuring elements*—again a rather abstract notion. Territorial capital and structuring elements (territorial structure) are notions that should be defined more precisely during the ongoing Rotterdam Process. Because they are relevant to the discussion in this chapter, the rest of this section looks briefly at what the documents produced in connection with the Rotterdam and Luxembourg meetings have to say about them.

Territorial Capital

At the Rotterdam and Luxembourg meetings, the EU ministers and the Commission issued a strong endorsement of policies seeking to bring about territorial cohesion in Europe and achieve the Lisbon/Gothenburg ambitions. But these policies must take into account the vast territorial diversity within the EU; generic measures applied uniformly across regions are no longer appropriate. It is here that the "scoping" papers by the Dutch and Luxembourg Presidencies adopt the notion of territorial capital developed by the OECD (2001) in its *Territorial Outlook of 2001*. The Luxembourg paper states: "Each region has a specific 'territorial capital' that is distinct from that of other areas and generates a higher return for specific kinds of investments than for others, since these are better suited to the area and use its assets and potential more effectively" (Luxembourg Presidency 2005, 2). And the Rotterdam paper declares: "Some of the most important and dynamic forces in terms of economic development are increasingly both localized and territorially specific. . . . Public policies aimed at promoting territorial development and limiting territorial disparities should first and foremost help areas to develop their territorial capital" (Dutch Presidency 2004, 6).

In defining territorial capital, the Dutch Presidency adopted the OECD's definition. A region's territorial capital is

> distinct from other areas and is determined by many factors [which] may include geographical location, size, factor of production endowment, climate, traditions, natural resources, quality of life or the agglomeration economies provided by its cities. Other factors may be "untraded interdependencies" such as understandings, customs and informal rules that enable economic actors to work together under conditions of uncertainty, or the solidarity, mutual assistance and co-opting of ideas that often develop in small and medium-size enterprises working in the same sector (social capital). Lastly there is an intangible factor, "something in the air", called "the environment" and which is the outcome of a combination of institutions, rules, practices, producers, researchers and policy-makers, that make a certain creativity and innovation possible. (OECD 2001, as quoted in Dutch Presidency 2004, 5)

Thus, the territorial capital of a region forms its endogenous potential. The idea is that every region has a specific territorial capital: "Territorial development policies (policies with a territorial approach to development) should first and foremost help areas to develop their territorial capital" (Luxembourg Presidency 2005, 2). If this territorial dimension is integrated into the Lisbon aims—the Luxembourg paper declares that implicitly the Lisbon aims already incorporate such a territorial dimension—territorial cohesion will be brought about, meaning balanced competitiveness and sustainable development in a territorial setting. In a way, territorial capital is thus a bridging concept, combining the grand issues of competitiveness, cohesion, and sustainability. The broad image of a European territorial model of society characteristic of the ESDP is therefore being maintained.

However, if the idea is to enrich the Lisbon/Gothenburg Strategy with a territorial dimension and thereby demonstrate the added value of a territorial approach, then some hard evidence is needed. The ESPON program now under way could provide such evidence. And yet the notion of territorial capital has more dimensions than are presently covered by the ESPON program. For example, ESPON falls short on social indicators, as pointed out by Davoudi in chapter 5 in this volume. Thus once the notion of territorial capital is endorsed by the member states during the Rotterdam Process, it would make sense for territorial capital to become the cornerstone of a future ESPON II program. In this way, the ESPON program would become more consistent; the current program is a mixed bag.

Territorial Structure

The Lisbon/Gothenburg aims are outside the realm of cooperation between member states and of the Commission in the field of spatial development. However, the notion of structuring elements lies very much within their sphere of influence. At the Rotterdam and Luxembourg meetings, agreement was reached on focusing territorial cooperation—Objective 3 of the future Structural Funds—on *trans-European structuring elements.* Such elements include European-wide networks, including their connection to secondary networks (transport, energy, and information communications technology infrastructure; ecological structures; maritime links; water networks; and urban networks), and cultural resources. Structuring elements—or territorial structure—encompass issues broader than services of general interest. Compared with the ESDP, nothing of fundamental importance has changed in the perception of problems surrounding the delivery of services of general interest. These problems occur just in rural areas and therefore should be the object of urban-rural partnerships (Luxembourg Presidency 2005, 4).

Thus, if the idea is to focus future EU policy such as the Structural Funds on the structuring elements of the European territory, then an important question arises: based on which guiding principles and on which strategic spatial concepts are these elements to be selected? In this respect, and as demonstrated, the fundamental goals and the policy guidelines of the ESDP are too broad and too general. The exception is polycentricity. However, this concept is still (at least in the ESDP) a sensitizing concept. It is in a way a clever compromise between the issues of territorial cohesion and competitiveness, but, in terms of territorial structure, it is rather underspecified. From this perspective, it was important to choose polycentricity as one of the key research themes of the ESPON program. The outcome of this program could be of critical importance in the search for the guiding principles to identify the structuring elements of the European territory.

At present, often very simple criteria are used to identify the areas that should be the targets of EU policies—the criteria used to allocate the Structural Funds are an example, especially the criterion for the designation of Objective 1 areas: 75 percent or less of the EU GDP per capita, adjusted for purchasing power parity. The outcome of the ESPON program could be used to develop more sophisticated criteria, starting with the need to observe a certain degree of territorial selectivity. The notion of territorial structure is therefore of great value in the search for policies to render territorial cooperation more concrete. Ultimately, then, one can arrive at territorial designations, a step not taken when the ESDP was drafted.

Indeed, such designations appear to be a prime concern of the

Rotterdam Process. European Territorial Co-operation (ETC) will be in large part "a continuation of the development of innovative approaches and the exchange and dissemination of best practices on common issues," just like the current Interreg IIIB programs. But ETC will mean more; it "will have to focus on *strategic projects*, i.e. projects that play a key role in structuring (parts of) a co-operation area by addressing the core issue that define the area" (Luxembourg Presidency 2005, 19, emphasis in the original). Some examples of strategic projects are given, such as the integrated development of metropolitan axes or coastal zones.

But defining territorial structure and selecting strategic projects cannot take place without some sort of conceptualization of space and territory. Projects can be declared "strategic" only if they are related to some sort of image of a territory. Territorial cooperation under the new Structural Funds will most likely involve visioning, provided that the new ETC objective of the Structural Funds is not defined too narrowly, which seems to be the case in the present proposals by the Commission (CEC 2005). It even remains to be seen whether the notion of structuring elements fits into the approach proposed by the Commission.

◼ Conclusions

The European Spatial Development Perspective, although thought to be a milestone on a road that ultimately could lead to some sort of territorial governance within the European Union, could hardly be called a vision. Apart from the concept of polycentricity, which in itself can be interpreted in many ways, the ESDP does not give a vision of Europe's territorial structure. Key players in the ESDP process equated vision with a master plan, and so the route to articulating spatial concepts, let alone maps, was not taken.

Meanwhile, after a period of five years the ministers responsible for spatial development and the European Commission have resumed their regular meetings, the so-called Rotterdam Process. The idea is to make headway along two trajectories: first, to influence the wider political discussion on how to bring about territorial cohesion in the light of the Lisbon/Gothenburg ambitions, and, second, to create consensus on the goals and central issues of territorial cooperation, if and when this becomes the new Objective 3 of the Structural Funds.

To make such headway, it seems essential to unravel Europe's territorial structure and to develop some sort of spatial visions. To avoid the misconception that "visioning" means drawing up of a master plan, a new visual language must be created that allows various interpretations, comparable with how written texts often function. Visioning, visualization, and scenario building will have to become priorities in the years ahead. In some of the present transnational cooperation areas, efforts are under way to launch new visioning processes. ESPON could play an important role here, because it has brought together much of the empirical research and created many maps illustrating the enormous territorial diversity in Europe. There is, then, great potential for evidence-based visioning. It is important, though, to keep in mind the use of visioning. It should be directed at creating new strategic spatial concepts. Such concepts set the frames for policy making and concrete decision making, but are in themselves not the same as making concrete territorial decisions. In this phaseology of European territorial governance, visions can only serve as guidance and not as a prescription for selecting strategic projects, for example. Territorial structure should not to be equated with the spaces and places where certain concrete actions take place. Thus, the future is for fuzzy spatial concepts and visions.

References

Bengs, C. 2000. From conservation to convelopment. *Built Environment* 26(1):13–20.

CEC—Commission of the European Communities. 1991. *Europe 2000: Outlook for the development of the Community's territory.* Luxembourg: Office for Official Publications of the European Communities.

———. 1994. *Europe 2000+: Co-operation for European territorial development.* Luxembourg: Office for Official Publications of the European Communities.

———. 1999. *European Spatial Development Perspective: Towards balanced and sustainable development of the territory of the EU.* Luxembourg: Office for Official Publications of the European Communities.

———. 2005. *Cohesion policy in support of growth and jobs: Community Strategic Guidelines, 2007–2013 (communication from the Commission).* COM (2005) 0299. Brussels, 5 July.

Davoudi, S. 2003. Polycentricity in European spatial planning: From an analytical tool to a normative agenda? *European Planning Studies* 11(8):979–999.

Davoudi, S., and M. Wishardt. 2005. The polycentric turn in the Irish spatial strategy. *Built Environment* 31(2):122–132.

de Vries, J. 2002. *Grenzen verkend: Internationalisering van de ruimtelijke planning in de Benelux* [Exploring borders: The internationalization of spatial planning in the Benelux]. Stedelijke en Regionale Verkenningen 27. Delft: DUP Science.

Dühr, S. 2005. European spatial planning and cartographic representations. Ph.D. diss., University of the West of England, Bristol.

Duinen, L. van. 2004. Planning imagery: The emergence and development of new planning concepts in Dutch national spatial policy. Ph.D. diss., University of Amsterdam.

Dutch Presidency. 1997. *European Spatial Development Perspective: First Official Draft.* Presented at the Informal Meeting of Ministers Responsible for Spatial Planning of the Member States of the European Union, Noordwijk, June 1997.

———. 2004. *Exploiting Europe's territorial diversity for sustainable economic growth.* Discussion paper for the EU Informal Ministerial Meeting on Territorial Cohesion, Rotterdam, November 29.

Faludi, A., ed. 2002. *European spatial planning.* Cambridge, MA: Lincoln Institute of Land Policy.

———. 2005. Polycentric territorial cohesion policy. In Territorial cohesion, A. Faludi, ed., special issue, *Town Planning Review* 76(1):107–118.

Faludi, A., and B. Waterhout. 2005. The usual suspects: The Rotterdam Informal Ministerial Meeting on Territorial Cohesion. *Tijdschrift voor Economische en Sociale Geografie* 96(3):338–342.

Fleischer, T. 2004. *Comments on services of general interest and territorial and social cohesion.* Contribution to the international conference on "Services of General Interest in an

Enlarged European Union," organized in Budapest by the TEPSA Members Study Group for European Policies (Belgium), Institute for World Economics (Hungary), and the Initiative pour des services d'utilité publique en Europe (Belgium) with the support of the European Commission, 21–22 October.

Healey, P. 1996. The communicative turn in planning theory and its implications for spatial strategy formation. *Environment and Planning B* 23:217–234.

———. 2006. *Collaborative planning: Shaping places in fragmented societies.* (First edition 1997) London: Macmillan.

Jensen, O. B., and T. Richardson. 2004. *Making European space mobility, power and territorial identity.* London and New York: Routledge.

Kunzmann, K. R. 1993. Geodesign: Chance oder gefahr? *Informationen zur Raumentwicklung* 7:389–396.

Kunzmann, K. R., and M. Wegener. 1991. *The pattern of urbanisation in Western Europe, 1960–1990.* Report for the Directorate General XVI of the Commission of the European Communities. Berichte aus dem Institut für Raumplanung 28. Dortmund: Institut für Raumplanung Universität Dortmund (IRPUD).

Luxembourg Presidency. 2005. *Scoping document and summary of political messages for an assessment of "The territorial state and perspectives of the European Union: Towards a stronger European territorial cohesion in the light of the Lisbon and Gothenburg ambitions."* Endorsed for further development by the Ministers for Spatial Development and the European Commission at the Informal Ministerial Meeting for Regional Policy and Territorial Cohesion, Luxembourg, 20–21 May.

OECD—Organisation for Economic Co-operation and Development. 2001. *Territorial outlook 2001.* Paris: OECD Publications.

Rein, M., and D. Schön. 1986. Frame-reflective policy discourse. *Beleidsanalyse* 15(4):4–18.

———. 1993. Reframing policy discourse. In *The argumentative turn in policy analysis and planning,* F. Fischer and J. Forester, eds., 145–166. London: UCL Press.

Shipley, R., and R. Newkirk. 1998. Visioning: Did anybody see where it came from? *Journal of Planning Literature* 12(4):407–416.

———. 1999. Vision and visioning in planning: What do these terms really mean? *Environment and Planning B* 26:573–592.

Vermeersch, C. 1994. *Structuurplanning: Instrument voor het denken over de vormgeving aan de ruimtelijke structuur* [Structure planning: Instrument for thinking about the design of spatial structure]. Brugge: Die Keure.

Williams, R. H. 1996. *European Union spatial policy and planning.* London: Paul Chapman Publishing.

Zonneveld, W. 1991. *Conceptvorming in de ruimtelijke planning: Patronen en processen* [Conceptualisation in spatial planning: Patterns and processes]. Planologische Studies No. 9a. Amsterdam: Planologisch en Demografisch Instituut Universiteit van Amsterdam.

———. 2005a. Expansive spatial planning: The new European transnational spatial visions. *European Planning Studies* 13(1):137–155.

———. 2005b. Multiple visioning: New ways of constructing transnational spatial visions. *Environment and Planning C* 23(1):41–62.

Contributors

EDITOR

Andreas Faludi
Professor
OTB Research Institute for Housing,
  Urban and Mobility Studies
Delft University of Technology
Delft, The Netherlands

AUTHORS

John Bachtler
Professor
European Policy Studies
Director
European Policies Research Center
  (EPRC)
University of Strathclyde
Glasgow, Scotland

Roberto Camagni
Professor
Department of Management, Economics
  and Industrial Engineering
Politecnico di Milano
Milan, Italy

Armando Carbonell
Senior Fellow
Lincoln Institute of Land Policy
Cambridge, Massachusetts, USA

Simin Davoudi
Professor
Environmental Policy and Planning
Director of Social Systems
Institute for Research on Environment and
  Stability
Newcastle University
Newcastle, United Kingdom

Jean-François Drevet
Retired
Directorate General for Regional Policy
European Commission
Brussels, Belgium

Jean Peyrony
Director of Developments
Mission opérationnelle transfrontalière
Délégation à l'Aménagement du Territoire
  et à l'Action Régionale (DATAR)
Paris, France

Laura Polverari
Research Fellow
European Policies Research Center
  (EPRC)
University of Strathclyde
Glasgow, Scotland

Jacques Robert
Director
Agence Européene "Territoires et
  Synergies" (TERSYN)
Strasbourg, France

Gabriele Tatzberger
Research Fellow
Austrian Institute for Regional and Spatial
    Planning (ÖIR)
Vienna, Austria

Bas Waterhout
Researcher
OTB Research Institute for Housing,
    Urban and Mobility Studies
Delft University of Technology
Delft, The Netherlands

Wil Zonneveld
Senior Lecturer
OTB Research Institute for Housing,
    Urban and Mobility Studies
Delft University of Technology
Delft, The Netherlands

Index

About the Lincoln Institute of Land Policy

The Lincoln Institute of Land Policy is a private operating foundation whose mission is to improve the quality of public debate and decisions in the areas of land policy and land-related taxation in the United States and around the world. The Institute's goals are to integrate theory and practice to better shape land policy and to provide a nonpartisan forum for discussion of the multidisciplinary forces that influence public policy. This focus on land derives from the Institute's founding objective—to address the links between land policy and social and economic progress—that was identified and analyzed by political economist and author Henry George.

The work of the Institute is organized in four departments: Valuation and Taxation, Planning and Urban Form, Economic and Community Development, and International Studies. We seek to inform decision making through education, research, demonstration projects, and the dissemination of information through publications, our Web site, and other media. Our programs bring together scholars, practitioners, public officials, policy advisers, and involved citizens in a collegial learning environment. The Institute does not take a particular point of view, but rather serves as a catalyst to facilitate analysis and discussion of land use and taxation issues—to make a difference today and to help policy makers plan for tomorrow.

The Lincoln Institute of Land Policy is an equal opportunity institution.

L LINCOLN INSTITUTE
OF LAND POLICY

113 Brattle Street
Cambridge, MA 02138-3400 USA

Phone: 1-617-661-3016 x127 or 1-800-LAND-USE (800-526-3873)
Fax: 1-617-661-7235 or 1-800-LAND-944 (800-526-3944)
E-mail: help@lincolninst.edu
Web: www.lincolninst.edu